STORY-LIVES OF
MASTER MUSICIANS

STORY-LIVES OF
MASTER MUSICIANS

by

Harriette Brower

YESTERDAY'S CLASSICS

ITHACA, NEW YORK

ISBN: 978-1-63334-159-3

Yesterday's Classics, LLC
PO Box 339
Ithaca, NY 14851

FOREWORD

The preparation of this volume began with a period of delightful research work in a great musical library. As a honey-bee flutters from flower to flower, culling sweetness from many blossoms, so the compiler of such stories as these must gather facts from many sources—from biography, letters, journals and musical history. Then, impressed with the personality and individual achievement of each composer, the author has endeavored to present his life story.

While the aim has been to make the story-sketches interesting to young people, the author hopes that they may prove valuable to musical readers of all ages. Students of piano, violin or other instruments need to know how the great composers lived their lives. In every musical career described in this book, from the old masters represented by Bach and Beethoven to the musical prophets of our own day, there is a wealth of inspiration and practical guidance for the artist in any field. Through their struggles, sorrows and triumphs, divine melody and harmony came into being, which will bless the world for all time to come.

CONTENTS

CONTENTS

PALESTRINA

CHAPTER I

PALESTRINA

To learn something of the life and labors of Palestrina, one of the earliest as well as one of the greatest musicians, we must go back in the world's history nearly four hundred years. And even then we may not be able to discover all the events of his life as some of the records have been lost. But we have the main facts, and know that Palestrina's name will be revered for all time as the man who strove to make sacred music the expression of lofty and spiritual meaning.

Upon a hoary spur of the Apennines stands the crumbling town of Palestrina. It is very old now; it was old when Rome was young. Four hundred years ago Palestrina was dominated by the great castle of its lords, the proud Colonnas. Naturally the town was much more important in those days than it is to-day.

At that time there lived in Palestrina a peasant pair, Sante Pierluigi and his wife Maria, who seem to have been an honest couple, and not grindingly poor, since the will of Sante's mother has lately been found, in which she bequeathed a house in Palestrina to her two sons. Besides this she left behind a fine store of bed linen, mattresses and cooking utensils. Maria Gismondi also had a little property.

To this pair was born, probably in 1526, a boy whom they named Giovanni Pierluigi, which means John Peter Louis. This boy, from a tiniest child, loved beauty of sight and sound. And this is not at all surprising, for a child surrounded from infancy by the natural loveliness and glory of old Palestrina, would unconsciously breathe in a sense of beauty and grandeur.

It was soon discovered the boy had a voice, and his mother is said to have sold some land she owned to provide for her son's musical training.

From the rocky heights on which their town was built, the people of Palestrina could look across the Campagna—the great plain between—and see the walls and towers of Rome. At the time of our story, Saint Peter's had withstood the sack of the city, which happened a dozen years before, and Bramante's vast basilica had already begun to rise. The artistic life of Rome was still at high tide, for Raphael had passed away but twenty years before, and Michael Angelo was at work on his Last Judgment.

Though painting and sculpture flourished, music did not keep pace with advance in other arts. The leading musicians were Belgian, Spanish or French, and their music did not match the great achievements attained in the kindred art of the time—architecture, sculpture and painting. There was needed a new impetus, a vital force. Its rise began when the peasant youth John Peter

Louis descended from the heights of Palestrina to the banks of the Tiber.

It is said that Tomasso Crinello was the boy's master; whether this is true or not, he was surely trained in the Netherland manner of composition.

The youth, whom we shall now call Palestrina, as he is known by the name of his birthplace, returned from Rome at the age of eighteen to his native town, in 1544, as a practising musician, and took a post at the Cathedral of Saint Agapitus. Here he engaged himself for life, to be present every day at mass and vespers, and to teach singing to the canons and choristers. Thus he spent the early years of his young manhood directing the daily services and drumming the rudiments of music into the heads of the little choristers. It may have been dry and wearisome labor; but afterward, when Palestrina began to reform the music of the church, it must have been of great advantage to him to know so absolutely the liturgy, not only of Saint Peter's and Saint John Lateran, but also that in the simple cathedral of his own small hill-town.

Young Palestrina, living his simple, busy life in his home town, never dreamed he was destined to become a great musician. He married in 1548, when he was about twenty-two. If he had wished to secure one of the great musical appointments in Rome, it was a very unwise thing for him to marry, for single singers were preferred in nine cases out of ten. Palestrina did not seem to realize this danger to a brilliant career, and took his bride, Lucrezia, for pure love. She seems to have been a person after his own heart, besides having a comfortable dowry of her own. They had a happy union, which lasted for more than thirty years.

Although he had agreed to remain for life at the cathedral church of Saint Agapitus, it seems that such contracts could be broken without peril. Thus, after seven years of service, he once more turned his steps toward the Eternal City.

He returned to Rome as a recognized musician. In 1551 he became master of the Capella Giulia, at the modest salary of six scudi a month, something like ten dollars. But the young chapel master seemed satisfied. Hardly three years after his arrival had elapsed, when he had written and printed a book containing five masses, which he dedicated to Pope Julius III. This act pleased the pontiff, who, in January, 1555, appointed Palestrina one of the singers of the Sistine Chapel, with an increased salary.

It seems however, that the Sistine singers resented the appointment of a new member, and complained about it. Several changes in the Papal chair occurred at this time, and when Paul IV, as Pope, came into power, he began at once with reforms. Finding that Palestrina and two other singers were married men, he put all three out, though granting an annuity of six scudi a month for each.

The loss of this post was a great humiliation, which Palestrina found it hard to endure. He fell ill at this time, and the outlook was dark indeed, with a wife and three little children to provide for.

But the clouds soon lifted. Within a few weeks after this unfortunate event, the rejected singer of the Sistine Chapel was created Chapel Master of Saint John Lateran, the splendid basilica, where the young Orlandus Lassus had so recently directed the music. As Palestrina could still keep his six scudi pension, increased with the added salary of the new position, he was able to establish his family in a pretty villa on the Coelian Hill, where he could be near his work at the Lateran, but far enough removed from the turmoil of the city to obtain the quiet he desired, and where he lived in tranquillity for the next five years.

Palestrina spent forty-four years of his life in Rome. All the eleven popes who reigned during this long period honored Palestrina as a great musician. Marcellus II spent a part of his three weeks' reign in showing kindness to the young Chapel master, which the composer returned by naming for this pontiff a famous work, "Mass of Pope Marcellus." Pius IV, who was in power when the mass was performed, praised it eloquently, saying John Peter Louis of Palestrina was a new John, bringing down to the church militant the harmonies of that "new song" which John the Apostle heard in the Holy City. The musician-pope, Gregory XIII, to whom Palestrina dedicated his grandest motets, entrusted him with the sacred task of revising the ancient chant. Pope Sixtus V greatly praised his beautiful mass, "Assumpta est Maria" and promoted him to higher honors.

With this encouragement and patronage, Palestrina labored five years at the Lateran, ten years at Santa

Maria Maggiore and twenty three at Saint Peter's. At the last named it was his second term, of course, but it continued from 1571 to his death. He was happy in his work, in his home and in his friends. He also saved quite a little money and was able to give his daughter-in-law, in 1577, 1300 scudi; he is known indeed, to have bought land, vineyards and houses in and about Rome.

All was not a life of sunshine for Palestrina, for he suffered many domestic sorrows. His three promising sons died one after another. They were talented young men, who might have followed in the footsteps of their distinguished father. In 1580 his wife died also. Yet neither poignant sorrow, worldly glory nor ascetic piety blighted his homely affections. At the Jubilee of Pope Gregory XIII, in 1575, when 1500 pilgrims from the town of Palestrina descended the hills on the way to Rome, it was their old townsman, Giovanni Pierluigi, who led their songs, as they entered the Eternal City, their maidens clad in white robes, and their young men bearing olive branches.

It is said of Palestrina that he became the "savior of church music," at a time when it had almost been decided to banish all music from the service except the chant, because so many secular subjects had been set to music and used in church. Things had come to a very difficult pass, until at last the fathers turned to Palestrina, desiring him to compose a mass in which sacred words should be heard throughout. Palestrina, deeply realizing his responsibility, wrote not only one but three, which, on being heard, pleased greatly by their piety, meekness, and beautiful spirit. Feeling more sure of himself, Palestrina continued to compose masses, until he had created ninety-three in all. He also wrote many motets on the Song of Solomon, his Stabat Mater, which was edited two hundred and fifty years later by Richard Wagner, and his lamentations, which were composed at the request of Sixtus V.

Palestrina's end came February 2, 1594. He died in Rome, a devout Christian, and on his coffin were engraved the simple but splendid words: "Prince of Music."

Johann Sebastian Bach

CHAPTER II

JOHN SEBASTIAN BACH

Away back in 1685, almost two hundred and fifty years ago, one of the greatest musicians of the world first saw the light, in the little town of Eisenach, nestling on the edge of the Thuringen forest. The long low-roofed cottage where little Johann Sebastian Bach was born, is still standing, and carefully preserved.

The name Bach belonged to a long race of musicians, who strove to elevate the growing art of music. For nearly two hundred years there had been organists and composers in the family; Sebastian's father, Johann Ambrosius Bach was organist of the Lutheran Church in Eisenach, and naturally a love of music was fostered in the home. It is no wonder that little Sebastian should have shown a fondness for music almost from infancy. But, beyond learning the violin from his father, he had not advanced very far in his studies, when, in his tenth year he lost both his parents and was taken care of by his brother Christoph, fourteen years older, a respectable musician and organist in a neighboring town. To give his little brother lessons on the clavier, and send him to the Lyceum to learn Latin, singing and other school subjects seemed to Christoph to include all that could be expected of him. That his small brother possessed musical genius of the highest order, was an idea he could not grasp; or if he did, he repressed the boy with indifference and harsh treatment.

Little Sebastian suffered in silence from this coldness. Fortunately the force of his genius was too great to be crushed. He knew all the simple pieces by heart, which his brother set for his lessons, and he longed for bigger things. There was a book of manuscript music containing pieces by Buxtehude and Frohberger, famous masters of the time, in the possession of Christoph. Sebastian greatly desired to play the pieces in that book, but his brother kept it under lock and key in his cupboard, or bookcase. One day the child mustered courage to ask permission to take the book for a little while. Instead of yielding to the boy's request Christoph became angry, told him not to imagine he could study such masters as Buxtehude and Frohberger, but should be content to get the lessons assigned him.

The injustice of this refusal fired Sebastian with the determination to get possession of the coveted book at all costs. One moonlight night, long after every one had retired, he decided to put into execution a project he had dreamed of for some time.

Creeping noiselessly down stairs he stood before the bookcase and sought the precious volume. There it was with the names of the various musicians printed in large letters on the back in his brother's handwriting. To get his small hands between the bars and draw the book outward took some time. But how to get it out. After much labor he found one bar weaker than the others, which could be bent.

When at last the book was in his hands, he clasped it to his breast and hurried quickly back to his chamber. Placing the book on a table in front of the window, where the moonlight fell full upon it, he took pen and music paper and began copying out the pieces in the book.

This was but the beginning of nights of endless toil. For six months whenever there were moonlight nights, Sebastian was at the window working at his task with passionate eagerness.

At last it was finished, and Sebastian in the joy of possessing it for his very own, crept into bed without the precaution of putting away all traces of his work. Poor boy, he had to pay dearly for his forgetfulness. As he lay sleeping, Christoph, thinking he heard sounds in his brother's room, came to seek the cause. His glance, as he entered the room, fell on the open books. There was no pity in his heart for all this devoted labor, only anger that he had been outwitted by his small brother. He took both books away and hid them in a place where Sebastian could never find them. But he did not reflect that the boy had the memory of all this beautiful music indelibly printed on his mind, which helped him to bear the bitter disappointment of the loss of his work.

When he was fifteen Sebastian left his brother's roof and entered the Latin school connected with the Church of St. Michael at Lüneburg. It was found he had a beautiful soprano voice, which placed him with the scholars who were chosen to sing in the church service in return for a free education. There were two church schools in Lüneburg, and the rivalry between them was so keen, that when the scholars sang in the streets during the winter months to collect money for their support, the routes for each had to be carefully marked out, to prevent collision.

Soon after he entered St. Michael's, Bach lost his beautiful soprano voice; his knowledge of violin and clavier, however, enabled him to keep his place in the school. The boy worked hard at his musical studies, giving his spare time to the study of the best composers. He began to realize that he cared more for the organ than for any other instrument; indeed his love for it became a passion. He was too poor to take lessons, for he was almost entirely self-dependent—a penniless scholar, living on the plainest of fare, yet determined to gain a knowledge of the music he longed for.

One of the great organists of the time was Johann Adam Reinken. When Sebastian learned that this master played the organ in St. Katharine's Church in Hamburg, he determined to walk the whole distance thither to hear him. Now Hamburg was called in those days the "Paradise of German music," and was twenty-five good English miles from the little town of Lüneburg, but what did that matter to the eager lad? Obstacles only fired him to strive the harder for what he desired to attain.

The great joy of listening to such a master made him forget the long tramp and all the weariness, and spurred him on to repeat the journey whenever he had saved a few shillings to pay for food and lodging. On one occasion he lingered a little longer in Hamburg than usual, until his funds were well-nigh exhausted, and before him was the long walk without any food. As he trudged along he came upon a small inn, from the open door of which came a delightful savory odor. He could not resist looking in through the window. At that instant a window above was thrown open and a couple of herrings' heads were tossed into the road. The herring is a favorite article of food in Germany and poor Sebastian was glad to pick up these bits to satisfy the cravings of hunger. What was his surprise on pulling the heads to pieces to find each one contained a Danish ducat. When he recovered from his astonishment, he entered the inn and made a good meal with part of the money; the rest ensured another visit to Hamburg.

After remaining three years in Lüneburg, Bach secured a post as violinist in the private band of Prince Johann Ernst of Saxe-Weimar; but this was only to fill the time till he could find a place to play the instrument he so loved. An opportunity soon came. The old Thuringian town Arnstadt had a new church and a fine new organ. The consistory of the church were looking for a capable organist and Bach's request to be allowed to try the instrument was readily granted.

As soon as they heard him play they offered him the post, with promise of increasing the salary by a contribution from the town funds. Bach thus found himself at the age of eighteen installed as organist at a salary of fifty florins, with thirty thalers in addition for board and lodging, equal, all in all, to less than fifty dollars. In those days this amount was considered a fair sum for a young player. On August 14, 1708, the young organist entered upon his duties, promising solemnly to be diligent and faithful to all requirements.

The requirements of the post fortunately left him plenty of leisure to study. Up to this time he had done very little composing, but now he set about teaching himself the art of composition.

The first thing he did was to take a number of concertos written for the violin by Vivaldi, and set them for the harpsichord. In this way he learned to express himself and to attain facility in putting his thoughts on paper without first playing them on an instrument. He worked alone in this way with no assistance from any one, and often studied till far into the night to perfect himself in this branch of his art.

From the very beginning, his playing on the new organ excited admiration, but his artistic temperament frequently threatened to be his undoing. For the young enthusiast was no sooner seated at the organ to conduct the church music than he forgot that the choir and congregation were depending on him and would begin to improvise at such length that the singing had to stop altogether, while the people listened in mute admiration. Of course there were many disputes between the new organist and the elders of the church, but they overlooked his vagaries because of his genius.

Yet he must have been a trial to that well-ordered body. Once he asked for a month's leave of absence to visit Lübeck, where the celebrated Buxtehude was playing the organ in the Marien Kirche during Advent. Lübeck was fifty miles from Arnstadt, but the courageous boy made the entire journey on foot. He enjoyed the music at Lübeck so much that he quite forgot his promise to return in one month until he had stayed three. His pockets being quite empty, he thought for the first time of returning to his post. Of course there was trouble on his return, but the authorities retained him in spite of all, for the esteem in which they held his gifts.

Bach soon began to find Arnstadt too small and narrow for his soaring desires. Besides, his fame was growing and his name becoming known in the larger, adjacent towns. When he was offered the post of organist at St. Blasius at Mülhausen, near Eisenach, he accepted at once. He was told he might name his own salary. If Bach had been avaricious he could have asked a large sum, but he modestly named the small amount he had received at Arnstadt with the addition of certain articles of food which should be delivered at his door, gratis.

Bach's prospects were now so much improved that he thought he might make a home for himself. He had fallen in love with a cousin, Maria Bach, and they were married October 17, 1707.

The young organist only remained in Mülhausen a year, for he received a more important offer. He was invited to play before Duke Wilhelm Ernst of Weimar, and hastened thither, hoping this might lead to an appointment at Court. He was not disappointed, for the Duke was so delighted with Bach's playing that he at once offered him the post of Court organist.

A wider outlook now opened for Sebastian Bach, who had all his young life struggled with poverty, and privation. He was now able to give much time to composition, and began to write those masterpieces for the organ which have placed his name on the highest pinnacle in the temple of music.

In his comfortable Weimar home the musician had the quiet and leisure that he needed to perfect his art on all sides, not only in composition but in organ and harpsichord playing. He felt that he had conquered all difficulties of both instruments, and one day boasted to a friend that he could play any piece, no matter how difficult, at sight, without a mistake. In order to test this statement the friend invited him to breakfast shortly after. On the harpsichord were several pieces of music, one of which, though apparently simple, was really very difficult. His host left the room to prepare the breakfast, while Bach began to try over the music. All went well until he came to the difficult piece which he began quite boldly but stuck in the middle. It went no better after several attempts. As his friend entered, bringing the breakfast, Bach exclaimed:—"You are right. One cannot play everything perfectly at sight,—it is impossible!"

Duke Wilhelm Ernst, in 1714, raised him to the position of Head-Concert Master, a position which offered added privileges. Every autumn he used his annual vacation in traveling to the principal towns to give performances on organ and clavier. By such means he gained a great reputation both as player and composer.

On one of these tours he arrived in Dresden in time to learn of a French player who had just come to town. Jean Marchand had won a great reputation in France, where he was organist to the King at Versailles, and regarded as the most fashionable musician of the day. All this had made him very conceited and overbearing. Every one was discussing the Frenchman's wonderful playing and it was whispered he had been offered an appointment in Dresden.

The friends of Bach proposed that he should engage Marchand in a contest, to defend the musical honor of the German nation. Both musicians were willing; the King promised to attend.

The day fixed for the trial arrived; a brilliant company assembled. Bach made his appearance, and all was ready, but the adversary failed to come. After a considerable delay it was learned that Marchand had fled the city.

In 1717, on his return from Dresden, Bach was appointed Capellmeister to the young Prince Leopold of Anhalt-Cöthen. The Prince was an enthusiastic lover of music, and at Cöthen Bach led a happy, busy life. The Prince often journeyed to different towns to gratify his taste for music, and always took Bach with him. On one of these trips he was unable to receive the news that his wife had suddenly passed away, and was buried before he could return to Cöthen. This was a severe blow to the whole family.

Four years afterward, Bach married again, Anna Magdalena Wülkens was in every way suited for a musician's wife, and for her he composed many of the delightful dances which we now so greatly enjoy. He also wrote a number of books of studies for his wife and his sons, several of whom later became good musicians and composers.

Perhaps no man ever led a more crowded life, though outwardly a quiet one. He never had an idle moment. When not playing, composing or teaching, he would be found engraving music on copper, since that work was costly in those days. Or he would be manufacturing some kind of musical instrument. At least two are known to be of his invention.

Bach began to realize that the Cöthen post, while it gave him plenty of leisure for his work, did not give him the scope he needed for his art. The Prince had lately married, and did not seem to care as much for music as before.

The wider opportunity which Bach sought came when he was appointed director of music in the churches of St. Thomas and St. Nicholas in Leipsic, and Cantor of the Thomas-Schule there. With the Leipsic period Bach entered the last stage of his career, for he retained this post for the rest of his life. He labored unceasingly, in spite of many obstacles and petty restrictions, to train the boys under his care, and raise the standard of musical efficiency in the Schule, as choirs of both churches were recruited from the scholars of the Thomas School.

During the twenty-seven years of life in Leipsic, Bach wrote some of his greatest works, such as the Oratorios of St. Matthew and St. John, and the Mass in B Minor. It was the Passion according to St. Matthew that Mendelssohn, about a hundred years later discovered, studied with so much zeal, and performed in Berlin, with so much devotion and success.

Bach always preferred a life of quiet and retirement; simplicity had ever been his chief characteristic. He was always very religious; his greatest works voice the noblest sentiments of exaltation.

Bach's modesty and retiring disposition is illustrated by the following little incident. Carl Philip Emmanuel, his third son, was cembalist in the royal orchestra of Frederick the Great. His Majesty was very fond of music and played the flute to some extent. He had several times sent messages to Bach by Philip Emmanuel, that he would like to see him. But Bach, intent on his work, ignored the royal favor, until he finally received an imperative command, which could not be disobeyed. He then, with his son Friedmann, set out for Potsdam.

The King was about to begin the evening's music when he learned that Bach had arrived. With a smile he turned to his musicians: "Gentlemen, old Bach has come." Bach was sent for at once, without having time to change his traveling dress. His Majesty received him with great kindness and respect, and showed him through the palace, where he must try the

Silbermann pianofortes, of which there were several. Bach improvised on each and the King gave a theme which he treated as a fantasia, to the astonishment of all. Frederick next asked him to play a six part fugue, and then Bach improvised one on a theme of his own. The King clapped his hands, exclaiming over and over, "Only one Bach! Only one Bach!" It was a great evening for the master, and one he never forgot.

Just after completing his great work, The Art of Fugue, Bach became totally blind, due no doubt, to the great strain he had always put upon his eyes, in not only writing his own music, but in copying out large works of the older masters. Notwithstanding this handicap he continued at work up to the very last. On the morning of the day on which he passed away, July 28, 1750, he suddenly regained his sight. A few hours later he became unconscious and passed in sleep.

Bach was laid to rest in the churchyard of St. John's at Leipsic, but no stone marks his resting place. Only the town library register tells that Johann Sebastian Bach, Musical Director and Singing Master of the St. Thomas School, was carried to his grave July 30, 1750.

But the memory of Bach is enduring, his fame immortal and the love his beautiful music inspires increases from year to year, wherever that music is known, all over the world.

CHAPTER III

GEORGE FREDERICK HANDEL

WHILE little Sebastian Bach was laboriously copying out music by pale moonlight, because of his great love for it, another child of the same age was finding the greatest happiness of his life seated before an old spinet, standing in a lumber garret. He was trying to make music from those half dumb keys. No one had taught him how to play; it was innate genius that guided his little hands to find the right harmonies and bring melody out of the old spinet.

The boy's name was George Frederick Handel, and he was born in the German town of Halle, February 23, 1685. Almost from infancy he showed a remarkable fondness for music. His toys must be able to produce musical sounds or he did not care for them. The child did not inherit a love for music from his father, for Dr. Handel, who was a surgeon, looked on music with contempt, as something beneath the notice of a gentleman. He had decided his son was to be a lawyer, and refused to allow him to attend school for fear some one might teach him his notes. The mother was a sweet

Georg Friedrich Händel

gentle woman, a second wife, and much younger than her husband, who seemed to have ruled his household with a rod of iron.

When little George was about five, a kind friend, who knew how he longed to make music, had a spinet sent to him unbeknown to his father, and placed in a corner of the old garret. Here the child loved to come when he could escape notice. Often at night, when all were asleep, he would steal away to the garret and work at the spinet, mastering difficulties one by one. The strings of the instrument had been wound with cloth to deaden the sound, and thus made only a tiny tinkle.

After this secret practising had been going on for some time, it was discovered one night, when little George was enjoying his favorite pastime. He had been missed and the whole house went in search. Finally the father, holding high the lantern in his hand and followed by mother and the rest of the inmates, reached the garret, and there found the lost child seated at his beloved spinet, quite lost to the material world. There is no record of any angry outburst on the father's part and it is likely little George was left in peace.

One day when the boy was seven years old, the father was about to start for the castle of the Duke of Saxe-Weissenfels, to see his son, a stepbrother of George, who was a *valet de chambre* to the Duke. Little George begged to go too, for he knew there was music to be heard at the castle. In spite of his father's refusal he made up his mind to go if he had to run every step of the way. So watching his chance, he started to run after the coach in which his father rode. The child had no idea it was a distance of forty miles. He strove bravely to keep pace with the horses, but the roads were rough and muddy. His strength beginning to fail, he called out to the coachman to stop. His father, hearing the boy's voice, looked out of the window. Instead of scolding the little scamp roundly, he was touched by his woebegone appearance, had him lifted into the coach and carried on to Weissenfels.

George enjoyed himself hugely at the castle. The musicians were very kind to him, and his delight could hardly be restrained when he was allowed to try the beautiful organ in the chapel. The organist stood behind him and arranged the stops, and the child put his fingers on the keys that made the big pipes speak. During his stay, George had several chances to play; one was on a Sunday at the close of the service. The organist lifted him upon the bench and bade him play. Instead of the Duke and all his people leaving the chapel, they stayed to listen. When the music ceased the Duke asked: "Who is that child? Does anybody know his name?" The organist was sent for, and then little George was brought. The Duke patted him on the head, praised his playing and said he was sure to become a good musician. The organist then remarked he had heard the father disapproved of his musical studies. The Duke was greatly astonished. He sent for the father and after speaking highly of the boy's talent, said that to place any obstacle in the child's way would be unworthy of the father's honorable profession.

And so it was settled that George Frederick should

devote himself to music. Frederick Zachau, organist of the cathedral at Halle, was the teacher chosen to instruct the boy on the organ, harpsichord and violin. He also taught him composition, and showed him how different countries and composers differed in their ideas of musical style. Very soon the boy was composing the regular weekly service for the church, besides playing the organ whenever Zachau happened to be absent. At that time the boy could not have been more than eight years old.

After three years' hard work his teacher told him he must seek another master, as he could teach him nothing more. So the boy was sent to Berlin, to continue his studies. Two of the prominent musicians there were Ariosti and Buononcini; the former received the boy kindly and gave him great encouragement; the other took a dislike to the little fellow, and tried to injure him. Pretending to test his musicianship, Buononcini composed a very difficult piece for the harpsichord and asked him to play it at sight. This the boy did with ease and correctness. The Elector was delighted with the little musician, offered him a place at Court and even promised to send him to Italy to pursue his studies. Both offers were refused and George returned to Halle and to his old master, who was happy to have him back once more.

Not long after this the boy's father passed away, and as there was but little money left for the mother, her son decided at once that he must support himself and not deprive her of her small income. He acted as deputy organist at the Cathedral and Castle of Halle, and a few years later, when the post was vacant, secured it at a salary of less than forty dollars a year and free lodging. George Frederick was now seventeen and longed for a broader field. Knowing that he must leave Halle to find it, he said good-by to his mother, and in January 1703, set out for Hamburg to seek his fortune.

The Opera House Orchestra needed a supplementary violin. It was a very small post, but he took it, pretending not to be able to do anything better. However a chance soon came his way to show what he was capable of. One day the conductor, who always presided at the harpsichord, was absent, and no one was there to take his place. Without delay George came forward and took his vacant seat. He conducted so ably, that he secured the position for himself.

The young musician led a busy life in Hamburg, filled with teaching, study and composition. As his fame increased he secured more pupils, and he was not only able to support himself, but could send some money to his mother. He believed in saving money whenever he could; he knew a man should not only be self supporting, but somewhat independent, in order to produce works of art.

Handel now turned his attention to opera, composing "Almira, Queen of Castile," which was produced in Hamburg early in January 1705. This success encouraged him to write others; indeed he was the author of forty operas, which are only remembered now by an occasional aria. During these several years of hard work he had looked forward to a journey to

Italy, for study. He was now a composer of some note and decided it was high time to carry out his cherished desire.

He remained some time in Florence and composed the opera "Rodrigo," which was performed with great success. While in Venice he brought out another opera, "Agrippina," which had even greater success. Rome delighted him especially and he returned for a second time in 1709. Here he composed his first oratorio, the "Resurrection," which was produced there. Handel returned to Germany the following year. The Elector of Hanover was kind to him, and offered him the post of Capellmeister, with a salary of about fifteen hundred dollars. He had long desired to visit England, and the Elector gave him leave of absence. First, however, he went to Halle to see his mother and his old teacher. We can imagine the joy of the meeting, and how proud and happy both were at the success of the young musician. After a little time spent with his dear ones, he set out for England.

Handel came to London, preceded by the fame of his Italian success. Italian opera was the vogue just then in the English capital, but it was so badly produced that a man of Handel's genius was needed to properly set it before the people. He had not been long on English soil when he produced his opera "Rinaldo," at the Queen's Theater; it had taken him just two weeks to compose the opera. It had great success and ran night after night. There are many beautiful airs in "Rinaldo," some of which we hear to-day with the deepest pleasure. "Lascia ch'jo pianga" and "Cara si's sposa" are two of them. The

Londoners had welcomed Handel with great cordiality and with his new opera he was firmly established in their regard. With the young musician likewise there seemed to be a sincere affection for England. He returned in due time to his duties in Hanover, but he felt that London was the field for his future activities.

It was not very long after his return to Germany that he sought another leave of absence to visit England, promising to return within a "reasonable time." London received him with open arms and many great people showered favors upon him. Lord Burlington invited him to his residence in Piccadilly, which at that time consisted of green fields. The only return to be made for all this social and home luxury was that he should conduct the Earl's chamber concerts. Handel devoted his abundant leisure to composition, at which he worked with much ardor. His fame was making great strides, and when the Peace of Utrecht was signed and a Thanksgiving service was to be held in St. Paul's, he was commissioned to compose a Te Deum and Jubilate. To show appreciation for his work and in honor of the event, Queen Anne awarded Handel a life pension of a thousand dollars.

The death of the Queen, not long after, brought the Elector of Hanover to England, to succeed her as George I. It was not likely that King George would look with favor on his former Capellmeister, who had so long deserted his post. But an opportunity soon came to placate his Majesty. A royal entertainment, with decorated barges on the Thames was arranged.

An orchestra was to furnish the music, and the Lord Chamberlain commissioned Handel to compose music for the fête. He wrote a series of pieces, since known as "Water Music." The king was greatly delighted with the music, had it repeated, and learning that Handel conducted in person, sent for him, forgave all and granted him another pension of a thousand dollars. He was also appointed teacher to the daughters of the Prince of Wales, at a salary of a thousand a year. With the combined sum (three thousand dollars) which he now received, he felt quite independent, indeed a man of means.

Not long after this Handel was appointed Chapel master to the Duke of Chandos, and was expected to live at the princely mansion he inhabited. The size and magnificence of The Cannons was the talk of the country for miles around. Here the composer lived and worked, played the organ in the chapel, composed church music for the service and wrote his first English oratorio, "Esther." This was performed in the Duke's chapel, and the Duke on this occasion handed the composer five thousand dollars. Numerous compositions for the harpsichord belong to this period, among them the air and variations known as "The Harmonious Blacksmith." The story goes that Handel was walking to Cannons through the village of Edgeware, and being overtaken by a heavy shower, sought shelter in the smithy. The blacksmith was singing at his work and his hammer kept time with his song. The composer was struck with the air and its accompaniment, and as soon as he reached home, wrote out the tune with the variations. This story has been disputed, and it is not known whether it is true or not.

When Handel first came to London, he had done much to encourage the production of opera in the Italian style. Later these productions had to be given up for lack of money, and the King's Theater remained closed for a long time. Finally a number of rich men formed a society to revive opera in London. The King subscribed liberally to the venture. Handel was at once engaged as composer and impressario. He started work on a new opera and when that was well along, set out for Germany, going to Dresden to select singers. On his return he stopped at Halle, where his mother was still living, but his old teacher had passed away.

The new opera "Radamisto" was ready early in 1720, and produced at the Royal Academy of Music, as the theater was now called. The success of the production was tremendous. But Handel, by his self-will had stirred up envy and jealousy, and an opposition party was formed, headed by his old enemy from Hamburg, Buononcini, who had come to London to try his fortunes. A test opera was planned, of which Handel wrote the third act, Buononcini the second and a third musician the first. When the new work was performed, the third act was pronounced by the judges much superior to the second. But Buononcini's friends would not accept defeat, and the battle between all parties was violent. Newspapers were full of it, and many verses were written. Handel cared not a whit for all this tempest, but calmly went his way.

In 1723, his opera "Ottone" was to be produced. The great singer Cuzzoni had been engaged, but the capricious lady did not arrive in England till the rehearsals were far advanced, which of course did not please the composer. When she did appear she refused to sing the aria as he had composed it. He flew into a rage, took her by the arm and threatened to throw her out of the window unless she obeyed. The singer was so frightened by his anger that she sang as he directed, and made a great success of the aria.

Handel's industry in composing for the Royal Academy of Music was untiring. For the first eight years from the beginning of the Society's work he had composed and produced fourteen operas. During all this time, his enemies never ceased their efforts to destroy him. The great expense of operatic production, the troubles and quarrels with singers, at last brought the Academy to the end of its resources. At this juncture, the famous "Beggar's Opera," by John Gay, was brought out at a rival theater. It was a collection of most beautiful melodies from various sources, used with words quite unworthy of them. But the fickle public hailed the piece with delight, and its success was the means of bringing total failure to the Royal Academy. Handel, however, in spite of the schemes of his enemies, was determined to carry on the work with his own fortune, He went again to Italy to engage new singers, stopping at Halle to see his mother who was ill. She passed away the next year at the age of eighty.

Handel tried for several years to keep Italian opera

going in London, in spite of the lack of musical taste and the opposition of his enemies; but in 1737, he was forced to give up the struggle. He was deeply in debt, his whole fortune of ten thousand pounds had been swept away and his health broken by anxiety. He would not give up; after a brief rest, he returned to London to begin the conflict anew. The effort to re-awaken the English public's interest in Italian opera seemed useless, and the composer at last gave up the struggle. He was now fifty-five, and began to think of turning his attention to more serious work. Handel has been called the father of the oratorio; he composed at least twenty-eight works in this style, the best known being "Samson," "Israel in Egypt," "Jephtha," "Saul," "Judas Maccabæus" and greatest of all, the "Messiah."

The composer conceived the idea of writing the last named work in 1741. Towards the end of this year he was invited to visit Ireland to make known some of his works. On the way there he was detained at Chester for several days by contrary winds. He must have had the score of the "Messiah" with him, for he got together some choir boys to try over a few of the choral parts. "Can you sing at sight?" was put to each boy before he was asked to sing. One broke down at the start. "What de devil you mean!" cried the impetuous composer, snatching the music from him. "Didn't you say you could sing at sight?"

"Yes sir, but not at *first* sight."

The people of Dublin warmly welcomed Handel, and the new oratorio, the "Messiah," was performed at

Music Hall, with choirs of both cathedrals, and with some concertos on the organ played by the composer. The performance took place, April 13, 1742. Four hundred pounds were realized, which were given to charity. The success was so great that a second performance was announced. Ladies were requested to come without crinoline, thereby providing a hundred more seats than at the first event.

The Irish people were so cordial, that the composer remained almost a year among them. For it was not till March 23, 1743, that the "Messiah" was performed in London. The King was one of the great audience who heard it. All were so deeply impressed by the Hallelujah chorus, that with the opening words, "For the Lord God omnipotent reigneth," the whole audience, including the King, sprang to their feet, and remained standing through the entire chorus. From that time to this it has always been the custom to stand during this chorus, whenever it is performed.

Once started on this line of thought, one oratorio after another flowed from his prolific pen, though none of them proved to be as exalted in conception as the "Messiah." The last work of this style was "Jephtha," which contains the beautiful song, "Waft her, angels." While engaged in composing this oratorio, Handel became blind, but this affliction did not seem to lessen his power for work. He was now sixty-eight, and had conquered and lived down most of the hostility that had been so bitter against him. His fortunes also constantly improved, so that when he passed away he left twenty thousand pounds.

The great composer was a big man, both physically and mentally. A friend describes his countenance as full of fire; "when he smiled it was like the sun bursting out of a black cloud. It was a sudden flash of intelligence, wit and good humor, which illumined his countenance, which I have hardly ever seen in any other." He could relish a joke, and had a keen sense of humor. Few things outside his work interested him; but he was fond of the theater, and liked to go to picture sales. His fiery temper often led him to explode at trifles. No talking among the listeners could be borne by him while he was conducting. He did not hesitate to visit violent abuse on the heads of those who ventured to speak while he was directing and not even the presence of royalty could restrain his anger.

Handel was always generous in assisting those who needed aid, and he helped found the Society for Aiding Distressed Musicians. His last appearance in public, was at a performance of the "Messiah," at Covent Garden, on April 6, 1759. His death occurred on the 14th of the same month, at the house in Brook Street where he had lived for many years. Thus, while born in the same year as Sebastian Bach, he outlived him by about a decade. He was buried in Westminster Abbey, and later a fine monument was erected to his memory. The most of his manuscripts came into the possession of King George III, and are preserved in the musical library of Buckingham Palace.

CHAPTER IV

CHRISTOPH WILLIBALD GLUCK

CHRISTOPH WILLIBALD GLUCK has been called the "regenerator of the opera" for he appeared just at the right moment to rescue opera from the deplorable state into which it had fallen. At that time the composers often yielded to the caprices of the singers and wrote to suit them, while the singers themselves, through vanity and ignorance, made such requirements that opera itself often became ridiculous. Gluck desired "to restrict the art of music to its true object, that of aiding the effect of poetry by giving greater expression to words and scenes, without interrupting the action or the plot." He wrote only operas, and some of his best works keep the stage to-day. They are simple in design yet powerful in appeal: very original and stamped with refinement and true feeling.

The boy Christoph, like many another lad who became a great musician, had a sorrowful childhood, full of poverty and neglect. His home was in the little town of Weissenwangen, on the borders of Bohemia, where he was born July 2, 1714. As a little lad he early manifested a love for music, but his parents were in very straitened circumstances and could not afford to pay for musical instruction. He was sent to one of the public schools. Fortunately the art of reading music from notes, formation of scales and fundamentals, was taught along with general school subjects.

While his father lived the boy was sure of sympathy and affection, though circumstances were of the poorest. But the good man passed away when the boy was quite young, and then matters were much worse. He was gradually neglected until he was at last left to shift for himself.

He possessed not only talent but perseverance and the will to succeed. The violoncello attracted him, and he began to teach himself to play it, with no other help than an old instruction book. Determination conquered many difficulties however, and before long he had made sufficient progress to enable him to join a troop of traveling minstrels. From Prague they made their way to Vienna.

Arrived in Vienna, that rich, gay, laughter-loving city, where the people loved music and often did much for it, the youth's musical talent together with his forlorn appearance and condition won sympathy from a few generous souls, who not only provided a home and took care of his material needs, but gave him also the means to continue his musical studies. Christoph was overcome with gratitude and made the best possible use of his opportunities. For nearly two years he gave himself up to his musical studies.

Italy was the goal of his ambition, and at last the opportunity to visit that land of song was within his grasp. At the age of twenty-four, in the year 1738, Gluck bade adieu to his many kind friends in Vienna, and set out to complete his studies in Italy. Milan was his objective point. Soon after arriving there he had the good fortune to meet Padre Martini, the celebrated master of musical theory. Young Gluck at once placed himself under the great man's guidance and labored diligently with him for about four years. How much he owed to the careful training Martini was able to give, was seen in even his first attempts at operatic composition.

At the conclusion of this long period of devoted study, Gluck began to write an opera, entitled "Artaxerxes." When completed it was accepted at the Milan Theater, brought out in 1741 and met with much success. This success induced one of the managers in Venice to offer him an engagement for that city if he would compose a new opera. Gluck then produced "Clytemnestra." This second work had a remarkable success, and the managers arranged for the composition of another opera, which was "Demetrio," which, like the others was most favorably received.

Gluck now had offers from Turin, so that the next two years were spent between that city and Milan, for which cities he wrote five or six operas. By this time the name of Gluck had become famous all over Italy; indeed his fame had spread to other countries, with the result that tempting offers for new operas flowed in to him from all directions. Especially was a London manager, a certain Lord Middlesex, anxious to entice the young composer from Italy to come over to London, and produce some of his works at the King's Theater in the Haymarket.

The noble manager made a good offer too, and Gluck felt he ought to accept. He reached London in 1745, but owing to the rebellion which had broken out in Scotland all the theaters were closed, and the city in more or less confusion. However a chance to hear the famous German composer, who had traveled such a distance, was not to be lost, and Lord Middlesex besought the Powers to re-open the theater. After much pleading his request was finally granted. The opening opera, written on purpose to introduce Gluck to English audiences, was entitled "La Caduta del Giganti,"—"Fall of the Giants"—and did not seem to please the public. But the young composer was undaunted. His next opera, "Artamene," pleased them no better. The mind of the people was taken up at that period with politics and political events, and they cared less than usual for music and the arts. Then, too, Handel, at the height of his fame, was living in London, honored and courted by the aristocracy and the world of fashion.

Though disappointed at his lack of success, Gluck remained in England several years, constantly composing operas, none of which seemed to win success. At last he took his way quietly back to Vienna. In 1754, he was invited to Rome, where he produced several operas, among them "Antigone"; they were all successful, showing the Italians appreciated his work. He now proceeded to Florence, and while there became acquainted with an Italian poet, Ranieri di Calzabigi. They were mutually attracted to each other, and on parting had sworn to use their influence and talents to reform Italian opera.

Gluck returned to Vienna, and continued to compose operas. In 1764, "Orfeo" was produced,—an example of the new reform in opera! "Orfeo" was received most favorably and sung twenty-eight times, a long run for those days. The singing and acting of Guadagni made the opera quite the rage, and the work began to be known in England. Even in Paris and Parma it became a great favorite. The composer was now fifty, and his greatest works had yet—with the exception or "Orfeo"—to be written. He began to develop that purity of style which we find in "Alceste," "Iphigénie en Tauride" and others. "Alceste" was the second opera on the reformed plan which simplified the music to give more prominence to the poetry. It was produced in Vienna in 1769, with the text written by Calzabigi. The opera was ahead of "Orfeo" in simplicity and nobility, but it did not seem to please the critics. The composer himself wrote: "Pedants and critics, an infinite multitude, form the greatest obstacle to the progress of art. They think themselves entitled to pass a verdict on 'Alceste' from some informal rehearsals, badly conducted and executed. Some fastidious ear found a vocal passage too harsh, or another too impassioned, forgetting that forcible expression and striking contrasts are absolutely necessary. It was likewise decided in full conclave, that this style of music was barbarous and extravagant."

In spite of the judgment of the critics, "Alceste"

increased the fame of Gluck to a great degree. Paris wanted to see the man who had revolutionized Italian opera. The French Royale Académie had made him an offer to visit the capital, for which he was to write a new opera for a début. A French poet, Du Rollet, living in Vienna, offered to write a libretto for the new opera, and assured him there was every chance for success in a visit to France. The libretto was thereupon written, or rather arranged from Racine's "Iphigénie en Aulide," and with this, Chevalier Gluck, lately made Knight of the papal order of the Golden Spur, set out for Paris.

And now began a long season of hard work. The opera "Iphigénie" took about a year to compose, besides a careful study of the French language. He had even more trouble with the slovenly, ignorant orchestra, than he had with the French language. The orchestra declared itself against foreign music; but this opposition was softened down by his former pupil and patroness, the charming Marie Antoinette, Queen of France.

After many trials and delays, "Iphigénie" was produced August 19, 1774. The opera proved an enormous success. The beautiful Queen herself gave the signal for applause in which the whole house joined. The charming Sophie Arnould sang the part of Iphigénie and seemed to quite satisfy the composer. Larrivée was the Agamemnon, and other parts were well sung. The French were thoroughly delighted. They fêted and praised Gluck, declaring he had discovered the music of the ancient Greeks, that he was the only man in Europe who could express real feelings in music. Marie Antoinette wrote to her sister: "We had, on the nineteenth, the first performance of Gluck's 'Iphigénie,' and it was a glorious triumph. I was quite enchanted, and nothing else is talked of. All the world wishes to see the piece, and Gluck seems well satisfied."

The next year, 1775, Gluck brought out an adaptation suitable for the French stage, of his "Alceste," which again aroused the greatest enthusiasm. The theater was crammed at every performance. Marie Antoinette's favorite composer was again praised to the skies, and was declared to be the greatest composer living.

But Gluck had one powerful opponent at the French Court, who was none other than the famous Madame du Barry, the favorite of Louis XV. Since the Queen had her pet musical composer, Mme. du Barry wished to have hers. An Italian by birth, she could gather about her a powerful Italian faction, who were bent upon opposition to the Austrian Gluck. She had listened to his praises long enough, and the tremendous success of "Alceste" had been the last straw and brought things to a climax. Du Barry would have some one to represent Italian music, and applied to the Italian ambassador to desire Piccini to come to Paris.

On the arrival of Piccini, Madame du Barry began activities, aided by Louis XV himself. She gathered a powerful Italian party about her, and their first act was to induce the Grand Opera management to make Piccini an offer for a new opera, although they had already made the same offer to Gluck. This breach of good faith led to a furious war, in which all Paris joined; it was fierce and bitter while it lasted. Even politics were forgotten for the time being. Part of the press took up one side and part the other. Many pamphlets, poems and satires appeared, in which both composers were unmercifully attacked. Gluck was at the time in Germany, and Piccini had come to Paris principally to secure the tempting fee offered him. The leaders of the feud kept things well stirred up, so that a stranger could not enter a cafe, hotel or theater without first answering the question whether he stood for Gluck or Piccini. Many foolish lies were told of Gluck in his absence. It was declared by the Piccinists that he went away on purpose, to escape the war; that he could no longer write melodies because he was a dried up old man and had nothing new to give France. These lies and false stories were put to flight one evening when the Abbé Arnaud, one of Gluck's most ardent adherents, declared in an aristocratic company, that the Chevalier was returning to France with an "Orlando" and an "Armide" in his portfolio.

"Piccini is also working on an 'Orlando,'" spoke up a follower of that redoubtable Italian.

"That will be all the better," returned the abbé, "for we shall then have an 'Orlando' and also an 'Orlandino.'"

When Gluck arrived in Paris, he brought with him the finished opera of "Armide," which was produced at the Paris Grand Opera on September 23, 1777. At first it was merely a *succès d'estime,* but soon became immensely popular. On the first night many of the critics were against the opera, which was called too noisy. The composer, however, felt he had done some of his best work in "Armide"; that the music was written in such style that it would not grow old, at least not for a long time. He had taken the greatest pains in composing it, and declared that if it were not properly rehearsed at the Opera he would not let them have it at all, but would retain the work himself for his own pleasure. He wrote to a friend: "I have put forth what little strength is left in me, into 'Armide'; I confess I should like to finish my career with it."

It is said the Gluck composed "Armide" in order to praise the beauty of Marie Antoinette, and she for her part showed the deepest interest in the success of the piece, and really "became quite a slave to it." Gluck often told her he "rearranged his music according to the impression it made upon the Queen."

"Great as was the success of 'Armide,'" wrote the Princess de Lamballe, "no one prized this beautiful work more highly than the composer of it. He was passionately enamored of it; he told the Queen the air of France had rejuvenated his creative powers, and the sight of her majesty had given such a wonderful impetus to the flow of ideas, that his composition had become like herself, angelic, sublime."

The growing success of "Armide" only added fuel to the flame of controversy which had been stirred up. To cap the climax, Piccini had finished his opera, which was duly brought out and met with a brilliant reception. Indeed its success was greater than that won by "Armide," much to the delight of the Piccinists. Of course the natural outcome was that the other party should do something to surpass the work of their rivals. Marie Antoinette was besought to prevail on Gluck to write another opera.

A new director was now in charge of the Opera House. He conceived the bright idea of setting the two composers at work on the same subject, which was to be "Iphigénie en Tauride." This plan made great commotion in the ranks of the rival factions, as each wished to have their composer's work performed first. The director promised that Piccini's opera should be first placed in rehearsal. Gluck soon finished his and handed it in, but the Italian, trusting to the director's word of honor, was not troubled when he heard the news, though he determined to complete his as soon as possible. A few days later, when he went to the Opera House with his completed score, he was horrified to find the work of his rival already in rehearsal. There was a lively scene, but the manager said he had received orders to produce the work of Gluck at once, and he must obey. On the 18th of May, 1779, the Gluck opera was first performed. It produced the greatest excitement and had a marvelous success. Even Piccini succumbed to the spell, for the music made such an impression on him that he did not wish his own work to be brought out.

The director, however, insisted, and soon after the second Iphigénie appeared. The first night the opera did not greatly please; the next night proved a comic tragedy, as the prima donna was intoxicated. After a couple of days' imprisonment she returned and sang well. But the war between the two factions continued till the death of Gluck, and the retirement of Piccini.

The following year, in September, Gluck finished a new opera, "Echo et Narcisse," and with this work decided to close his career, feeling he was too old to write longer for the lyric stage. He was then nearly seventy years old, and retired to Vienna, to rest and enjoy the fruits of all his years of incessant toil. He was now rich, as he had earned nearly thirty thousand pounds. Kings and princes came to do him honor, and to tell him what pleasure his music had always given them.

Gluck passed away on November 15, 1787, honored and beloved by all. The simple beauty and purity of his music are as moving and expressive to-day as when it was written, and the "Michael of Music" speaks to us still in his operas, whenever they are adequately performed.

CHAPTER V

JOSEF HAYDN

In Josef Haydn we have one of the classic composers, a sweet, gentle spirit, who suffered many privations in early life, and through his own industrious efforts rose to positions of respect and honor, the result of unremitting toil and devotion to a noble ideal. Like many of the other great musicians, through hardship and sorrow he won his place among the elect.

Fifteen leagues south of Vienna, amid marshy flats along the river Leitha, lies the small village of Rehrau. At the end of the straggling street which constitutes the village, stood a low thatched cottage and next to it a wheelwright's shop, with a small patch of greensward before it. The master wheelwright, Mathias Haydn, was sexton, too, of the little church on the hill. He was a worthy man and very religious. A deep love for music was part of the man's nature, and it was shared to a large extent by his wife Maria. Every Sunday evening he would bring out his harp, on which he had taught himself to play, and he and his wife would sing songs and hymns, accompanied by the harp. The children, too, would add their voices to the concert.

The little boy Josef, sat near his father and watched his playing with rapt attention. Sometimes he would take two sticks and make believe play the violin, just as he had seen the village schoolmaster do. And when he sang hymns with the others, his voice was sweet and true. The father watched the child with interest, and a new hope rose within him. His own life had been a bitter disappointment, for he had been unable to satisfy his longing for a knowledge of the art he loved. Perhaps Josef might one day become a musician—indeed he might even rise to be Capellmeister.

Little Josef was born March 31, 1732. The mother had a secret desire that the boy should join the priesthood, but the father, as we have seen, hoped he would make a musical career, and determined, though poor in this world's goods, to aid him in every possible way.

About this time a distant relative, one Johann Mathias Frankh by name, arrived at the Haydn cottage on a visit. He was a schoolmaster at Hainburg, a little town four leagues away. During the regular evening concert he took particular notice of Josef and his toy violin. The child's sweet voice indicated that he had the makings of a good musician. At last he said: "If you will let me take Sepperl, I will see he is properly taught; I can see he promises well."

The parents were quite willing and as for little Sepperl, he was simply overjoyed, for he longed to learn more about the beautiful music which filled his soul. He went with his new cousin, as he called Frankh, without any hesitation, and with the expectation that his childish day dreams were to be realized.

A new world indeed opened to the six year old boy, but it was not all beautiful. Frankh was a careful and strict teacher; Josef not only was taught to sing well, but learned much about various instruments. He had school lessons also. But his life in other ways was hard and cheerless. The wife of his cousin treated him with the utmost indifference, never looking after his clothing or his well being in any way. After a time his destitute and neglected appearance was a source of misery to the refined, sensitive boy, but he tried to realize that present conditions could not last forever, and he bravely endeavored to make the best of them. Meanwhile the training of his voice was well advanced and when not in school he could nearly always be found in church, listening to the organ and the singing. Not long after, he was admitted to the choir, where his sweet young voice joined in the church anthems. Always before his mind was a great city where he knew he would find the most beautiful music—the music of his dreams. That city was Vienna, but it lay far away. Josef looked down at his ragged clothing and wondered if he would ever see that magical city.

One morning his cousin told him there would be a procession through the town in honor of a prominent citizen who had just passed away. A drummer was needed and the cousin had proposed Josef. He showed the boy how to make the strokes for a march, with the result that Josef walked in the procession and felt quite proud of this exhibition of his skill. The very drum

51

he used that day is preserved in the little church at Hainburg.

A great event occurred in Josef's prospects at the end of his second year of school life at Hainburg. The Capellmeister, Reutter by name, of St. Stephen's cathedral in Vienna, came to see his friend, the pastor of Hainburg. He happened to say he was looking for a few good voices for the choir. "I can find you one at least," said the pastor; "he is a scholar of Frankh, the schoolmaster, and has a sweet voice."

Josef was sent for and the schoolmaster soon returned leading him by the hand.

"Well my little fellow," said the Capellmeister, drawing him to his knee, "can you make a shake?"

"No sir, but neither can my cousin Frankh."

Reutter laughed at this frankness, and then proceeded to show him how the shake was done. Josef after a few trials was able to perform the shake to the entire satisfaction of his teacher. After testing him on a portion of a mass the Capellmeister was willing to take him to the Cantorei or Choir school of St. Stephen's in Vienna. The boy's heart gave a great leap. Vienna, the city of his dreams. And he was really going there! He could scarcely believe in his good fortune. If he could have known all that was to befall him there, he might not have been so eager to go. But he was only a little eight-year-old boy, and childhood's dreams are rosy.

Once arrived at the Cantorei, Josef plunged into his studies with great fervor, and his progress was most rapid. He was now possessed with a desire to compose, but had not the slightest idea how to go about such a feat. However, he hoarded every scrap of music paper he could find and covered it with notes. Reutter gave no encouragement to such proceedings. One day he asked what the boy was about, and when he heard the lad was composing a "Salve Regina," for twelve voices, he remarked it would be better to write it for two voices before attempting it in twelve. "And if you must try your hand at composition," added Reutter more kindly, "write variations on the motets and vespers which are played in church."

As neither the Capellmeister nor any of the teachers offered to show Josef the principles of composition, he was thrown upon his own resources. With much self denial he scraped together enough money to buy two books which he had seen at the second hand bookseller's and which he had longed to possess. One was Fox's "Gradus ad Parnassum," a treatise on composition and counterpoint; the other Matheson's "The Complete Capellmeister." Happy in the possession of these books, Josef used every moment outside of school and choir practise to study them. He loved fun and games as well as any boy, but music always came first. The desire to perfect himself was so strong that he often added several hours each day to those already required, working sixteen or eighteen hours out of the twenty-four.

And thus a number of years slipped away amid these happy surroundings. Little Josef was now a likely lad of about fifteen years. It was arranged that his younger brother Michael was to come to the Cantorei. Josef looked eagerly forward to this event, planning how he would help the little one over the beginning and show him the pleasant things that would happen to him in the new life. But the elder brother could not foresee the sorrow and privation in store for him. From the moment Michael's pure young voice filled the vast spaces of the cathedral, it was plain that Josef's singing could not compete with it. His soprano showed signs of breaking, and gradually the principal solo parts, which had always fallen to him, were given to the new chorister. On a special church day, when there was more elaborate music, the "Salve Regina," which had always been given to Josef, was sung so beautifully by the little brother, that the Emperor and Empress were delighted, and they presented the young singer with twenty ducats.

Poor Josef! He realized that his place was virtually taken by the brother he had welcomed so joyously only a short time before. No one was to blame of course; it was one of those things that could not be avoided. But what actually caused him to leave St. Stephen's was a boyish prank played on one of the choir boys, who sat in front of him. Taking up a new pair of shears lying near, he snipped off, in a mischievous moment, the boy's pigtail. For this jest he was punished and then dismissed from the school. He could hardly realize it, in his first dazed, angry condition. Not to enjoy the busy life any more, not to see Michael and the others and have a comfortable home and sing in the Cathedral. How he lived after that he hardly knew. But several miserable days went by. One rainy night a young man whom he had known before, came upon him near the Cathedral, and was struck by his white, pinched face. He asked where the boy was living. "Nowhere—I am starving," was the reply. Honest Franz Spangler was touched at once.

"We can't stand here in the rain," he said. "You know I haven't a palace to offer, but you are welcome to share my poor place for one night anyway. Then we shall see."

It was indeed a poor garret where the Spanglers lived, but the cheerful fire and warm bread and milk were luxuries to the starving lad. Best of all was it to curl up on the floor, beside the dying embers and fall into refreshing slumber. The next morning the world looked brighter. He had made up his mind not to try and see his brother; he would support himself by music. He did not know just how he was going to do this, but determined to fight for it *and never give in.*

Spangler, deeply touched by the boy's forlorn case, offered to let him occupy a corner of his garret until he could find work, and Josef gratefully accepted. The boy hoped he could quickly find something to do; but many weary months were spent in looking for employment and in seeking to secure pupils, before there was the slightest sign of success. Thinly clad as he was and with the vigorous appetite of seventeen, which was scarcely ever appeased, he struggled on, hopeful that spring would bring some sort of good cheer.

But spring came, yet no employment was in sight. His sole earnings had been the coppers thrown to him as he stood singing in the snow covered streets, during the long cold winter. Now it was spring, and hope rose within him. He had been taught to have simple faith in God, and felt sure that in some way his needs would be met.

At last the tide turned slightly. A few pupils attracted by the small fee he charged, took lessons on the clavier; he got a few engagements to play violin at balls and parties, while some budding composers got him to revise their manuscripts for a small fee. All these cheering signs of better times made Josef hopeful and grateful. One day a special piece of good fortune came his way. A man who loved music, at whose house he had sometimes played, sent him a hundred and fifty florins, to be repaid without interest whenever convenient.

This sum seemed to Haydn a real fortune. He was able to leave the Spanglers and take up a garret of his own. There was no stove in it and winter was coming on; it was only partly light, even at midday, but the youth was happy. For he had acquired a little worm-eaten spinet, and he had added to his treasures the first six sonatas of Emmanuel Bach.

On the third floor of the house which contained the garret, lived a celebrated Italian poet, Metastasio. Haydn and the poet struck up an acquaintance, which resulted in the musician's introduction to the poet's favorite pupil, Marianne Martinez. Also through Metastasio, Haydn met Nicolo Porpora, an eminent teacher of singing and composition. About this time another avenue opened to him. It was a fashion in Vienna to pick up a few florins by serenading prominent persons. A manager of one of the principal theaters in Vienna, Felix Kurz, had recently married a beautiful woman, whose loveliness was much talked of. It occurred to Haydn to take a couple of companions along and serenade the lady, playing some of his own music. Soon after they had begun to play the house door opened and Kurz himself stood there in dressing gown and slippers. "Whose music was that you were playing?" he asked. "My own," was the answer. "Indeed; then just step inside." The three entered, wondering. They were presented to Madame, then were given refreshments. "Come and see me to-morrow," said Kurz when the boys left; "I think I have some work for you."

Haydn called next day and learned the manager had written a libretto of a comic opera which he called "The Devil on two Sticks," and was looking for some one to compose the music. In one place there was to be a tempest at sea, and Haydn was asked how he would represent that. As he had never seen the sea, he was at a loss how to express it. The manager said he himself had never seen the ocean, but to his mind it was like this, and he began to toss his arms wildly about. Haydn tried every way he could think of to represent the ocean, but Kurz was not satisfied. At last he flung his hands down with a crash on each end of the keyboard and brought them together in the middle. "That's it, that's it," cried the manager and embraced the youth excitedly. All went well with the rest of the opera. It was finished and produced, but did not make much stir, a fact which was not displeasing to the composer, as he was not proud of his first attempt.

His acquaintance with Porpora promised better things. The singing master had noticed his skill in playing the harpsichord, and offered to engage him as accompanist. Haydn gladly accepted at once, hoping to pick up much musical knowledge in this way. Old Porpora was very harsh and domineering at first, treating him more like a valet than a musician. But at last he was won over by Haydn's gentleness and patience, until he was willing to answer all his questions and to correct his compositions. Best of all he brought Haydn to the attention of the nobleman in whose house he was teaching, so that when the nobleman and his family went to the baths of Mannersdorf for several months, Haydn was asked to go along as accompanist to Porpora.

The distinguished musicians he met at Mannersdorf were all very kind to him and showed much interest in his compositions, many of which were performed during this visit. The nobleman, impressed with Haydn's desire to succeed, allotted him a pension of a sum equal to fifteen dollars a month. The young musician's first act on receiving this was to buy himself a neat suit of black.

Good fortune followed him on his return to Vienna. More pupils came, until he was able to raise his prices and move into better lodgings. A wealthy patron of music, the Countess of Thun, sent for him to come and see her. She had heard one of his clavier sonatas played, found it charming and wished to see the composer. Her manner was so sympathetic, that Haydn was led to tell her the story of his struggles. Tears came into her eyes as she listened. She promised her support as friend and pupil, and Haydn left her with a happy, grateful heart.

His compositions were heard in the best musical circles in Vienna, and the future was bright with promise. A wealthy music patron persuaded him to write a string quartet, the first of many to follow. Through this man he received, in 1759, an appointment of music director to a rich Bohemian, Count Morzin, who had a small orchestra at his country seat. In the same year the first Symphony was composed.

As brighter days dawned, Haydn procured all the works on theory obtainable, and studied them deeply. He had mastered the difficulties of the "Gradus," one of the books purchased years before, and without any outside help had worked out his musical independence, uninfluenced by any other musician. He was now twenty-six, and his fame was growing. Meanwhile an affair of the heart had great influence on his life. Sometime previously Haydn had been engaged to give lessons on the harpsichord to two daughters of a wig-maker named Keller. An attachment soon sprang up between the teacher and the younger of the girls. His poverty had stood in the way of making his feelings known. But as prosperity began to dawn, he grew courageous and asked the maiden to become his wife. His disappointment was keen when he found the girl had in the meantime decided to take the veil. The wig-maker proved to be a matchmaker, for when he learned how matters stood he urged the composer to take the sister, who was only three years older. The gentle Haydn was unable to withstand the pressure brought to bear, and consented. After his bride was his he found he had won a virago, one who cared nothing for art or for her husband's ideals, if only she could have enough money to spend.

The composer was in sad straits for a while, but fortunately a way opened by means of which he could be free. Count Morzin, where he had conducted the orchestra, was obliged to reduce his establishment and dismissed his band and its director. As soon as this was known, the reigning Prince of Hungary, Paul Anton Esterházy offered Haydn the post of assistant Capellmeister at his country seat of Eisenstadt. The head Capellmeister, Werner, was old, but the Prince kept him on account of his long service. Haydn, however, was to have entire control of the orchestra, and also of most of the musical arrangements.

Haydn was blissfully happy over the realization of his highest hopes. In his wildest dreams he had never imagined such magnificence as he found at the palace of Eisenstadt. The great buildings, troops of servants, the wonderful parks and gardens, with their flowers, lakes and fountains almost made him believe he was in fairyland. Of course there would be some hard work, though it would not seem hard amid such fascinating surroundings and there would be plenty of leisure for his own creative activities. Best of all his wife could not be with him.

Prince Paul Anton passed away after a year and his brother Nikolaus succeeded him. He advanced Haydn still further, and increased his salary. Werner, the old

Capellmeister, died in 1766, and Haydn succeeded to the full title. This was the father's dream for his boy Josef, and it had been abundantly realized. His mother had passed away, but his father was living, and had come, on one occasion, to Eisenstadt to see him. His brother Michael who had now become Concertmeister in Salzburg, spent several happy days with him also.

The summer residence of Prince Nikolaus at Esterházy had been rebuilt, enlarged and was more magnificent than Eisenstadt. The music was more elaborate. The Prince was so fond of the life there that he postponed his return to town till late in the autumn.

In order to give him a hint through music, Haydn composed what he called the "Farewell Symphony," in which, toward the close each pair of players in turn rose, extinguished their candles and passed out, until only the first violinist remained. He last of all blew out his light and left, while Haydn prepared to follow. The Prince at last understood, and treating the whole as a joke, gave orders for the departure of the household.

In 1790 Haydn lost the master to whom he was so devotedly attached. He received a pension of a thousand florins on condition that he would retain his post. But Prince Anton, who succeeded his brother, cared nothing for music; Haydn was not obliged to live at the palace and returned to Vienna. Several attempts had already been made to induce him to visit London, but he always had refused. Now there seemed to be no obstacle in the way. One day a visitor called. "My name is Salomon; I have come from London to fetch you; we will settle terms tomorrow." On the sail from Calais to Dover, the composer first saw the sea and was reminded of his boyish efforts to describe it in tones.

London welcomed Haydn warmly, for his fame had preceded him and his music was familiar. The first concert was given March 11, 1790 at the Hanover Square Rooms, and was a great success. This was followed by a series of concerts, and at last a benefit for the composer on May 16, which was an ovation and realized three hundred and fifty pounds. He heard the "Messiah" for the first time and when, at the "Hallelujah Chorus," the audience sprang to its feet, he burst into tears, exclaiming "He is the master of us all!"

At Oxford, in July, he received the honorary degree of Doctor of Music, and three great concerts were given in his honor, with special performers brought from London. In fact the whole visit to England had been such a success that he repeated the trip in 1794, and received even greater honors. His symphonies were heard on all London programs. He was the lion of the season, and was frequently invited to Buckingham Palace to play for the King and Queen, who always urged him to live in England. Haydn was now sixty-five; he had composed quantities of music, but his greatest work, "The Creation," was not yet written. While in London, Salomon had shown him a poem founded on "Paradise Lost," written years before in the hope that Handel would use it for an oratorio. Haydn decided to try his hand at oratorio on this subject. As he went on, it grew to be a labor of love and prayer. It was finished and performed in Vienna, March 19, 1799, and made a profound impression. The composer at once began work on a second oratorio, founded on Thompson's "Seasons." The desire for work was strong within, but his health was failing. " 'The Seasons' gave me my finishing stroke," he often remarked to friends.

Haydn was acknowledged on every hand as the father of instrumental music. He laid great stress on melody. "It is the air which is the charm of music," he said, "and it is the air which is the most difficult to produce. The invention of a fine melody is a work of genius."

Full of years and honors, respected and beloved, Father Haydn passed away. As Vienna was at that time in the hands of the French, he was given a very simple burial. In 1820 Prince Esterházy had the remains reinterred in the upper parish church at Eisenstadt, where a simple stone with Latin inscription is placed in the wall above the vault to mark the spot.

CHAPTER VI

WOLFGANG MOZART

THE early December dusk was closing in over the quaint old city of Salzburg. Up on the heights above the town the battlements of the great castle caught a reflection of the last gleams of light in the sky. But the narrow streets below were quite in shadow.

In one of the substantial looking houses on a principal thoroughfare, called the Getreide Gasse, lights gleamed from windows on the third floor. Within, all was arranged as if for some special occasion. The larger room, with its three windows looking on the street, was immaculate in its neatness. The brass candlesticks shone like gold, the mahogany table was polished like a mirror, the simple furniture likewise. For today was Father Mozart's birthday and the little household was to celebrate the event.

Mother Mozart had been busy all day putting everything in order while Nannerl, the seven year old daughter, had been helping. Little Wolfgang, now three years old, in his childish eagerness to be as busy as the others, had only hindered, and had to be reprimanded once in a while. One could never be vexed with the little elf, even if he turned somersaults in new clean clothes, or made chalk figures all over the living-room chairs. He never meant to do any harm, and was always so tenderhearted and lovable, it was hard to scold him.

And this was the Father's birthday, about the most important of all the family celebrations. Already the roast on the spit was nearing perfection, while in the oven a fine cake was browning.

When all was ready and Leopold Mozart had received the good wishes of the little household, baby Wolfgang was mounted on a footstool to recite a poem in honor of the occasion. When he had finished it he stood quietly a moment then reaching out his tiny arms, clasped them tightly about his father's neck, and said:

"Dear papa, I love you very, very much; after God, next comes my papa."

Leopold Mozart was a musician and held the post of Vice-Capellmeister. Music was honored in this simple home, and when two of the Court musicians, friends of Father Mozart, came in to join the festivities on this birthday night, a toast was drunk to the honor of *Musica,* the divine goddess of tones.

"I wonder if even a little of my own musical knowledge and love for the art will overflow upon the two dear children," remarked Father Mozart, gazing down tenderly on the little ones.

"Why not," answered the mother; "you long ago promised to begin lessons with Nannerl; can she not start this very night?"

"Yes, indeed, Papachen, may I not learn to play the piano? I promise to work very hard."

"Very well," answered the father; "you shall see I am grateful for all the love you have showed me tonight, and I will begin to teach Nannerl at once."

"I want to learn music too," broke in little Wolfgang, looking at his father with beaming eyes.

Every one laughed at this, while the father said baby Wolfgang would have to grow some inches before he could reach the keys.

The lesson began, and the little girl showed both quickness and patience to grasp the ideas. No one at first noticed the tiny child who planted himself at his sister's elbow, the light of the candles falling on his delicate, sensitive features and bright brown hair. His glance never left Nannerl's fingers as they felt hesitatingly among the white and black keys, while his ear easily understood the intervals she tried to play.

When the little girl left the piano, or the harpsichord, as it was called in those days, Wolfgang slipped into her place and began to repeat with his tiny fingers what his father had taught her. He sought the different intervals, and when at last he found them, his little face beamed with joy. In a short time he was able to play all the simple exercises that had been given his sister.

The parents listened to their wonder-child with ever increasing astonishment, mingled with tears of emotion. It was plain to be seen that Wolfgang must have lessons as well as Nannerl. And what joy it would be to teach them both.

It was a happy household that retired that night. Nannerl was happy because she at last had the chance to take piano lessons. Wolfgang, little "Starbeam," dreamed of the wonderful Goddess of Music, who carried him away to fairyland which was filled with beautiful music. The parents were filled with joy that heaven had granted them such blessings in their children.

The musical progress of the children was quite re-markable. Marianne, which was Nannerl's real name, soon began to play very well indeed, while little Wolfgang hardly had to be told anything in music, for he seemed to know it already. The father would write Minuets for the little girl to study; her tiny brother would learn them in half an hour. Soon Wolfgang was able to compose his own Minuets. Several have come down to us which he wrote when he was five years old; and they are quite perfect in form and style.

One day Father Mozart brought home Schachtner, the Court trumpeter, to dinner. Coming suddenly into the living-room, they found the tiny elf busily writing at his father's desk.

"Whatever are you doing, Wolferl?" cried his father, gazing at the ink stained fingers of his little son and then at the paper covered with blots.

"Oh, Papa, a piano sonata, but it isn't finished yet."

"Never mind that," said Leopold Mozart, "let us see it, it must be something very fine." Taking up the paper the father and his friend looked at it curiously. The sheets were bedaubed with ink stains that almost concealed the notes. For the child had thrust his pen each time to the bottom of the ink well, so that frequent blots on the paper were the result. These did not trouble him in the least, for he merely rubbed his hand over the offending blot and proceeded with his writing.

At first the two friends laughed heartily to see how the little composer had written the notes over smudges, but soon the father's eyes filled with happy tears.

"Look, my dear Schachtner!" he cried. "See how correct and orderly it all is, all written according to rule. Only one could never play it for it seems to be too difficult."

"But it's a sonata, Papa, and one must practice it first, of course, but this is the way it should go."

He sprang to the piano and began to play. The small fingers could not master the more intricate parts, but gave sufficient idea of how he intended the piece to sound.

They stood in speechless astonishment at this proof of the child's powers; then Leopold Mozart caught up the little composer and kissing him cried, "My Wolfgang, you will become a great musician."

Wolfgang, not content with merely learning the piano, begged to study the violin also. His violin lessons had hardly begun when one evening his father and two friends were about to play a set of six trios, composed by Wentzl, one of the players. Wolfgang begged to be allowed to play the second violin. Needless to say his request was refused. At last he was told he might sit next to Schachtner and make believe play, though he must make no sound.

The playing began, when before long it was seen the boy was actually playing the second violin part and doing it correctly. The second violin ceased bowing in amazement and allowed Wolfgang to go on alone. After this he was permitted to play all the second violin part of the whole six pieces. Emboldened by this success, he volunteered to attempt the first violin part, an offer which was greeted with laughter; but nothing daunted, he took up his violin and began. There were mistakes here and there, of course, but he persisted to the end, to the astonishment of all.

Three years had passed swiftly by since little Wolfgang Mozart began to study music the night of his father's fortieth birthday. He had made marvelous progress and already the fame of his powers had passed beyond the narrow limits of his native town. Leopold Mozart had no means other than the salary which he received from the Court. His children's musical gifts induced the father to turn them to advantage, both to supply the family needs and to provide the children a broad education in music. He determined to travel with the children. A first experiment in January, 1762, had proved so successful that the following September they set out for Vienna. Wolfgang was now six years old and Marianne eleven.

At Linz they gave a successful concert and every

one was delighted with the playing of the children. From here they continued their journey as far as the monastery of Ips, where they expected to stay for the night. It had been a wonderful day, spent in sailing down the majestic Danube, till they reached the grey old building with its battlemented walls. Soon after they arrived, Father Mozart took Wolfgang into the chapel to see the organ.

The child gazed with awe at the great pipes, the keyboard and the pedals. He begged his father to explain their working, and then as the father filled the great bellows the tiny organist pushed aside the organ bench, stood upon the pedals and trod them, as though he had always known how. The monks in the monastery hastened to the chapel, holding their breath as one pointed to the figure of a tiny child in the organ loft. Was it possible, they asked themselves, that a child could produce such beautiful music? They remained rooted to the spot, till Wolfgang happened to see them and crept meekly down from his perch.

All the rest of the journey to Vienna, Wolfgang was the life of the party, eager to know the name and history of everything they met. At the custom-house on the frontier, he made friends with the officials by playing for them on his violin, and thus secured an easy pass for the party.

Arrived at Vienna, Leopold Mozart found the fame of the children's playing had preceded them. A kind and gracious welcome awaited the little party when they went to the palace of Schonbrunn. The Emperor

Franz Josef took to Wolfgang at once, was delighted with his playing and called him his "little magician." The boy's powers were tested by being required to read difficult pieces at sight, and playing with one finger, as the Emperor jestingly asked him to do. Next, the keyboard was covered with a cloth, as a final test, but little Wolfgang played as finely as before, to the great delight of the company who applauded heartily. The little magician was so pleased with the kindness of both the Emperor and Empress that he returned it in his own childish way, by climbing into the lap of the Empress and giving her a hug and a kiss, just as though she were his own mother. He was also greatly attracted by the little Princess Marie Antoinette, a beautiful child of about his own age, with long fair curls and laughing blue eyes. The two struck up an immediate friendship.

After the favor shown them, at Court, the gifted children became the rage in Vienna society. Invitations poured in from every side, and many gifts. Those bestowed by the royal family were perhaps the most valued. Wolfgang's present was a violet colored suit, trimmed with broad gold braid, while Nannerl received a pretty white silk dress. Each of the children also received a beautiful diamond ring from the Emperor. A portrait of the boy in his gala suit, which was painted at the time, is still preserved.

The following year the Mozarts took the children on a longer journey, this time with Paris in view. They stopped at many towns and cities on the way. At Frankfort the first performance was so successful that three more were given. A newspaper of the time says "little Mozart is able to name all notes played at a distance, whether single or in chords, whether played on the piano, or any other instrument, bell, glass or clock." The father offered as an additional attraction that Wolfgang would play with the keyboard covered.

The family stayed five months in Paris; the children played before the Court at Versailles, exciting surprise and enthusiasm there and wherever they appeared. From Paris they traveled to London, in April, 1764.

Leopold Mozart's first care on reaching the great English metropolis was to obtain an introduction at Court. King George III and the Queen were very fond of music, and it was not long before an invitation came for the children to attend at the Palace. The King showed the greatest interest in Wolfgang, asking him to play at sight difficult pieces by Bach and Handel. Then the boy, after accompanying the Queen in a song, selected the bass part in a piece by Handel, and improvised a charming melody to it. The King was so impressed that he wished him to play the organ, in the playing of which Wolfgang won a further triumph.

The King's birthday was to be celebrated on June 4 and London was crowded with people from all parts of the country. Leopold Mozart had chosen June 5 as the date for his first public concert. The hall was filled to overflowing; one hundred guineas being taken in. Many of the assisting performers would take no fee for their services, which added to the father's gratitude and happiness.

Not long after this Leopold Mozart fell ill, and the

little family moved to Chelsea, for the quiet and good air. Later they were given another reception at Court, where, after Wolfgang's wonderful performances, the children won much applause by playing some piano duets composed by the boy—a style of composition then quite new.

In July, 1765, the family left London and traveled in Holland, after which came a second visit to Paris, where they added to their former triumphs, in addition to playing in many towns on the way back. Finally the long tour was brought to a close by the return to Salzburg in November, 1766.

At the period of musical history in which the gifted boy lived, a musician's education was not complete unless he went to Italy, for this country stood first as the home of music. Leopold Mozart had made a couple of trips to Vienna with his children, the account of which need not detain us here. He had decided that Wolfgang must go to Italy, and breathe in the atmosphere of that land of song. And so in December, 1769, father and son set out for the sunny south, with high hopes for success.

Mozart's happy nature was jubilant over the journey. He watched eagerly the peasants as they danced on the vine-clad terraces, overlooking the deep blue lakes,—or listened as they sang at their work in the sunny fields. He gazed at the wonderful processions of priests through narrow streets of the towns, but above all there was the grand music in the cathedrals.

The young musician had plenty of work to do, more than most boys of thirteen. For, besides the concerts he had to give, he was set difficult problems by the various professors who wished to test his powers. The fame of his playing constantly spread, so the further he traveled into Italy there were more demands to hear him. At Roveredo, where it was announced he would play the organ in St. Thomas's Church, the crowd was so great he could scarcely get to the organ-loft. The vast audience listened spellbound, and then refused to disperse till they had caught a glimpse of the boy player. At Verona he had another triumph; one of his symphonies was performed, and his portrait was ordered to be painted.

When they reached Milan the Chief musician of the city subjected the boy to severe tests, all of which he accomplished to the astonishment and delight of everybody. It was at Bologna however, where he met the most flattering reception. Here was the home of the famous Padre Martini, the aged composer of church music. Father Martini was almost worshiped by the Italians; he was a most lovable man and looked up to as a great composer. He had long ago given up attending concerts, so that every one was astonished when he was present in the brilliant audience gathered at Count Pallavicini's mansion to listen to the boy's playing. Wolfgang did his best, for he realized the importance of the event. Father Martini took the boy to his heart at once, invited him to visit him as often as possible during his stay, and gave him several fugue subjects to work out. These the boy accomplished with ease, and the Padre declared he was perfectly satisfied with his knowledge of composition.

The journey to Rome was now continued, and for Wolfgang it was a succession of triumphs. At Florence he played before the Court of the Archduke Leopold, and solved every problem put to him by the Court music director as easily as though he were eating a bit of bread.

It was Holy Week when young Mozart and his father entered Rome, and the city lay under the spell of the great festival of the year. They soon joined the throngs that filled the vast temple of St. Peter's, to which all turn during this solemn season. After attending a service and viewing the treasures of the Cathedral, they turned their steps to the Sistine Chapel, which contains the wonderful painting of the Last Judgment by Michael Angelo. It was here that the celebrated Miserere by Allegri was performed. Wolfgang had been looking forward to this moment all through the latter part of his journey. His father had told him how jealously guarded this music was; it could never be performed in any other place, and the singers could never take their parts out of the chapel. He was intensely eager to hear this work. And indeed it would be difficult to imagine anything more beautiful and impressive than the singing of the Miserere, which means "Have Mercy." It follows the solemn service called Tenebrae, (Darkness) during which the six tall candles on the altar are extinguished one by one,—till but one is left, which is removed to a space behind the altar. Then in almost complete darkness the Miserere begins. A single voice is heard singing the antiphon, or short introduction,— and then comes silence, a silence so profound that the listener scarcely dares to breathe for fear of disturbing it. At length the first sad notes of the supplication are heard, like the softest wailing of an anguished spirit; they gradually gain force till the whole building seems to throb with the thrilling intensity of the music.

The young musician was profoundly moved; the father too, was much affected by the solemn service. Neither spoke as they left the chapel and sought their lodgings. After they had retired the boy could not sleep; his thoughts were filled with the wonderful music he had heard. He arose, lit the lamp, and got out pens and music paper. He worked industriously the long night through. When morning dawned the boy sat with his beautiful head upon his folded arms, asleep, while before him on the table lay a score of the Miserere of Allegri, entirely written from memory.

The next day, Good Friday, the Miserere was performed for the second time. Wolfgang, the boy of fourteen, who had performed the wonderful feat of writing this work out after one hearing, again attended the service, keeping the score in his hat, and found his work was nearly perfect, needing but a couple of trifling corrections.

The news of this startling feat gained for the young musician a cordial welcome into the houses of the great in Rome; during their stay father and son were fêted to their hearts' content.

At Naples, their next stopping place, Wolfgang played before a brilliant company, and excited so much astonishment, that people declared his power in playing came from a ring he wore on his finger. "He wears a charm," they cried. Mozart smiled, took off the ring and played more brilliantly than ever. Then the enthusiasm was redoubled. The Neapolitans showed them every attention and honor. A carriage was provided for their use, and we have an account of how they drove through the best streets, the father wearing a maroon-colored coat with light blue facings, and Wolfgang in one of apple green, with rose-colored facings and silver buttons.

It was indeed a wonderful tour which they made in Italy, though there is not time to tell of many things that happened. On their return to Rome, the Pope gave him the order of the Golden Spur, which made him Chevalier de Mozart. Arriving at Bologna the young musician was made a member of the Accademia Filharmonica. The test for this admission was setting an antiphon in four parts. Wolfgang was locked in a room till the task should be finished. To the astonishment of everybody he asked to be let out at the end of half an hour,—having completed the work.

The travelers now proceeded to Milan, where Mozart was to work on his first opera, for which he had received a commission. It was a great task for a boy to accomplish and we find the young composer writing to his mother and sister to pray for his success. The opera was called "Mitridate," and was finished after three months' hard work. The first performance was given in Milan, December 26, 1770, and was conducted by Wolfgang himself. It was a proud, happy day for the father, indeed for the whole family. "Mitridate" succeeded beyond their hopes; it was given twenty times before crowded houses; and its success brought an election to the Accademia, and also a commission to write a dramatic Serenata for an approaching royal wedding. This work also was a great success. The Empress who had commissioned Mozart to compose the work was so pleased, that besides the promised fee, she gave the composer a gold watch with her portrait set in diamonds on the back.

Sunshine and success had followed the gifted boy through all his travels; but now shadows and disappointments were to come, due to jealousy, intrigue and indifference of those in power who might have helped him but failed to recognize his genius. Shortly after the return of the father and son to their home town of Salzburg, their protector and friend, the good Archbishop of Salzburg, died. His successor was indifferent to art and held in contempt those who followed it as a profession. He persistently refused to appoint the young musician to any office worthy his talent or to recognize his gifts in any way. While Mozart remained at home in Salzburg, hoping his prospects would improve, he worked at composing with untiring diligence. By the time he was twenty-one he had accumulated a mass of music that embraced every branch of the art. He had a growing reputation as a composer but no settled future. He had the post of concertmaster, it is true, but the salary was but a trifle and he was often pressed for money. Leopold therefore decided to undertake another professional tour with his son. The Archbishop however prevented the father leaving Salzburg. So the only course left open was to allow Wolfgang and his mother to travel together. They set out on the morning of September 23, 1777. Wolfgang's spirits rose as the town of Salzburg faded into the haze of that September morning; the sense of freedom was exhilarating; he had escaped the place associated in his mind with tyranny and oppression, to seek his fortune in new and wider fields.

At Munich where they first halted, Wolfgang sought an engagement at the Elector's Court. He had an audience at the Nymphenburg, a magnificent palace on the outskirts of the city. The Elector said there was no vacancy; he did not know but later it might be possible to make one, after Mozart had been to Italy and had made a name for himself. With these words the Elector turned away. Mozart stood as if stunned. To Italy, when he had concertized there for about seven years, and had been showered with honors! It was too much. He shook off the dust of Munich and he and his mother went on to Mannheim. Here was a more congenial atmosphere. The Elector maintained a fine orchestra, and with the conductor, Cannabich, Mozart became great friends, giving music lessons to his daughter. But he could not seem to secure a permanent appointment at Court, worthy his genius and ability. Money became more scarce and the father and sister must make many sacrifices at home to send money to maintain mother and son. With the best of intentions Wolfgang failed to make his way except as a piano teacher. The father had resorted to the same means of securing the extra sums required, and wrote quite sharply to the son to bestir himself and get something settled for the future.

For the young genius, Mannheim possessed a special attraction of which the father knew nothing. Shortly after their arrival in the city, Wolfgang became acquainted with the Weber family. The two oldest daughters, Aloysia, fifteen, and Constanza, fourteen, were charming girls just budding into womanhood. Aloysia had a sweet, pure voice, and was studying for the stage; indeed she had already made her debut in opera. It was not at all strange that young Mozart, who often joined the family circle, should fall in love with the girl's fair beauty and fresh voice, should write songs for her and teach her to sing them as he wished. They were much together and their early attraction fast ripened into love. Wolfgang formed a project for helping the Webers, who were in rather straitened circumstances, by undertaking a journey to Italy in company with Aloysia and her father; he would write an opera in which Aloysia should appear as prima donna. Of this brilliant plan he wrote his father, saying they could stop in Salzburg on the way, when the father and Nannerl could meet the fair young singer, whom they would be sure to love.

Leopold Mozart was distracted at news of this project. He at once wrote, advising his son to go to Paris and try there to make a name and fame for himself. The son dutifully yielded at once. With a heavy heart he prepared to leave Mannheim, where he had spent such a happy winter, and his love dream came to an end. It was a sad parting with the Weber household, for they regarded Wolfgang as their greatest benefactor.

The hopes Leopold Mozart had built on Wolfgang's success in Paris were not to be realized. The enthusiasm he had aroused as a child prodigy was not awarded to the matured musician. Three months passed away in more or less fruitless endeavor. Then the mother, who had been his constant companion in these trials and travels, fell seriously ill. On July 3, 1778, she passed away in her son's arms.

Mozart prepared to leave Paris at once, and his father was the more willing, since the Archbishop of Salzburg offered Wolfgang the position of Court organist, at a salary of 500 florins, with permission to absent himself whenever he might be called upon to conduct his own operas. Leopold urged Wolfgang's acceptance, as their joint income would amount to one thousand florins a year—a sum that would enable them to pay their debts and live in comparative comfort.

To Mozart the thought of settling down in Salzburg under the conditions stated in his father's letter was distasteful, but he had not the heart to withstand his father's appeal. He set out from Paris at once, promising himself just one indulgence before entering the bondage which lay before him, a visit to his friends the Webers at Mannheim. When he arrived there he found they had gone to Munich to live. Therefore he pushed on to Munich. The Weber family received him as warmly as of old, but in Aloysia's eyes there was only a friendly greeting, nothing more. A few short months had cooled her fickle attachment for the young composer. This discovery was a bitter trial to Wolfgang and he returned to his Salzburg home saddened by disappointed love and ambition.

Here in his old home he was cheered by a rapturous welcome; it was little short of a triumph, this greeting and homage showered on him by father, sister and friends. In their eyes his success was unshadowed by failure; to them he was Mozart the great composer, the genius among musicians. He was very grateful for these proofs of affection and esteem, but he had still the same aversion to Salzburg and his Court duties. So it was with new-kindled joy that he set out once more for Munich, in November, 1780, to complete and produce the opera he had been commissioned to write for the carnival the following year.

The new opera, "Idomeneo," fulfilled the high expectations his Munich friends had formed of the composer's genius. Its reception at the rehearsals proved success was certain, and the Elector who was present, joined the performers in expressing his unqualified approval. At home the progress of the work was followed with deepest interest. The first performance of "Idomeneo" took place on January 29, 1781. Leopold and Marianne journeyed to Munich to witness Wolfgang's triumph. It was a proud, happy moment for all three; the enthusiastic acclaim which shook the theater seemed to the old father, who watched with swimming eyes the sea of waving hands around him, to set the seal of greatness on his son's career.

The Archbishop, under whom Mozart held the meager office we have spoken of, grew more overbearing in his treatment; he was undoubtedly jealous that great people of Vienna were so deferential to one of his servants, as he chose to call him. At last the rupture came; after a stormy scene Mozart was dismissed from his service, and was free.

Father Mozart was alarmed when he heard the news of the break, and endeavored to induce Wolfgang to reconsider his decision and return to Salzburg. But the son took a firm stand for his independence. "Do not ask me to return to Salzburg," he wrote his father; "ask me anything but that."

And now came a time of struggling for Mozart. His small salary was cut off and he had but one pupil. He had numerous friends, however, and soon his fortunes began to mend. He was lodging with his old friends the Webers. Aloysia, his former beloved, had married; Madame Weber and her two unmarried daughters were now in Vienna and in reduced circumstances. Mozart's latest opera, "The Elopement," had brought him fame both in Vienna and Prague, and he had the patronage of many distinguished persons, as well as that of Emperor Josef.

Mozart had now decided to make a home for himself, and chose as his bride Constanza Weber, a younger sister of Aloysia, his first love. In spite of Leopold Mozart's remonstrance, the young people were married August 16, 1782.

Constanza, though a devoted wife, was inexperienced in home keeping. The young couple were soon involved in many financial troubles from which there seemed no way out, except by means of some Court appointment. This the Emperor in spite of his sincere interest in the composer, seemed disinclined to give.

Mozart now thought seriously of a journey to London and Paris, but his father's urgent appeal that he would wait and exercise patience, delayed him. Meanwhile he carried out an ardent desire to pay a visit to his father and sister in Salzburg, to present to them his bride. It was a very happy visit, and later on, when Mozart and his wife were again settled in Vienna, they welcomed the father on a return visit. Leopold found his son immersed in work, and it gladdened his heart to see the appreciation in which his playing and compositions were held. One happy evening they spent with Josef Haydn who, after hearing some of Mozart's quartets played, took the father aside, saying: "I declare before God, as a man of honor, that your son is the greatest composer I know, either personally or by reputation. He has taste, but more than that the most consummate knowledge of the art of composition."

This happy time was to be the last meeting between father and son. Soon after Leopold's return to Salzburg, he was stricken with illness, and passed away May 28, 1787. The news reached the composer shortly after he had achieved one of the greatest successes of his life. The performances of his latest opera, "The Marriage of Figaro," had been hailed with delight by enthusiastic crowds in Vienna and Prague; its songs were heard at every street corner, and village ale house. "Never was anything more complete than the triumph of Mozart and his 'Nozze di Figaro,'" wrote a singer and friend.—"And for Mozart himself, I shall never forget his face when lighted up with the glowing rays of genius; it is as impossible to describe as to paint sunbeams."

Despite the success of Figaro, Mozart was still a poor man, and must earn his bread by giving music lessons. Finally the Emperor, hoping to keep him in Germany, appointed him Chamber-composer at a salary of about eighty pounds a year. It must have seemed to Mozart and his friends a beggarly sum for the value his Majesty professed to set upon the composer's services to art. "Too much for the little I am asked to produce, too little for what I could produce," were the bitter words he penned on the official return stating the amount of his salary.

Mozart was inclined to be somewhat extravagant in dress and household expenditure, also very generous to any one who needed assistance. These trials, added to the fact that his wife was frequently in ill health, and not very economical, served to keep the family in continual straits. Occasionally they were even without fire or food, though friends always assisted such dire distress. Mozart's father had declared procrastination was his son's besetting sin. Yet the son was a tireless worker, never idle. In September, 1787, he was at Prague, writing the score of his greatest opera, "Don Giovanni"; the time was short, as the work was to be produced October 29. On the evening of the 28th it was found he had not yet written the overture. It only had to be written down, for this wonderful genius had the music quite complete in his head. He set to work, while his wife read fairy tales aloud to keep him awake, and gave him strong punch at intervals. By seven o'clock next morning the score was ready for the copyist. It was played in the evening without rehearsal, with the ink scarcely dry on the paper.

Even the successes of "Don Giovanni," which was received with thunders of applause, failed to remedy his desperate financial straits. Shortly after this his pupil and patron, Prince Karl Lichnowsky, proposed he should accompany him to Berlin. Mozart gladly consented, hoping for some betterment to his fortunes. The King of Prussia received him with honor and respect and offered him the post of Capellmeister, at a salary equal to about three thousand dollars. This sum would have liberated him from all his financial embarrassments, and he was strongly tempted to accept. But loyalty to his good Emperor Josef caused him to decline the offer.

The month of July, 1791, found Mozart at home in Vienna at work on a magic opera to help his friend Salieri, who had taken a little theater in the suburb of Wieden. One day he was visited by a stranger, a tall man, who said he came to commission Mozart to compose a Requiem. He would neither give his own name nor that of the person who had sent him.

Mozart was somewhat depressed by this mysterious commission; however he set to work on the Requiem at once. The composing of both this and the fairy opera was suddenly interrupted by a pressing request that he would write an opera for the coronation of Leopold II at Prague. The ceremony was fixed for September 6, so no time was to be lost. Mozart set out at once for Prague. The traveling carriage was at the door. As he was about to enter it, the mysterious stranger suddenly appeared and enquired for the Requiem. The composer could only promise to finish on his return, when hastily entering his carriage, he drove away.

The new opera, "La Clemenza di Tito," was finished in time and performed, but was received somewhat indifferently. Mozart returned to Vienna with spirits depressed and body exhausted by overwork. However, he braced himself anew, and on September 30th, the new fairy opera, the "Magic Flute," was produced, and its success increased with each performance.

The Requiem was not yet finished and to this work Mozart now turned. But the strain and excitement he had undergone for the past few months had done their work: a succession of fainting spells overcame him, and the marvelous powers which had always been his seemed no longer at his command. He feared he would not live to complete the work. "It is for myself I am writing the Requiem," he said sadly to Constanza, one day.

On the evening of December 4, friends who had gathered at his bedside, handed him, at his desire, the score of the Requiem, and, propped up by pillows he tried to sing one of the passages. The effort was too great; the manuscript slipped from his nerveless hand and he fell back speechless with emotion. A few hours later, on the morning of December 5, 1791, this great master of whom it was prophesied that he would cause

all others to be forgotten, passed from the scene of his
many struggles and greater triumphs.

LUDWIG VAN BEETHOVEN

CHAPTER VII

LUDWIG VAN BEETHOVEN

THE Shakespeare of the realm of music, as he has been called, first saw the light on December 16, 1770, in the little University town of Bonn, on the Rhine. His father, Johann Beethoven, belonged to the court band of the Elector of Cologne. The family were extremely poor. The little room, where the future great master was born, was so low, that a good-sized man could barely stand upright in it. Very small it was too, and not very light either, as it was at the back of the building and looked out on a walled garden.

The fame of young Mozart, who was acclaimed everywhere as a marvelous prodigy, had naturally reached the father's ears. He decided to train the little Ludwig as a pianist, so that he should also be hailed as a prodigy and win fame and best of all money for the poverty-stricken family. So the tiny child was made to practice scales and finger exercises for hours together. He was a musically gifted child, but how he hated those everlasting tasks of finger technic, when he longed to join his little companions, who could run and play in the sunshine. If he stopped his practice to rest and dream a bit, the stern face of his father would appear at the doorway, and a harsh voice would call out, "Ludwig! what are you doing? Go on with your exercises at once. There will be no soup for you till they are finished."

The father, though harsh and stern, wished his boy to have as thorough a knowledge of music as his means would permit. The boy was also sent to the public school, where he picked up reading and writing, but did not make friends very quickly with the other children. The fact was the child seemed wholly absorbed in music; of music he dreamed constantly; in the companionship of music he never could be lonely.

When Ludwig was nine his father, regarding him with satisfaction and some pride, declared he could teach him no more—and another master must be found. Those childhood years of hard toil had resulted in remarkable progress, even with the sort of teaching he had received. The circumstances of the family had not improved, for poverty had become acute, as the father became more and more addicted to drink. Just at this time, a new lodger appeared, who was something of a musician, and arranged to teach the boy in part payment for his room. Ludwig wondered if he would turn out to be a more severe taskmaster than his father had been. The times and seasons when his instruction was given were at least unusual. Tobias Pfeiffer, as the new lodger was called, soon discovered that father Beethoven generally spent his evenings at the tavern. As an act of kindness, to keep his drunken landlord out of the way of the police, Tobias used to go to the tavern late at night and bring him safely home. Then he would go to the bedside of the sleeping boy, and awake him by telling him it was time for practice. The two would go to the living room, where they would play together for several hours, improvising on original themes and playing duets. This went on for about a year; meanwhile Ludwig studied Latin, French, Italian and logic. He also had organ lessons.

Things were going from bad to worse in the Beethoven home, and in the hope of bettering these unhappy conditions, Frau Beethoven undertook a trip through Holland with her boy, hoping that his playing in the homes of the wealthy might produce some money. The tour was successful in that it relieved the pressing necessities of the moment, but the sturdy, independent spirit of the boy showed itself even then. "The Dutch are very stingy, and I shall take care not to trouble them again," he remarked to a friend.

The boy Ludwig could play the organ fairly well, as he had studied it with Christian Neefe, who was organist at the Court church. He also could play the piano with force and finish, read well at sight and knew nearly the whole of Bach's "Well-Tempered Clavichord." This was a pretty good record for a boy of 11, who, if he went on as he had begun, it was said, would become a second Mozart.

Neefe was ordered to proceed with the Elector and Court to Münster, which meant to leave his organ in Bonn for a time. Before starting he called Ludwig to him and told him of his intended absence. "I must have an assistant to take my place at the organ here. Whom do you think I should appoint?" Seeing the boy had no inkling of his meaning, he continued: "I have thought of an assistant, one I am sure I can trust,—and that is you, Ludwig."

The honor was great, for a boy of eleven and a half. To conduct the service, and receive the respect and deference due the position, quite overwhelmed the lad. Honors of this kind were very pleasant, but, alas, there was no money attached to the position, and this was what the straitened family needed most sorely. The responsibilities of the position and the confidence of Neefe spurred Ludwig on to a passion of work which nothing could check. He began to compose; three sonatas for the pianoforte were written about this time. Before completing his thirteenth year, Ludwig obtained his first official appointment from the Elector; he became what is called cembalist in the orchestra, which meant that he had to play the piano in the orchestra, and conduct the band at rehearsals. With this appointment there was no salary attached either, and it was not until a year later when he was made second organist to the Court, under the new Elector, Max Franz, that he began to receive a small salary, equal to about sixty-five dollars a year. We have seen that the straits of the family had not prevented Ludwig from pursuing his musical studies with great ardor. With his present attainments and his ambition for higher achievements, he longed to leave the little town of Bonn, and see something of the great world. Vienna was the center of the musical life of Germany; the boy dreamed of this magical city by day as he went about his routine of work, and by night as he lay on his poor narrow cot. Like Haydn, Vienna was the goal of his ambition. When a kind friend, knowing his great longing, came forward with an offer to pay the expenses of the journey, the lad knew his dream was to become a reality. In Vienna he would see the first composers of the day; best of all he would see and meet the divine Mozart, the greatest of them all.

Ludwig, now seventeen, set out for the city of his dreams with the brightest anticipations. On his arrival in Vienna he went at once to Mozart's house. He was received most kindly and asked to play, but Mozart seemed preoccupied and paid but little attention. Ludwig, seeing this stopped playing and asked for a theme on which to improvise. Mozart gave a simple theme, and Beethoven, taking the slender thread, worked it up with so much feeling and power, that Mozart, who was now all attention and astonishment, stepped into the next room, where some friends were waiting for him, and said, "Pay attention to this young man; he will make a noise in the world some day."

Shortly after his return home he was saddened by the loss of his good, kind, patient mother, and a few months later his little sister Margaretha passed away. No doubt these sorrows were expressed in some of his most beautiful compositions. But brighter days followed the dark ones. He became acquainted with the Breuning family, a widow lady and four children, three boys and a girl, all young people. The youngest boy and the girl became his pupils, and all were very fond of him. He would stay at their house for days at a time and was always treated as one of the family. They were cultured people, and in their society Beethoven's whole nature expanded. He began to take an interest in the literature of his own country and in English authors as well. All his spare time was given to reading and composition. A valuable acquaintance with the young Count Von Waldstein was made about this time. The Count called one day and found the composer at his old worn out piano, surrounded by signs of abject poverty. It went to his heart to see that the young man, whose music he so greatly admired should have to struggle for the bare necessities of life while he himself enjoyed every luxury. It seemed to him terribly unjust. He feared to offend the composer's self-respect by sending him money, but shortly after the call Beethoven was made happy by the gift of a fine new piano, in place of his old one. He was very grateful for this friendship and later dedicated to the Count one of his finest sonatas, the Op. 53, known as the "Waldstein Sonata."

With a view of aiding the growth of the opera, and operatic art, the Elector founded a national theater, and Beethoven was appointed viola player in the orchestra besides still being assistant organist in the chapel. In July, 1792, the band arranged a reception for Haydn, who was to pass through Bonn on his way from London, where he had had a wonderful success, to his home in Vienna. Beethoven seized the opportunity to show the master a cantata he had just composed. Haydn praised the work and greatly encouraged the young musician to go forward in his studies. The Elector, hearing of Haydn's words of praise, felt that Beethoven should have the chance to develop his talents that he might be able to produce greater works. Therefore he decided to send the young composer, at his own expense, to study strict counterpoint with Haydn. He was now twenty-two and his compositions already published had brought him considerable fame and appreciation in his vicinity. Now he was to have wider scope for his gifts.

He bade farewell to Bonn in November of this year and set out a second time for the city of his dreams— Vienna. He was never to see Bonn again. He arrived in Vienna comparatively unknown, but his fine piano playing and wonderful gift for improvising greatly impressed all who heard him. He constantly played in the homes of the wealthy aristocracy. Many who heard him play, engaged lessons and he was well on the road to social success. Yet his brusque manners often antagonized his patrons. He made no effort to please or conciliate; he was obstinate and self-willed. In spite of all this, the innate nobleness and truth of his character retained the regard of men and women belonging to the highest ranks of society. With the Prince and Princess Lichnowsky Beethoven shortly became very intimate, and was invited to stay at the Palace. The Princess looked after his personal comfort with as motherly an affection as Madame Breuning had done. The etiquette of the Palace however, offended Ludwig's love of Bohemianism, especially the dressing for dinner at a certain time. He took to dining at a tavern quite frequently, and finally engaged lodgings. The Prince and his good lady, far from taking offense at this unmannerly behavior, forgave it and always kept for Beethoven a warm place in their hearts, while he, on his part was sincere in his affection for his kind friends.

Beethoven began his lessons with Haydn, but they did not seem to get on well together. The pupil thought the master did not give him enough time and attention. When Haydn went to England, about a year after the lessons began, Beethoven studied with several of the best musicians of the city, both in playing and composition. Albrechtsberger, one of these, was a famous contrapuntist of his time, and the student gained much from his teaching. The young musician was irresistible when he seated himself at the piano to extemporize. "His improvisating was most brilliant and striking," wrote Carl Czerny, a pupil of Beethoven. "In whatever company he might be, he knew how to produce such an effect upon the listeners that frequently all eyes would be wet, and some listeners would sob; there was something wonderful in his expressive style, the beauty and originality of his ideas and his spirited way of playing." Strange to say the emotion he roused in his hearers seemed to find no response in Beethoven himself. He would sometimes laugh at it, at other times he would resent it, saying, "We artists don't want tears, we want applause." These expressions however only concealed his inner feelings—for he was very sympathetic with those friends he loved. His anger, though sharp, was of short duration, but his suspicions of those whose confidence he had won by his genius and force of character, were the cause of much suffering to himself and others.

Beethoven in appearance was short and stockily

built; his face was not at all good looking. It is said he was generally meanly dressed and was homely, but full of nobility, fine feeling and highly cultivated. The eyes were black and bright, and they dilated, when the composer was lost in thought, in a way that made him look inspired. A mass of dark hair surmounted a high broad forehead. He often looked gloomy, but when he smiled it was with a radiant brightness. His hands were strong and the fingers short and pressed out with much practise. He was very particular about hand position when playing. As a conductor he made many movements, and is said to have crouched below the desk in soft passages; in crescendos he would gradually lift himself up until at the loudest parts he would rise to his full height with arms extended, even springing into the air, as though he would float in space.

Beethoven as a teacher, showed none of the impatience and carelessness that were seen in his personal habits. He insisted on a pupil repeating the passage carefully a number of times, until it could be played to his satisfaction. He did not seem to mind a few wrong notes, but the pupil must not fail to grasp the meaning or put in the right expression, or his anger would be aroused. The first was an accident, the other would be a lack of knowledge of feeling.

Beethoven loved nature as much or more than any musician ever did. How he hailed the spring because he knew the time would soon come when he could close the door of his lodgings in the hot city, and slip away to some quiet spot and hold sweet communion with nature. A forest was a paradise, where he could ramble among the trees and dream. Or he would select a tree where a forking branch would form a seat near the ground. He would climb up and sit in it for hours, lost in thought. Leaning against the trunk of a lime tree, his eyes fixed upon the network of leaves and branches above him, he sketched the plan of his oratorio "The Mount of Olives"; also that of his one-opera "Fidelio," and the third Symphony, known as the "Eroica." He wrote to a friend, "No man loves the country more than I. Woods, trees and rocks give the response which man requires. Every tree seems to say 'Holy, holy.'"

Already, as a young man, symptoms of deafness began to appear, and the fear of becoming a victim of this malady made the composer more sensitive than ever. He was not yet thirty when this happened, and believing his life work at an end, he became deeply depressed. Various treatments were tried for increasing deafness; at one time it seemed to be cured by the skill of Dr. Schmidt, to whom out of gratitude he dedicated his Septet, arranged as a Trio. By his advice the composer went for the summer of 1820 to the little village of Heiligenstadt (which means Holy City) in the hope that the calm, sweet environment would act as a balm to his troubled mind. During this period of rest and quiet his health improved somewhat, but from now on he had to give up conducting his works, on account of his deafness.

It may be thought that one so reticent and retiring, of such hasty temper and brusque manners, would scarcely be attracted to women. But Beethoven, it is said, was very susceptible to the charm of the opposite sex. He was however, most careful and high-souled in all his relations with women. He was frequently in love, but it was usually a Platonic affection. For the Countess Julie Guicciardi he protested the most passionate love, which was in a measure returned. She was doubtless his "immortal beloved," whose name vibrates through the Adagio of the "Moonlight Sonata," which is dedicated to her. He wrote her the most adoring letters; but the union, which he seemed to desire so intensely, was never brought about, though the reason is not known. For Bettina von Arnim, Goethe's little friend, he conceived a tender affection. Another love of his was for the Countess Marie Erdödy, to whom he dedicated the two fine Trios, Op. 70, but this was also a purely Platonic affection. The composer was unfortunate in his attachments, for the objects were always of a much higher social standing than himself. As he constantly associated with people of rank and culture, it was natural that the young girl nobly born, with all the fascinations of the high bred aristocrat, should attract him far more than the ordinary woman of his own class. And thus it happened that several times he staked his chances of happiness on a love he knew could never be consummated. Yet no one needed a kind, helpful, sympathetic wife more than did our poet-musician. She would have soothed his sensitive soul when he suffered from fancied wrongs, shielded him from intrusion, shared his sorrows and triumphs, and attended to his house-keeping arrangements, which were always in a sad state of confusion. This blissful state was seemingly not for him. It was best for the great genius to devote himself wholly to his divine art, and to create those masterpieces which will always endure.

In 1804 Beethoven completed one of his greatest symphonies, the "Eroica." He made a sketch, as we have seen, two years before. He had intended it to honor Napoleon, to whose character and career he was greatly attracted. But when Napoleon entered Paris in triumph and was proclaimed Emperor, Beethoven's worship was turned to contempt. He seized the symphony, tore the little page to shreds and flung the work to the other end of the room. It was a long time before he would look at the music again, but finally, he consented to publish it under the title by which it is now known.

When we consider the number and greatness of Beethoven's compositions we stand aghast at the amount of labor he accomplished. "I live only in my music," he wrote, "and no sooner is one thing done than the next is begun. I often work at two or three things at once." Music was his language of expression, and through his music we can reach his heart and know the man as he really was. At heart he was a man capable of loving deeply and most worthy to be loved.

Of the composer's two brothers, one had passed away and had left his boy Carl, named after himself, as a solemn charge, to be brought up by Uncle Ludwig as his own son. The composer took up this task generously and unselfishly. He was happy to have the little lad near him, one of his own kin to love. But as Carl grew to young manhood he proved to be utterly unworthy of all this affection. He treated his good uncle shamefully, stole money from him, though he had been always generously supplied with it, and became a disgrace to the family. There is no doubt that his nephew's dissolute habits saddened the master's life, estranged him from his friends and hastened his death.

How simple and modest was this great master, in face of his mighty achievements! He wrote to a friend in 1824: "I feel as if I had scarcely written more than a few notes." These later years had been more than full of work and anxiety. Totally deaf, entirely thrown in upon himself, often weak and ill, the master kept on creating work after work of the highest beauty and grandeur.

Ludwig van Beethoven passed from this plane March 26, 1827, having recently completed his fifty-sixth year, and was laid to rest in the Währing Cemetery near Vienna. Unlike Mozart, he was buried with much honor. Twenty thousand people followed him to his grave. Among them was Schubert, who had visited him on his deathbed, and was one of the torch bearers. Several of the Master's compositions were sung by a choir of male voices, accompanied by trombones. At the grave Hummel laid three laurel wreaths on the casket.

CHAPTER VIII

CARL MARIA VON WEBER

As we have already seen in the life stories of a number of musicians, the career they were to follow was often decided by the father, who determined to form them into wonder children, either for monetary gain or for the honor and glory of the family. The subject of this story is an example of such a preconceived plan.

Franz Anton von Weber, who was a capable musician himself, had always cherished the desire to give a wonder child to the world. In his idea wonder children need not be born such, they could be made by the proper care and training. He had been a wealthy man, but at the time of our story, was in reduced circumstances, and was traveling about Saxony at the head of a troupe of theatrical folk, called "Weber's Company of Comedians."

Little Carl Maria Friedrich Ernst, to give his full name, was born December 18, 1786, at Eutin, a little town in Lower Saxony. He was the first child of a second marriage, and before the baby boy could speak, his career had been planned; the father had made up his mind to develop his son into an extraordinary musical genius. It is not recorded what his young mother, a delicate girl of seventeen, thought about it; probably her ideas for her baby son did not enter into the father's plan. Mother and child were obliged to follow in the train of the wandering comedians, so baby Carl was brought up amid the properties of stage business. Scenery, canvas, paints and stage lights were the materials upon which Carl's imagination was fed. He learned stage language with his earliest breath; it is no wonder he turned to writing for the stage as to the manner born.

As a child, he was neither robust nor even healthy, which is not surprising, since he was not allowed to run afield with other children, enjoying the sweet air of nature, the flowers, the sunshine and blue sky. No, he must stay indoors much of the time and find his playmates among cardboard castles and painted canvas streets. This treatment was not conducive to rosy cheeks and strong, sturdy little legs. Then, before the delicate child was six years old, a violin was put into his hand, and if his progress on it was thought to be too slow by his impatient father, he was treated to raps and blows by way of incentive to work yet harder. His teachers, too, were continually changing, as the comedians had to travel about from place to place. After awhile he was taken in hand by Michael Haydn, a brother of the great Josef. Michael was a famous musician himself and seldom gave lessons to any one. But he was interested in Carl and took charge of his musical education for some time.

It was not long before Carl Maria's genius began definitely to show itself, for he started to write for the lyric stage. Two comic operas appeared, "The Dumb Girl of the Forest," and "Peter Schmoll and his Neighbors." They were both performed, but neither made a hit.

When Carl was seventeen, the father decided he should go to Vienna, for there he would meet all the great musicians of the time. The boy was at the most impressionable age: he was lively, witty, with pleasant manners and amiable disposition; he soon became a favorite in the highest musical circles. It was a gay life and the inexperienced youth yielded to its allurements. In the meantime he did some serious studying under the famous Abbé Vogler. The following year the Abbé recommended him to the conductorship of the Breslau Opera House. This was a very difficult post for a boy of eighteen, and he encountered much jealousy and opposition from the older musicians, who did not relish finding themselves under the leadership of such a youth. A year served to disgust him with the work and he resigned. During the year he had found time to compose most of his opera "Rubezahl."

For the next few years there were many "ups and downs" in Carl's life. From Breslau he went to Carlsruhe, and entered the service of Prince Eugene. For about a year he was a brilliant figure at the Court. Then war clouds gathered and the gay Court life came to an end. Music under the present conditions could no longer support him, as the whole social state of Germany had altered. The young composer was forced to earn his livelihood in some way, and now became private secretary to Prince Ludwig of Wurtemburg, whose Court was held at Stuttgart. The gay, dissolute life at the

Court was full of temptation for our young composer, yet he found considerable time for composition; his opera "Sylvana" was the result, besides several smaller things. During the Stuttgart period, his finances became so low, that on one occasion he had to spend several days in prison for debt. Determined to recruit his fortunes, he began traveling to other towns to make known his art. In Mannheim, Darmstadt and Baden, he gave concerts, bringing out in each place some of his newer pieces, and earning enough at each concert to last a few weeks, when another concert would keep the wolf from the door a little longer.

In 1810, when he was twenty-four, he finished his pretty opera "Abu Hassan," which, on the suggestion of his venerable master, Vogler, he dedicated to the Grand Duke. The Duke accepted the dedication with evident pleasure, and sent Carl a purse of gold, in value about two hundred dollars. The opera was performed on February 6, 1811, and its reception was very gratifying to the composer. The Grand Duke took one hundred and twenty tickets and the performance netted over two hundred florins clear profit. It was after this that Carl Maria went on a tour of the principal German cities and gave concerts in Munich, Prague, Berlin, Dresden and other places. He was everywhere welcomed, his talents and charming manners winning friends everywhere. Especially in Prague he found the highest and noblest aristocracy ready to bid him welcome.

Weber paid a visit to Liebich, director of the Prague theater, almost as soon as he arrived in town. The invalid director greeted him warmly.

"So, you are *the* Weber! I suppose you want me to buy your operas. One fills an evening, the other doesn't. Very well, I will give fifteen hundred florins for the two. Is it a bargain?" Weber accepted, and promised to return the next spring to conduct the operas. He kept his promise, and the result was much better than he ever dreamed. For beyond the performance of his operas, he was offered the post of music director of the Prague theater, which post was just then vacant. The salary was two thousand florins, with a benefit concert at a guaranteed sum of one thousand more, and three months leave of absence every year. This assured sum gave young Weber the chance of paying his debts and starting afresh, which, he writes "was a delight to him."

The composer now threw himself heart and soul into improving the orchestra placed in his charge. Before long he had drilled it to a high state of excellence. Many new operas were put on the stage in quick succession. Thus Weber worked on with great industry for three years. The success he achieved created enemies, and perhaps because of intrigues, envy and ill feeling which had arisen, he resigned his post in 1816. The three years in Prague had been fruitful in new compositions. Several fine piano sonatas, a set of "National Songs," and the Cantata, "Kampf und Sieg," (Struggle and Victory). This last work soon became known all over Germany and made the gifted young composer very popular. During this period Weber became engaged to Caroline Brandt, a charming singer, who created the title rôle in his opera of "Sylvana."

Weber had many kind, influential friends in Prague,

who admired his zeal and efficiency as music director. One of them, Count Vitzhum, did all he could to secure Weber for Dresden. On Christmas morning, 1816, he received the appointment. He wrote to Caroline: "Long did I look on Count Vitzhum's letter without daring to open it. Did it contain joy or sorrow? At length I took courage and broke the seal. It was joy! I am Capellmeister to his Majesty the King of Saxony. I must now rig myself out in true Court style. Perhaps I ought to wear a pigtail to please the Dresdeners. What do you say? I ought at least to have an extra kiss from you for this good news."

He went to Dresden, and at first looked over the situation. On nearer view the prospect was not as bright as it had appeared at first. There was a rival faction, strongly opposed to his plans for the promotion of German opera. There had never been anything tolerated at Dresden but Italian opera, and there were many talented Italian singers to interpret them. Weber was encouraged by a new national spirit, which he felt would favor German opera, and was determined to conquer at all costs. He finally succeeded, for, as he wrote to a friend, "The Italians have moved heaven, earth and hell also, to swallow up the whole German opera and its promoter. But they have found in me a precious tough morsel; I am not easily swallowed." It was the same kind of fight that Handel waged in England, and that Gluck fought against the Piccinists.

"Joseph and his Brethren," by Mehul, was the first opera to be taken up by the new conductor. He drilled the orchestra much more carefully than they had been accustomed, and while, in the beginning, some were sulky at the strictness they were subjected to, yet they finally saw the justice of it and at last took pride in doing their work well. "Joseph" was brought out January 30, 1817. The King and Court were present, and everything passed off well, indeed remarkably well. His majesty was greatly pleased and did not cough once during the whole performance, as he used to do when things did not go to suit him.

In spite of Italian opposition which still continued, Weber's efforts to establish German opera kept right on, until at last it became a State institution, and the composer was appointed musical director for life. With this bright prospect in view he was able to wed his beloved Caroline. They were married on November 4. A quotation from his diary shows the talented musician had become a serious, earnest man. "May God bless our union, and grant me strength and power to make my beloved Lina as happy and contented as my inmost heart would desire. May His mercy lead me in all things."

Weber was now entering the most prolific and brilliant period of his life. His music became richer, more noble and beautiful. The happy union with Caroline seemed to put new life and energy into him, and as a result his works became quickly known all over Europe. His mind was literally teeming with original themes, which crowded each other, struggling to be expressed. First there was the "Mass in E flat," a beautiful, original work; then a festal Cantata, "Nature and Love," written to celebrate the Queen of Saxony's birthday. After this the "Jubilee Cantata," composed to celebrate the fiftieth anniversary of the reign of Augustus, of Saxony. The Italian faction prevented a performance of the whole work, and only the Overture was given. When the entire work was heard it made a great sensation. Now came a Jubilee Mass and some piano pieces, among them the charming and famous "Invitation to the Dance," with which every one is familiar. While writing all these works, the composer was busy with one of his greatest operas, "Der Freischütz." On May 8, 1820, a hundred years ago, the score of "Der Freischütz," was sent to the director of the Berlin theater, and directly put in rehearsal. The rehearsals had not proceeded very far before Weber, the tireless ceaseless worker, had finished his important opera, "Preciosa," which was also despatched to Berlin. "Preciosa" was brought out before "Der Freischütz," which was just as it should be, as the public needed to be educated up to the "Freischütz" music. "Preciosa" was founded on a Spanish story, "The Gypsy of Madrid," and Weber has written for it some of his most charming melodies, full of Spanish color, life and vivacity. Nowadays the opera is neglected, but we often hear the overture. It is to be noted that the overtures to each of Weber's operas contain the leading themes and melodies of the operas themselves, showing with what skill the artist wrought. When Weber's widow presented the original score of "Der Freischütz" to the Royal Library in Berlin, it was found there was not a single erasure or correction in the whole work.

On June 18, 1821, came the first performance of Weber's masterpiece, "Der Freischütz." The theater was beseiged for hours by eager crowds, and when the doors were at last opened, there was a grand rush to enter. The whole house from pit to galleries was soon filled, and when the composer entered the orchestra, there was a roar of applause, which it seemed would never end. As the performance proceeded, the listeners became more charmed and carried away, and at the close there was a wild scene of excitement. The success had been tremendous, and the frequent repetitions demanded soon filled the treasury of the theater. Everybody was happy, the composer most of all. The melodies were played on every piano in Germany and whistled by every street urchin. Its fame spread like lightning over Europe, and quickly reached England. In London the whole atmosphere seemed to vibrate with its melodies. In Paris, however, it did not please on first hearing, perhaps because it was so thoroughly German. But somewhat later, when renamed "Robin des Bois,"— "Robin of the Forest,"—it was performed some three hundred and fifty times before being withdrawn.

Weber kept ever at work. Two years after the production of "Der Freischütz" the opera of "Euryanthe" was completed. The libretto was the work of a half demented woman, Helmine von Chezy, but Weber set out to produce the best opera he was capable of, and to this story he has joined some wonderful music. It was his favorite work; he wrote to his beloved wife two hours before the first performance: "I rely on God and my 'Euryanthe.'" The opera was produced at the Kärnthnertor Theater, in Vienna, on October 25, 1823. The composer, though weak and ill, made the long journey to the great city, that he might personally introduce his favorite to the Viennese. He wrote his wife after the performance: "Thank God, as I do, beloved wife, for the glorious success of 'Euryanthe.' Weary as I am, I must still say a sweet good night to my beloved Lina, and cry Victory! All the company seemed in a state of ecstasy; singers, chorus, orchestra;—all were drunk, as it were, with joy."

The title rôle was taken by Henrietta Sontag, a young girl, still in her teens, though giving high promise of the great things she achieved a few years later. Strange to say, a short time after its first appearance, "Euryanthe" failed to draw. One reason might have been laid to the poor libretto, another to the rumor, started, it is said, by no less an authority than the great master Beethoven, that the music of the opera was "only a collection of diminished sevenths."

The composer lost no time in laying his score before Beethoven, who said he should have visited him *before*, not *after* the performance. He advised him to do what he himself had done to "Fidelio," cut out nearly a third of the score. Weber took this advice, and remade parts of the opera, where he deemed it necessary.

The strain of the production of "Euryanthe" told severely on the composer's delicate health, and he returned to Dresden in an exhausted state. There was no rest for him here, as official duties were pressing. The malady afflicting his lungs had made rapid progress and he began to fear he should not be long spared to his wife and little ones.

He shook off the apathy and took up his pen once

more. His fame was known all over Europe and many tempting offers came in from all directions. One of these was from Covent Garden Theater, London, in the summer of 1824, which resulted in a visit to the English capital. Charles Kemble, the director of Covent Garden, desired Weber to write a new opera for production there. "Oberon" was the subject at last decided upon; it was taken from an old French romance. Weber at once set to work on the music of this fairy opera, and with the exception of the overture, had finished the work in time to bring it to London in 1826. He was ill and suffering at the time he left home, February 7, and it seemed as though he were bidding a final good-by to his wife and little ones.

Arrived in London, Sir George Smart invited him to take up his residence in his house. Here he had every comfort, a beautiful piano too was placed at his disposal by one of the first makers in London. "No King could be served with greater love and affection in all things," he wrote; "I cannot be sufficiently grateful to heaven for the blessings which surround me." Here he composed the beautiful Overture to "Oberon" which was only completed a few days before the first performance of the opera.

"Oberon" was given at Covent Garden on April 12. The house was packed from pit to dome, and the success was tremendous. Next morning the composer was in a highly nervous and exhausted state, but felt he must keep his promise to Kemble and conduct the first twelve performances of "Oberon." He was to have a benefit concert, and hoped through this to have a goodly sum to take back to his little family. Sad to relate, on the evening chosen, May 26, a heavy rain fell and the hall was nearly empty. After the concert he was so weak he had to be assisted from the room. The physician ordered postponement of the journey home, but he cried continually, "I must go to my own—I must! Let me see them once more and then God's will be done."

The next morning, when they came to call him, all was still in his chamber; he had passed away peacefully in sleep.

Weber was buried in London. His last wish—to return home,—was finally fulfilled. Eighteen years after, his remains were brought to Dresden, and the composer was at last at home.

CHAPTER IX

FRANZ SCHUBERT

In the old Lichtenthal quarter of the city of Vienna, in the vicinity of the fortifications, there still stands an old house. It is evidently a public house, for there hangs the sign—"At the Red Crab." Beside this there is a marble tablet fastened above the doorway, which says that Franz Schubert was born in this house. At the right of his name is placed a lyre crowned with a star, and at the left a laurel wreath within which is placed the date, January 31, 1797.

This then was the birthplace of the "most poetical composer who ever lived," as Liszt said of him; the man who created over six hundred songs, eight symphonies, operas, masses, chamber works and much beautiful piano music, and yet only lived to be thirty-one. It is almost unbelievable. Let us get a nearer view of this remarkable musician.

His father kept a school here; there were five children, four boys and a girl to provide for, and as there was nothing to depend on but the schoolmaster's pay, it is easy to see the family was in poor circumstances, though the wife managed most carefully to make ends meet. They were a very devoted family altogether. Little Franz early showed a decided fondness for music, and tried to pick out bits of tunes of his own by ear on an old dilapidated piano the family possessed. He made friends with a young apprentice who took him sometimes to a piano wareroom in the city, where he was allowed to play his little tunes on a fine piano.

When Franz was seven he began to have music lessons at home, the father teaching him violin and his big brother Ignaz, the piano. Franz, in his eagerness to learn soon outstripped his home teachers, and told them he could go on alone. It was then decided he should go to the parish choir master, Holzer, to learn piano, violin, organ, singing and thorough bass. Soon Holzer was astonished at the boy's progress. "Whenever I begin to teach him anything I find he knows it already; I never had such a pupil before." By the time Franz was eleven, his voice had come out so well that he was given the place of head soprano in the parish church, and played violin solos whenever they occurred in the service. He had even begun at home to compose and write down little piano pieces and songs. The parents considered that this remarkable talent should be cultivated further, if possible, in order that it might assist the slender purse of the family. There was a choir school, called the Convict, which trained its boys for the Imperial Chapel. If Franz could prove his ability to enter this school, he would receive free education in return for his services.

One fine morning in October, 1808, Franz in his homespun grey suit, spectacles shielding his bright, near-sighted eyes, his bushy black hair covered by an old fashioned hat, presented himself for examination by the Court Capellmeister and the singing master. The other boys jeered at his odd appearance, but he kept his good humor. When his turn came to sing, after solving all the problems given, his singing of the trial pieces was so astonishing that he was passed in at once, and ordered to put on the uniform of the imperial choristers.

The boy soon found plenty to fill his time and occupy his mind. There was the school orchestra, in which he was able to take a prominent place. There was daily practise, in which the boys learned the overtures and symphonies of Mozart and Haydn, and even Beethoven. He loved best Mozart's "Symphony in G minor," in which he said he heard angels singing. The leader of the orchestra was attracted to the lad's playing the very first day he entered, for he played with such precision and understanding. One day Franz mustered courage to talk a little to the big conductor, whose name was Spaun, and confessed he had composed quite a good deal already, adding he would like to do it every day, only he could not afford to get the music paper. Spaun received this burst of confidence with sympathy, and saw to it that the boy was, in the future, supplied with the necessary music paper.

Franz had soon made such progress on the violin, that he began to take the first violin parts and when the conductor was absent he was asked to lead the orchestra. Indeed by his deep earnestness and sincerity, as well as ability, the gifted boy had become a power in the school. When he went home to see his people, which could only be on Sundays and holidays, it was a happy reunion for all. If he brought home a new string quartet, the father would get out his 'cello, Ignaz and Ferdinand would take first and second violins and the young composer the viola. After it had been played through, then all the players discussed it and offered their criticism. Indeed Franz was composing at such an astonishing rate, that it was difficult to keep him supplied with music paper. One of his works of this time was a fantasia for four hands, in twelve movements. Then came a first attempt at song writing, a long affair which also contained twelve movements, and was in melancholy mood.

Five years the boy Franz Schubert remained at the Convict School and as he had decided to give himself entirely to music, there was no reason for his remaining longer in the school. At the end of the year 1813, he left, and his departure was celebrated by the composition of his first Symphony, in honor of Dr. Lang, the musical director. The lad, now seventeen, stood at the beginning of his career; he was full of hope and energy, and determined to follow in the footsteps of the great masters of music. Of all his compositions so far produced, his songs seemed to be the most spontaneous. He probably did not guess that he was to open up new paths in this field.

Hardly had he left the school when he was drafted for the army. This meant several years of virtual captivity, for conscription could not be avoided. The only other thing he could do was to return home and become a teacher in his father's school. He chose the lesser evil and qualified at once to become his father's assistant, which would also assure him a certain amount of leisure. We can imagine him installed as teacher of the infant class, and realize how distasteful was the daily round of school work, and how he longed to have it over, that he might put on paper all the lovely themes that had come to him through the school day. Other bright spots were the happy hours he spent with the Grob family, who lived also in the district of Lichtenthal. The family consisted of a mother, a son and daughter. They were all musical. Therese Grob had a fine voice and she enjoyed the songs Schubert brought her to sing, while her brother Heinrich could play both piano and 'cello. Many evenings filled with music were passed by the young people. His friends at the Convict too, welcomed each new piece he wrote. Nor did he forget his old master Holzer, the organist of the little church where the composer himself regularly attended. During 1814, Schubert composed his first mass, which was performed October 16. It excited so much interest that it was repeated ten days later at the Augustine church. Franz conducted, the choir was led by Holzer, Ferdinand sat at the organ, and Therese sang the soprano solos. In the audience sat old Salieri, Court Capellmeister of Vienna, with whom Beethoven had studied. Salieri praised Schubert for his work, and said that he should become his pupil. He kept his word and gave the young composer daily lessons for some time. The father was so proud and happy that he bought a five octave piano for his boy, to celebrate the event.

Schubert added many compositions to his list this

year, among them seventeen songs, including "Gretchen at the Spinning Wheel." His acquaintance with the poet Johann Mayrhofer, with whom he soon became intimate, was of benefit to both. The poet produced verses that his friend might set to music. The following year, 1815, he wrote a hundred and thirty-seven songs, to say nothing of six operas, and much music for church and piano. Twenty-nine of these songs were written in the month of August. One day in August eight songs were created; on another day seven. Some of the songs were quite long, making between twenty and thirty pages when printed.

A new friend came into Schubert's life the next year. His name was Franz Schober, and he intended entering the University in Vienna. Being a great lover of music and also familiar with some of Schubert's manuscript songs, he lost no time, on arriving in Vienna, in seeking out the composer. He found the young musician at his desk very busily writing. School work was over for the day, and he could compose in peace. The two young men became friends at once, for they felt the sympathetic bond between them. They were soon talking as though they had always known each other. In a few words Schubert told his new friend how he was situated at home, and how he disliked the daily drudgery of school teaching. On hearing of these trials Schober suggested they should make a home together, which arrangement would free the composer from the grinding life he was living and enable him to give his whole time to his art. The proposal delighted Franz, and the father willingly gave his consent. And so it came about that the composer was free at last, and took up his abode at his friend's lodgings. He insisted on giving him musical instruction, to make some return for all his kindness, though this did not last long, owing to the dislike Franz always had for teaching of any sort.

Schubert, at the age of twenty-four, had composed a great quantity of music, but none of it had as yet been published. He was almost unknown, and publishers were unwilling to undertake issuing the work of an unknown man. When his songs were performed by good artists, as had been done a number of times, they won instant recognition and success. Seeing that the publishers were unwilling to print the work of an unknown musician, two of Schubert's friends undertook to publish the "Erlking," one of his first songs, at their own risk. At the Sonnleithner mansion, where musicals were regularly held, the "Erlking" had been much applauded, and when it was decided to have it published, the decision was announced. A hundred copies were at once subscribed for and with this encouragement the engraving of the "Erlking" and "Gretchen at the Spinning Wheel" was forthwith begun. The pieces were sold by the music publishers on commission. The plan succeeded beyond expectation, so that other songs were issued in the same way, until, when seven had appeared the publishers were willing to risk the engraving of other songs themselves. Before all this had taken place, Johann Vogl, an admired opera singer in Vienna at the time, had learned Schubert's "Erlking," and had sung it in March, 1821, at a public concert patronized by royalty. The song was received with storms of applause.

Schober, who knew the singer, constantly talked to him about the gifts of his friend and begged him to come and see Schubert. At last one day he consented. They found the composer hard at work as usual, music sheets covering the floor as well as the table and chair. Vogl, used to the highest society, made himself quite at home and did his best to put Schubert at his ease, but the composer remained shy and confused. The singer began looking over some manuscripts. When he left he shook Schubert's hand warmly, remarking; "There is stuff in you, but you squander your fine thoughts instead of making the most of them."

Vogl had been much impressed by what he had seen that day, and repeated his visit. Before long the two were close friends. Schubert wrote to his brother: "When Vogl sings and I accompany him, we seem for the moment to be one." Vogl wrote of Schubert's songs that they were "truly divine inspirations."

Schubert's residence with his friend Schober only lasted six months, for Schober's brother came to live with him, and the composer had to shift for himself. Teaching was exceedingly distasteful to him, yet as his music did not bring in anything for years after he left home, he had to find some means of making a living. In these straits he accepted a position as music teacher in the family of Count Johann Esterházy. This meant that he must live with the family in their Vienna home in winter, and go with them to their country seat in the summer. The change from the free life he had enjoyed with his friends who idolized him and his beautiful music, to the etiquette of aristocratic life, was great. But there were many comforts amid his new surroundings; the family was musical, the duties were not heavy, and so Schubert was not unhappy.

At the Esterházy country estate of Zelész, he heard many Hungarian melodies sung or played by the gipsies, or by servants in the castle. He has employed some of these tunes in his first set of Valses. In his present position he had much leisure for composition. Indeed Franz Schubert's whole life was spent in giving out the vast treasures of melody with which he had been so richly endowed. These flowed from his pen in a constant stream, one beautiful work after another. He wrote them down wherever he happened to be and when a scrap of paper could be had. The exquisite song "Hark, Hark the Lark" was jotted down on the back of a bill of fare, in a beer garden. The beautiful works which he produced day after day brought him little or no money, perhaps because he was so modest and retiring, modestly undervaluing everything he did. He had no desire to push himself, but wrote because impelled to by the urge within. So little did he sometimes value his work that a fine composition would be tucked away somewhere and quite forgotten. His physical strength was not robust enough to stand the strain of constant composition. Then too, when funds were very low, as they often were, he took poor lodgings, and denied himself the necessary nourishing food. If he could have had a dear companion to look after his material needs and share his aims and aspirations, his earthly life might have been prolonged for many a year. With no one to advise him, and often pressed with hunger and poverty, he was induced to sell the copyrights of twelve of his best songs, including the "Erlking" and the "Wanderer," for a sum equal to about four hundred dollars. It is said the publishers made on the "Wanderer" alone, up to the year 1861, a sum of about five thousand five hundred dollars. It is true that "everything he touched turned to music," as Schumann once said of him. The hours of sleep were more and more curtailed, for he wrote late at night and rose early the next day. It is even said he slept in his spectacles, to save the trouble and time of putting them on in the morning.

In Schubert's boyhood, the music of Mozart influenced him most. This is seen in his earlier compositions. Beethoven was a great master to him then, but as time went on the spell of his music always grew stronger. In 1822, he wrote and published a set of variations on a French air, and dedicated them to Beethoven. He greatly desired to present them in person to the master he adored, but was too shy to go alone. Diabelli, the publisher, finally went with him. Beethoven was courteous but formal, pushing paper and pencil toward his guest, as he was totally deaf. Schubert was too shy to write a single word. However he produced his Variations. Beethoven seemed pleased with the dedication, and looked through the music. Soon he found something in it he did not approve of and pointed it out. The young author, losing his presence of mind, fled from the house. But Beethoven really liked the music and often played it to his nephew.,

Five years later, during his last illness, a, collection of some sixty of Schubert's songs was placed in his hands. He turned them over and over with amazement and delight. "Truly Schubert has the divine fire," he exclaimed. He wanted to see the composer of such beautiful music. Schubert came and was allowed to have a talk with him first, before other friends who were waiting. When Schubert paid another visit to the bedside of the master, it was almost the end of his life, though he could recognize all who stood about him. Overcome with emotion, Schubert left the room.

A couple of weeks after this Schubert was one of the torch bearers who accompanied the great master to the last resting place. Little did the young man of thirty dream that he would soon follow after. His life at this time was full of disappointments. He had always longed to write for the lyric stage. He composed numerous operas; but they were always rejected, for one reason or another. The last, "Fierabras," which was on the point of being produced, was finally given up. The composer became very dejected, and believed himself to be the most unfortunate, the most miserable being on earth. But, fortunately for Schubert, his cheerfulness again asserted itself and the stream of production resumed its flow. With his temperament, at one moment he would be utterly despairing, the next his troubles would seem to be forgotten, and he would be writing a song, a symphony or a sonata. At all events, constant work filled his days. The last year of his life was productive of some of his finest works.

About the end of October, 1828, he began to show signs of a serious breakdown. He was living at the home of his brother Ferdinand, in one of the suburbs of the city. Although he revived a little during the early part of November, so that he could resume walks in the neighborhood, the weakness increased, and eleven days passed without food or drink. Lingering till the nineteenth of November, he passed peacefully away, still in his early manhood. The old father, the schoolmaster at the old home, hoped to have his son buried in the little cemetery near by. But Ferdinand knew his brother's wish, to be placed near Beethoven in Währinger Cemetery. The monument, erected by his friends and admirers the following year, bears, above the name, this inscription:

"Music has here entombed a rich treasure, but much fairer hopes."

CHAPTER X

FELIX
MENDELSSOHN-BARTHOLDY

MENDELSSOHN has often been named "Felix the Happy," and he truly deserved the title. Blest with a most cheerful disposition, with the power to make friends of every one he met, and wherever he went, the son of a rich banker, surrounded with everything that wealth could give, it was indeed no wonder that Felix Mendelssohn was happy. He did not have to struggle with poverty and privation as most of the other great musicians were forced to do. Their music was often the expression of struggle and sorrow. He had none of these things to bear; he was carefree and happy, and his music reflects the joyous contentment of his life.

The Mendelssohn family originally lived in Hamburg. Their house faced one of the fine squares of the city, with a handsome church on the opposite side. The building is still there and well preserved, although the principal story is used as public dining rooms. A large tablet has been placed above the doorway, with a likeness of the composer encircled by a wreath of laurel. Here little Felix was born, February 3, 1809. There were other children, Fanny a year or two older, then after Felix came Rebekka and little Paul. When French soldiers occupied the town in 1811, life became very unpleasant for the German residents, and whoever could, sought refuge in other cities and towns. Among those who successfully made their escape was the Mendelssohn-Bartholdy family, the second name belonged to the family and was used to distinguish their own from other branches of the Mendelssohn family. With his wife and children, Abraham Mendelssohn fled to Berlin, and made his home for some years with the grandmother, who had a house on the Neue Promenade, a fine broad street, with houses only on one side, the opposite side descended in a grassy slope to the canal, which flowed lazily by.

It was a happy life the children led, amid ideal surroundings. Felix very early showed a great fondness for music, and everything was done to foster his budding talent. With his sister Fanny, to whom he was devotedly attached, he began to have short music lessons from his mother when he was only four years old. Their progress was so satisfactory, that after a while, professional musicians were engaged to teach them piano, violin and composition, as a regular part of their education. Besides these, they must study Greek, Latin, drawing and school subjects. With so much study to be done each day, it was necessary to begin work at five o'clock in the morning. But in spite of hard work all were happy, and as for Felix nothing could dampen the flow of his high spirits; he enjoyed equally work and play, giving the same earnest attention to each. Both he and Fanny were beginning to compose, and Felix's attempts at improvising upon some comical incident in their play time would call forth peals of laughter from the inseparable children.

Soon more ambitious attempts at composition were made, the aim being to write little operas. But unless they could be performed, it was useless to try and make operas. This was a serious difficulty; but Felix was deeply in earnest in whatever he undertook, and decided he must have an orchestra to try out his operatic efforts. It looked like an impossibility, but love and money can accomplish wonders. A small orchestra was duly selected from among the members of the Court band. The lad Felix was to conduct these sedate musicians, which he did modestly but without embarrassment, standing on a footstool before his men, waving the baton like a little general. Before the first performance was quite ready, Felix felt there must be some one present who could really judge of the merits of his little piece. Who would do so better than his old professor of thorough bass and composition, Carl Zelter, the director of the Berlin Singakademie. Zelter agreed to accept this delicate office, and a large number of friends were invited for the occasion.

This was only the beginning of a series of weekly musical evenings at the Mendelssohn home. Felix, with his dark curls, his shining eyes, and charming manners, was the life of anything he undertook. He often conducted his little pieces, but did not monopolize the time. Sometimes all four children took part, Fanny at the piano, Rebekka singing, Paul playing the 'cello and Felix at the desk. Old Zelter was generally present, and though averse to praising pupils, would often say a few words of encouragement at the close.

Felix was at this time but little more than twelve years old. He had within the last year composed fifty or sixty pieces, including a trio for piano and strings, containing three movements, several sonatas for the piano, some songs and a musical comedy in three scenes, for piano and voices. All these were written with the greatest care and precision, and with the date of each neatly added. He collected his pieces into volumes; and the more work he did the more neatly he wrote.

The boy Felix had a wonderful gift for making friends. One day he suddenly caught sight of Carl Maria von Weber walking along the streets of Berlin, near his home. He recognized the famous composer at once, as he had lately visited his parents. The boy's dark eyes glowed with pleasure at the recognition, and tossing back his curls, he sprang forward and threw his arms about Weber's neck, begging him to go home with him. When the astonished musician recovered himself, he presented the boy to Jules Benedict, his young friend and pupil who walked at his side, saying, "This is Felix Mendelssohn." For response Felix, with a bright look, seized the young man's hand in both his own. Weber stood by smiling at the boy's enthusiasm. Again Felix besought them to come home with him, but Weber had to attend a rehearsal. "Is it for the opera?" the boy cried excitedly.

"Yes," answered the composer.

"Does he know all about it?" asked Felix, pointing to Benedict.

"Indeed he does," answered the composer laughing, "or if he doesn't he ought to for he has been bored enough with it already." The boy's eyes flashed.

"Then *you* will come with me to my home, which is quite near, will you not?" There was no refusing those appealing dark eyes. Felix again embraced Weber, and then challenged his new friend, Mr. Benedict, to race him to the door of his house. On entering he dragged the visitor upstairs to the drawing-room, exclaiming, "Mama, Mama, here is a gentleman, a pupil of Carl Weber, who knows all about the new opera, 'Der Freischütz?'"

The young musician received a warm welcome, and was not able to leave until he had played on the piano all the airs he could remember from the wonderful new opera, which Weber had come to Berlin to superintend. Benedict was so pleased with his first visit that he came again. This time he found Felix writing music and asked what it was. "I am finishing my new quartet for piano and strings," was the simple reply. To say that Benedict was surprised at such an answer from a boy of twelve hardly expresses what he felt. It was quite true he did not yet know Felix Mendelssohn. "And now," said the boy, laying down his pen, "I will play to you, to prove how grateful I am that you played to us last time." He then sat down at the piano and played correctly several melodies from "Der Freischütz," which Benedict had played on his first visit. After that they went into the garden, and Felix for the moment, became a rollicking boy, jumping fences and climbing trees like a squirrel.

Toward the close of this year, 1821, his teacher Zelter

announced he intended going to Weimar, to see Goethe, the aged poet of Weimar, and was willing to take Felix with him. The poet's house at Weimar was indeed a shrine to the elect, and the chance of meeting the object of so much hero worship, filled the impressionable mind of Felix with reverential awe. Zelter on his part, felt a certain pride in bringing his favorite pupil to the notice of the great man, though he would not have permitted Felix to guess what he felt for anything he possessed.

When they arrived, Goethe was walking in his garden. He greeted both with kindness and affection, and it was arranged that Felix should play for him next day. Zelter had told Goethe much about his pupil's unusual talents, but the poet wished to prove these accounts by his own tests. Selecting piece after piece of manuscript music from his collection, he asked the boy to play them at sight. He was able to do so with ease, to the astonishment of the friends who had come in to hear him. They were more delighted when he took a theme from one of the pieces and improvised upon it. Withholding his praise, Goethe announced he had a final test, and placed on the music desk a sheet which seemed covered with mere scratches and blotches. The boy laughingly exclaimed, "Who could ever read such writing as that?" Zelter rose and came to the piano to look at this curiosity. "Why, it is Beethoven's writing; one can see that a mile off! He always wrote as if he used a broomstick for a pen, then wiped his sleeve over the wet ink!"

The boy picked out the strange manuscript bit by

bit; when he came to the end he cried, "Now I will play it through for you," which he did without a mistake. Goethe was well pleased and begged Felix to come every day and play, while he was in the city. The two became fast friends; the poet treated him as a son, and at parting begged he would soon return to Weimar, that they might again be together. During the following summer the whole family made a tour through Switzerland, much to the delight of Felix, who enjoyed every moment. There was little time for real work in composition, but a couple of songs and the beginning of a piano quartet were inspired by the view of Lake Geneva and its exquisite surroundings.

When Felix returned to Berlin, he had grown much, physically as well as mentally. He was now tall and strong, his curling locks had been clipped, and he seemed at a single bound to have become almost a man. His happy, boyish spirits, however, had not changed in the least. About this time the family removed from their home on the Neue Promenade, to a larger and more stately mansion, No. 3 Leipsiger Strasse, then situated on the outskirts of the town, near the Potsdam Gate. As those who know the modern city realize, this house, now no longer a private residence, stands in the very heart of traffic and business. The rooms of the new home were large and elegant, with a spacious salon suitable for musicals and large functions. A fine garden or park belonged to the house, where were lawns shaded by forest trees, winding paths, flowering shrubs and arbors in shady nooks, offering quiet retreats. Best of all there was a garden house, with a central hall, which would hold several hundred people, having long windows and glass doors looking out upon the trees and flowers. Sunday concerts were soon resumed and given in the garden house, where, on week days the young people met, with friends and elders, to play, and act and enjoy the social life of the home. The mansion and its hospitality became famous, and every great musician, at one time or another, came to pay his respects and become acquainted with this art-loving family.

At a family party in honor of Felix's fifteenth birthday, his teacher Zelter saluted him as no longer an apprentice, but as an "assistant" and member of the Brotherhood of Art. Very soon after this the young composer completed two important works. The first was an Octet for strings. He was not yet seventeen when the Octet was finished, which was pronounced the most fresh and original work he had yet accomplished. It marked a distinct stage in the gifted youth's development. The composition which followed was the beautiful "Midsummer Night's Dream" music. He and his sister Fanny had lately made the acquaintance of Shakespeare through a German translation, and had been fascinated by this fairy play. The young people spent much of their time in the lovely garden that summer, and amid these delightful surroundings the music was conceived.

The Overture was first to spring into being. When it was written out, Felix and Fanny often played it as a duet. In this form the composer-pianist Moscheles heard it and was impressed by its beauty. The fascinating Scherzo and dreamy Nocturne followed. When all were elaborated and perfected, the complete work was performed by the garden house orchestra for a crowded audience, who abundantly expressed their delight. Sir G. Macfarren has said of it: "No one musical work contains so many points of harmony and orchestration that are novel yet none of them have the air of experiment, but all seem to have been written with a certainty of their success."

And now a great plan occupied Mendelssohn's mind, a project which had been forming for some time; this was nothing less than to do something to arouse people to know and appreciate the great works of Johann Sebastian Bach. Two years before Felix had been presented with a manuscript score of Bach's "Passion according to St. Matthew," which Zelter had allowed to be copied from the manuscript preserved in the Singakademie. The old man was a devoted lover of Bach's music, and had taught his pupil in the same spirit. When Felix found himself the possessor of this wonderful book, he set to work to master it, until he knew every bit of it by heart. As he studied it deeply he was more and more impressed with its beauty and sublimity. He could hardly believe that this great work was unknown throughout Germany, since more than a hundred years had passed since it had been written. He determined to do something to arouse people from such apathy.

Talking the matter over with musicians and friends, he began to interest them in the plan to study the music of the Passion. Soon he had secured sixteen good voices, who rehearsed at his home once a week. His enthusiasm fired them to study the music seriously, and before very long they were anxious to give a public performance. There was a splendid choir of nearly four hundred voices conducted by Zelter, at the Singakademie; if he would only lend his chorus to give a trial performance, under Mendelssohn's conducting, how splendid that would be! But Felix knew that Zelter had no faith in the public taking any interest in Bach, so there was no use asking. This opinion was opposed by one of his little choir, named Devrient, who insisted that Zelter should be approached on the subject. As he himself had been a pupil of Zelter, he persuaded Mendelssohn to accompany him to the director's house.

Zelter was found seated at his instrument, enveloped by a cloud of smoke from a long stemmed pipe. Devrient unfolded the plan of bringing this great work of Bach to the knowledge of the public. The old man listened to their plea with growing impatience, until he became quite excited, rose from his chair and paced the floor with great strides, exclaiming, "No, it is not to be thought of—it is a mad scheme." To Felix argument then seemed useless and he beckoned his friend to come away, but Devrient refused to move, and kept up his persuasive argument. Finally, as though a miracle had been wrought, Zelter began to weaken, and at last gave in, and besides promised all the aid in his power.

How this youth, not yet twenty, undertook the great task of preparing this masterpiece, and what he accomplished is little short of the marvelous. The public performance, conducted by Mendelssohn, took place March 11, 1829, with every ticket sold and more than a thousand persons turned away. A second performance was given on March 21, the anniversary of Bach's birth, before a packed house. These performances marked the beginning of a great Bach revival in Germany and England, and the love for this music has never been lost, but increases each year.

And now it seemed best for Felix to travel and see something of other countries. He had long wished to visit England, and the present seemed a favorable time, as his friends there assured him of a warm welcome. The pleasure he felt on reaching London was increased by the enthusiastic greeting he received at the hands of the musical public. He first appeared at a Philharmonic concert on May 25, when his Symphony in C minor was played. The next day he wrote to Fanny: "The success of the concert last night was beyond all I had ever dreamed. It began with my Symphony. I was led to the desk and received an immense applause. The Adagio was encored, but I went on; the Scherzo was so vigorously applauded that I had to repeat it. After the Finale there was lots more applause, while I was thanking the orchestra and shaking hands, till I left the room."

A continual round of functions interspersed with concerts at which he played or conducted, filled the young composer's time. The overture to "Midsummer Night's Dream" was played several times and always received with enthusiasm. On one occasion a friend was so careless as to leave the manuscript in a hackney coach on his way home and it was lost. "Never mind, I will write another," said Mendelssohn, which he was able to do, without making a single error.

When the London season closed, Mendelssohn and his friend Klingemann went up to Scotland, where he was deeply impressed with the varied beauty of the scenery. Perhaps the Hebrides enthralled him most, with their lonely grandeur. His impressions have been preserved in the Overture to "Fingal's Cave," while from the whole trip he gained inspiration for the Scottish Symphony.

On his return to London and before he could set out for Berlin, Felix injured his knee, which laid him up for several weeks, and prevented his presence at the home marriage of his sister Fanny, to William Hensel, the young painter. This was a keen disappointment to all, but Fanny was not to be separated from her family, as on Mendelssohn's return, he found the young couple had taken up their residence in the Gartenhaus.

Mendelssohn had been greatly pleased with his London visit, and though the grand tour he had planned was really only begun, he felt a strong desire to return to England. However, other countries had to be visited first. The following May he started south, bound for Vienna, Florence and Rome. His way led through Weimar and gave opportunity for a last visit to Goethe. They passed a number of days in sympathetic companionship. The poet always wanted music, but did not seem to care for Beethoven's compositions, which he said did not touch him at all, though he felt they were great, astonishing.

After visiting numerous German cities, Switzerland was reached and its wonderful scenery stirred Mendelssohn's poetic soul to the depths. Yet, though his passionate love of nature was so impressed by the great mountains, forests and waterfalls, it was the sea which he loved best of all. As he approached Naples, and saw the sea sparkling in the sun lighted bay, he exclaimed: "To me it is the finest object in nature! I love it almost more than the sky. I always feel happy when I see before me the wide expanse of water." Rome, of course, was a center of fascination. Every day he picked out some special object of interest to visit, which made that particular day one never to be forgotten. The tour lasted until the spring of 1832, before Mendelssohn returned to his home in Berlin, only to leave it shortly afterwards to return to London. This great city, in spite of its fogs, noises and turmoil, appealed to him more than the sunshine of Naples, the fascination of Florence or the beauty of Rome.

The comment on Mendelssohn that "he lived years where others only lived weeks," gives a faint idea of the fulness with which his time was occupied. It is only possible to touch on his activities in composition, for he was always at work. In May 1836 when he was twenty-seven, he conducted in Düsseldorf the first performance of his oratorio of "St. Paul." At this period he wrote many of those charming piano pieces which he called "Songs without Words." This same year brought deepest happiness to Mendelssohn, in his engagement to Cécile Jean-Renaud, the beautiful daughter of a French Protestant clergyman. The following spring they were married, a true marriage of love and stedfast devotion.

The greatest work of Mendelssohn's career was his

oratorio of "Elijah" which had long grown in his mind, until it was on the eve of completion in the spring of 1846. In a letter to the famous singer Jenny Lind, an intimate friend, he writes: "I am jumping about my room for joy. If my work turns out half as good as I fancy it is, how pleased I shall be."

During these years in which he conceived the "Elijah," his fame had spread widely. Honors had been bestowed on him by many royalties. The King of Saxony had made him Capellmeister of his Court, and Queen Victoria had shown him many proofs of personal regard, which endeared him more than ever to the country which had first signally recognized his genius.

It was Leipsic perhaps which felt the power of his genius most conclusively. The since famous Leipsic Conservatory was founded by him, and he was unceasing in his labors to advance art in every direction. He also found time to carry out a long cherished plan to erect, at the threshold of the Thomas School, Leipsic, a monument to the memory of Sebastian Bach.

Let us take one more glimpse of our beloved composer. It was the morning of August 26, 1846. The Town Hall of Birmingham, England, was filled with an expectant throng, for today the composer of the "Elijah" was to conduct his greatest work, for the first time before an English audience. When Mendelssohn stepped upon the platform, he was greeted by a deafening shout; the reception was overwhelming, and at the close the entire audience sprang to its feet in a frenzy of admiration. He wrote to his brother Paul that evening: "No work of mine ever went so admirably at the first performance, or was received with such enthusiasm both by musicians and public." During April the following year, four performances of the "Elijah" took place in Exeter Hall, the composer conducting, the Queen and Prince Albert being present on the second occasion. This visit to England which was to be his last, had used his strength to the limit of endurance, and there was a shadow of a coming breakdown. Soon after he rejoined his family in Frankfort, his sister Fanny suddenly passed away in Berlin. The news was broken to him too quickly, and with a shriek he fell unconscious to the floor.

From this shock he never seemed to rally, though at intervals for a while, he still composed. His death occurred November 4, 1847. It can be said of him that his was a beautiful life, in which "there was nothing to tell that was not honorable to his memory and profitable to all men."

Mendelssohn's funeral was imposing. The first portion was solemnized at Leipsic, attended by crowds of musicians and students, one of the latter bearing on a cushion a silver crown presented by his pupils of the Conservatory. Beside the crown rested the Order "Pour le Mérite," conferred on him by the King of Prussia. The band, during the long procession, played the E minor "Song without Words," and at the close of the service the choir sang the final chorus from Bach's "Passion." The same night the body was taken to Berlin and placed in the family plot in the old Dreifaltigkeit Kirchhof, beside that of his devoted sister Fanny.

CHAPTER XI

ROBERT SCHUMANN

MANY of the composers whose life stories we have read were surrounded by musical atmosphere from their earliest years; Robert Schumann seems to have been an exception. His father, August Schumann, was the son of a poor pastor, and the boy August was intended to be brought up a merchant. At the age of fifteen he was put into a store in Nonneburg. He was refined in his tastes, loved books, and tried even in boyhood to write poetry. He seemed destined, however, to live the life marked out for him, at least for a time. It grew so distasteful, that later he gave it up and, on account of extreme poverty, returned to his parents' home, where he had the leisure to write. At last he secured a position in a book store in Zeitz. In this little town he met the daughter of his employer. The engagement was allowed on the condition that he should leave the book store and set up his own business. But where was the money to come from? He left the store, returned home and in a year and a half had earned a thousand thalers, then quite a handsome sum.

He now claimed the hand of his chosen love and

established in the book business, labored so unceasingly, that the business increased. Then he moved to a more favorable location, choosing the mining town of Zwickau, in Saxony.

Here, this industrious, honorable man and his attractive, intelligent, but rather narrow and uneducated young wife lived out their lives, and brought up their children, of whom Robert, born June 8, 1810, was the youngest; before him there were three brothers and a sister. All passed away before Robert himself.

He was the so-called "handsome child" of the family, and much petted by the women. Besides his mother there was his god-mother, who was very fond of him, and at her home he would spend whole days and nights. As his talents developed, the boy became the spoilt darling of everybody. This lay at the foundation of his extreme susceptibility, even the obstinacy of his riper years.

Little Robert at six was sent to a popular private school and now for the first time mingled with a number of children of his own age. The first symptoms of ambition, the source of much of his later achievement, began to show itself, though quite unconsciously. It made him the life of all childish games. If the children played "soldiers," little Robert was always captain. The others loved his good nature and friendliness, and always yielded to him.

He was a good student in the primary school, but in no way distinguished himself in his studies. The following year he was allowed to take piano lessons of an old pedantic professor from Zwickau High School. This man had taught himself music, but had heard little of it. The kind of instruction he was able to give may be imagined, yet Robert was faithful all his life to this kind old friend.

In spite of inadequate guidance, music soon kindled the boy's soul. He began to try to make music himself, though entirely ignorant of the rules of composition. The first of these efforts, a set of little dances, were written during his seventh or eighth year. It was soon discovered that he could improvise on the piano; indeed he could sketch the disposition of his companions by certain figures on the piano, so exactly and comically that every one burst out laughing at the portraits. He was fond of reading too, much to his father's delight, and early tried his hand at authorship. He wrote robber plays, which he staged with the aid of the family and such of his youthful friends as were qualified. The father now began to hope his favorite son would become an author or poet; but later Robert's increasing love for music put this hope to flight.

The father happened to take his boy with him to Carlsbad in the summer of 1819, and here he heard for the first time a great pianist, Ignatz Moscheles. His masterful playing made a great impression on the nine year old enthusiast, who began now to wish to become a musician, and applied himself to music with redoubled zeal. He also made such good progress at school that at Easter 1820 he was able to enter the Zwickau Academy.

The love for music grew with each day. With a

boy of his own age, as devoted as himself to music, four-hand works of Haydn, Mozart and Beethoven, as well as pieces by Weber, Hummel and Czerny, were played almost daily. The greatest ecstasy was caused by the arrival of a Steck piano at the Schumann home, which showed that father Schumann endeavored to further his boy's taste for music. About this time Robert found by chance, the orchestral score of an old Italian overture. He conceived the bold idea of performing it. So a bit of an orchestra was gathered among the boys he knew, who could play an instrument. There were two violins, two flutes, a clarinet and two horns. Robert, who conducted with great fervor, supplied as best he could the other parts on the piano.

This effort was a great incentive to the boys, principally to Robert, who began to arrange things for his little band and composed music for the one hundred fiftieth Psalm. This was in his twelfth year.

August Schumann was more and more convinced that Providence had intended his son to become a musician, and though the mother struggled against it, he resolved to see that Robert had a musical education. Carl Maria von Weber, then living in Dresden, was written to, and answered he was willing to accept the boy as a student. The plan never came to anything however, for what reason is not known. The boy was left now to direct his own musical studies, just when he needed an expert guiding hand. He had no rivals in his native town, where he sometimes appeared as a pianist. It was no wonder he thought he was on the right road, and that he tried more than ever to win his mother's consent to his following music as a life work.

And now a great change took place in the lively, fun-loving boy. He seemed to lose his gay spirits and become reflective, silent and reserved. This condition of mind never left him, but grew into a deeper reserve as the years passed.

Two events deeply stirred Robert's nature with great force—the death of his father in 1826, and his acquaintance with the works of Jean Paul. The Jean Paul fever attacked him in all its transcendentalism, and this influence remained through life, with more or less intensity.

After his father left him, Robert found he must make a choice of a profession. His mother had set her heart on his making a study of law, while his heart was set on music. Yielding to her wishes for a time he went to Leipsic in March 1828 to prepare to enter the University as a student of law. He also gained consent to study piano at the same time, and began lessons with Frederick Wieck. The desire to study with Wieck was inspired by the piano playing of his little daughter, Clara, then nine years old, who had already gained a considerable degree of musical culture and promised to make her mark as a pianist.

Under his new teacher, Robert for the first time was obliged to study a rational system of technic and tone production. He was also expected to learn harmony correctly, but strangely enough he seemed to take no interest in it, even saying he thought such knowledge useless. He held to this foolish idea for some time, not giving it up till forced to by realizing his total ignorance of this branch of the art.

Robert now became greatly impressed by the genius of Franz Schubert. He eagerly played everything the master had composed for the piano, both for two and four hands, and Schubert's death during this year, filled him with profound grief. The young musical friends with whom Robert had become intimate, while living in Leipsic, shared his enthusiasm about his hero of German song, and they desired to enlarge their knowledge of Schubert's work. They did more, for they decided to take one representative composition and practise together till they had reached the highest perfection. The choice fell on the Trio in B flat major, Op. 99, whose beauties had greatly impressed them. After much loving labor the performance was well nigh perfect. Schumann arranged a musical party at which the Trio was played. Besides students and friends, Wieck was invited and given the seat of honor.

This musical evening was the forerunner of many others. Weekly meetings were held in Robert's room, where much music was played and discussed. The talk often turned to grand old Bach and his "Well-Tempered Clavichord," to which in those early days, he gave ardent study.

With all this music study and intercourse with musical friends there was very little time left for the study of law. Yet he still kept up appearances by attending the lectures, and had intended for some months to enter the Heidelberg University. This decision was put into execution in May 1829, when he started by coach for Heidelberg.

We find Robert Schumann at nineteen domiciled in the beautiful city of Heidelberg, and surrounded by a few musical friends, who were kindred spirits. With a good piano in his room, the "life of flowers," as he called it, began. Almost daily they made delightful trips in a one-horse carriage into the suburbs. For longer trips they went to Baden-Baden, Wurms, Spires and Mannheim. Whenever Robert went with his friends he always carried a small "dumb piano" on which he industriously practised finger exercises, meanwhile joining in the conversation. During the following August and September, Robert and two or three chosen companions made a delightful journey through Italy, the young man preparing himself by studying Latin, in which he became so fluent that he could translate poems from one language to the other.

The next winter Robert devoted himself to music more than ever—"played the piano much," as he says. His skill as a pianist gradually became known in Heidelberg and he frequently played in private houses. But he was not content with the regular study of the piano. He wanted to get ahead faster and invented some sort of a device to render his fourth finger more firm and supple. It did not have the desired effect however, but was the means in time of injuring his hands so that he never could attain the piano virtuosity he dreamed of.

Before starting on the trip to Italy just mentioned,

he felt that a decision must be reached about his music. It had become as the breath of life to him. He wrote his mother and laid bare his heart to her. "My whole life has been a twenty years struggle between poetry and prose, or let us say—between music and law. If I follow my own bent, it points, as I believe correctly, to music. Write yourself to Wieck at Leipsic and ask him frankly what he thinks of me and my plan. Beg him to answer at once and decisively." The letter was duly written to Wieck, who decided in favor of Robert and his plans.

Robert on hearing his decision was wild with joy. He wrote an exuberant letter to Wieck promising to be most submissive as a piano pupil and saying "whole pailfuls of very very cold theory can do me no harm and I will work at it without a murmur. I give myself up wholly to you."

With a heart full of hope, young Schumann returned to Leipsic, which he had gladly left more than a year before. It was during this early resumption of piano lessons with Wieck that he began the treatment which he thought would advance his technic in such a marvelously short time. He fastened his third finger into a machine, of his own invention, then practised unceasingly with the other four. At last he lost control over the muscles of the right hand, to his great distress. He now practised unremittingly with the left hand, which gained great facility, remarkable long after he had given up piano playing.

Under these difficulties piano lessons with Wieck had to be given up and were never resumed. He studied theory for a short time with Kupach, but soon relinquished this also. He was now free to direct his own path in music and to study—study, and compose.

One of the first pieces he wrote was "The Papillons"—"Butterflies,"—published as Op. 2. It was dedicated to his three sisters-in-law, of all of whom he was very fond. In the various scenes of the Butterflies there are allusions to persons and places known to the composer; the whimsical spirit of Jean Paul broods over the whole.

Robert began to realize more and more his lack of thorough theoretical knowledge and applied to Dorn, who stood high in the musical profession in Leipsic. On his introduction, in spite of his lame hand he played his "Abegg Variations," published as Op. 1, and Dorn was willing to accept the timid quiet youth as pupil. He studied with great ardor, going from the A. B. C. to the most involved counterpoint.

Thus passed two or three busy years. Part of the time Schumann had a room in the house of his teacher Wieck and thus was thrown more or less in the society of Clara Wieck, now a young girl of thirteen or fourteen. Later he gave up his room—though not his intimate relations with the family—and moved to a summer residence in Riedel's Garden, where he spent the days in music and the evenings with his friends.

The year 1833, was one of the most remarkable in his life so far. Not the least important event was the establishment of the "Neue Zeitschrift für Musik." Schumann himself says of this:—

"At the close of the year '33, a number of musicians, mostly young, met in Leipsic every evening, apparently by accident at first, but really for the interchange of ideas on all musical subjects. One day the young hot heads exclaimed: 'Why do we look idly on? Let's take hold and make things better.' Thus the new Journal for music began.

"The youthful, fresh and fiery tone of the Journal is to be in sharp contrast to the characterless, worn-out Leipsic criticism. The elevation of German taste, the encouragement of young talent must be our goal. We write not to enrich tradespeople, but to honor artists."

Schumann took up arms in favor of the younger generation of musicians and helped make the fame of many now held in the world's highest esteem. Sometimes, he admits, his ardor carried him too far in recognition of youthful talent, but in the main he was very just in his estimates. We do not forget how his quick commendation aided Brahms.

The young musicians who founded the paper had formed themselves also into an alliance, which they called the Davidsbündlerschaft. The idea of this alliance, which was derived from David's war with the Philistines, seemed to exist only in the mind of Schumann himself. It gave him a chance to write under the name of different characters, chief of whom were Florestan and Eusebius, between whom stood Master Raro. In Florestan Schumann expressed the powerful, passionate side of his nature, and in Eusebius the mild and dreamy side.

He wrote to a friend: "Florestan and Eusebius are my double nature, which I would gladly—like Raro—melt down into one man." As time passed however, he made less and less use of these fanciful images until they finally seemed to fade out of his mind.

An important event of 1834, was Schumann's acquaintance with Ernestine von Fricken, who came to Leipsic from the little town of Asch, on the Bohemian border. She lived at the Wiecks', expecting to become a pianist under Papa Wieck's tuition. Schumann became greatly interested in Ernestine and for some time he had in mind an engagement with her. The noble "Études Symphoniques" were written this year. The theme was suggested by Ernestine's father. The "Carnival" was partly written in this year, but not completed till the following year. In this collection of charming short pieces he brings in the characters of his dreams,—Florestan, Eusebius, Chiarina (Clara), Estrella (Ernestine). There is the March against the Philistines, and the titles of many other of the little pieces are characteristic. It is a true Schumann composition, full of his traits. Here we have the sweet, graceful, elegant and the very humorous and comical finale.

The tone creations of 1835 consist of the two Sonatas, F sharp minor, Op. 11 and G minor, Op. 22, which are held by pianists to be among his most interesting and poetical works.

By the next year Schumann had suffered a deep sorrow in the loss of his mother, and also his love for Ernestine began to cool, until the partial bond was amicably dissolved. Meanwhile his affection for Clara Wieck, who was just budding into womanhood, began to ripen into devoted love. This, too, was the beginning of the long struggle for the possession of his beloved, since the father had opposed such a connection from beginning to end. Schumann wrote a friend in 1839: "Truly from the struggle Clara has cost me, much music has been caused and created; the Concerto, Sonatas, Davidsbündler Dances, Kreisleriana and Novellettes are the result." Beyond the compositions just mentioned, he relieved his oppressed heart by a composition rich in meaning—nothing less than the great Fantaisie, Op. 17. He meant to contribute the profits from its sale to the fund for the erection of a monument to Beethoven. The titles to the three movements were "Ruins," "Triumphal Arch," "Starry Crown." He afterwards gave up the whole idea, and dedicated the work to Franz Liszt.

Schumann lived a quiet, busy life, and if he could have gained the consent of Clara's father for their union, he would have been supremely happy. He feared the principal reason of Wieck's refusal was that the young man should earn more money first, before thinking of settling down with a wife. Robert therefore reverted more seriously to a plan he had thought of, to go to Vienna, and move his paper to that city, hoping to better his fortunes. He felt, too, that he ought to travel, as he had remained in Leipsic for eight years without change.

Thus, by the end of September, 1838, Schumann started for Vienna with many high hopes. A friend invited him to remain at his house, which was of much advantage. He made many calls and visits, saw musicians and publishers, and really learned to know the city for itself. He found it would not be profitable for him to publish the Journal there, also that the Austrian capital was a no more propitious place to make one's fortune than the smaller town of Leipsic. However he was able to compose a number of works which have become among the best known and beloved of all, including the "Arabesque," "Faschingsschwank," or "Carnival Strains from Vienna," the "Night Pieces," Op. 24, and other short compositions.

When Robert discovered Vienna was not the city to prosper in, he thought of a return to Leipsic, to win his bride. He came back in April, and succeeded, with the help of legal proceedings, in securing Clara's hand in marriage. This was in 1840. From now on Schumann began to write songs. In this one year he composed as many as a hundred and thirty-eight songs, both large and small. He writes at this time: "The best way to cultivate a taste for melody, is to write a great deal for the voice and for independent chorus."

He now began to express himself not only in song but in orchestral music. His first effort was the beautiful B flat major Symphony, which, with the songs of that time seems to embody all the happiness he enjoyed in winning his Clara. She proved a most admirable helpmate, trying to shield him from interruptions and annoyance of every sort, so he should have his time undisturbed for his work. Thus many of his best compositions came into being in the early years of wedded happiness.

This retirement was interrupted in 1844, by a long concert tour planned by Clara. She was firmly decided to go and made Robert solemnly promise to ,accompany her to St. Petersburg. He was loath to leave the quiet he loved, but it had to be done. Clara had great success everywhere, as a pianist, giving many recitals during their travels from place to place. From Russia the artist pair went to Helsingfors, Stockholm and Copenhagen. They started on their tour in January and did not reach home till the first of June.

Schumann now seemed to lose interest in the Journal and expressed a wish to withdraw from it and live only for his creative art. An alarming state of health—both mind and body—seemed to make this retirement desirable. Perhaps owing to this condition of health he decided to leave Leipsic for good and make his home in Dresden. He and his wife took formal leave of Leipsic in a Matinée musical given on the eighth of December.

But life in Dresden became even more strenuous and more racking than it had been in Leipsic. He threw himself into the labor of composing the epilogue of Goethe's "Faust" with such ardor that he fell into an intensely nervous state where work was impossible. However, with special medical treatment he so far recovered that he was able to resume the work, but still was not himself. We can divine from brief remarks he let drop from time to time, that he lived in constant fear—fear of death, insanity or disaster of some kind. He could not bear the sight of Sonnenstein, an insane asylum near Dresden. Mendelssohn's sudden death in

November, 1847, was a great shock and preyed on his mind.

Schumann had intervals of reprieve from these morbid dreams, and he again began to compose with renewed—almost abnormal—vigor and productiveness.

The artist pair took a trip to Vienna where Clara gave several concerts. They spent some weeks there and before returning to Dresden, gave two splendid concerts in Prague, where Schumann received a perfect ovation for his piano quintette and some songs. A little later the two artists made a trip north. In Berlin Robert conducted a performance of "Paradise and the Peri" at the Singakademie, while Clara gave two recitals.

This year of 1847 was a very active one outside of the musical journeys. The master composed several piano trios, much choral music, and began the opera "Genevieve," which was not completed however, until the middle of 1848. All the compositions of the previous year were perfectly lucid and sane. The opera unfortunately had a text from which all the beauty and romance had been left out.

The music, however, revealed a rare quality of creative power, combined with deep and noble feeling. Schumann's nature was more lyric than dramatic; he was not born to write for the stage. The lyric portions of his opera are much the best. He did not realize that he failed on the dramatic side in his work, indeed seemed quite unconscious of the fact.

"Genevieve" was given in Leipsic in June 1850, directed by the composer. Two more performances were given and then the work was laid away.

In 1848, Schumann, who loved children dearly and often stopped his more serious work to write for them, composed the "Album for the Young," Op. 68, a set of forty-two pieces. The title originally was: "Christmas Album for Children who like to play the Piano." How many children, from that day to this have loved those little pieces, the "Happy Farmer," "Wild Rider," "First Loss," "Reaper's Song," and all the rest. Even the great pianists of our time are not above performing these little classics in public. They are a gift, unique in musical literature, often imitated, but never equaled by other writers. Schumann wrote of them: "The first thing in the Album I wrote for my oldest child's birthday. It seems as if I were beginning my life as a composer anew, and there are traces of the old human here and there. They are decidedly different from 'Scenes from Childhood' which are retrospective glances by a parent, and for elders, while 'Album for the Young' contains hopes, presentiments and peeps into futurity for *the young.*"

After the children's Album came the music to Byron's "Manfred." This consists of an overture and fifteen numbers. The whole work, with one exception, is deep in thought and masterly in conception. The overture especially is one of his finest productions, surpassing other orchestral works in intellectual grandeur.

A choral club of sixty-seven members, of which Schumann was the director, inspired him to compose considerable choral music, and his compositions of this time, 1848-49, were numerous.

The intense creative activity of 1849 was followed by a period of rest when the artist pair made two trips from Dresden, early in 1850. Leipsic, Bremen, and Hamburg were visited. Most of the time in Hamburg was spent with Jenny Lind, who sang at his last two concerts.

The late summer of 1850 brought Schumann an appointment of director of music in Düsseldorf, left vacant by the departure of Ferdinand Hiller for Cologne. Schumann and his wife went to Düsseldorf the first week of September and were received with open arms. A banquet and concert were arranged, at which some of the composer's important works were performed. His duties in the new post were conducting the subscription concerts, weekly rehearsals of the Choral Club and other musical performances. He seemed well content with the situation and it did not require too much of his physical strength.

Outside of his official duties his passion for work again gained the ascendent. From November 2, to December 9, he sketched and completed the Symphony in E flat in five parts, a great work, equal to any of the other works in this form.

From this time on, one important composition followed another, until increasing illness foreshadowed the sad catastrophe of the early part of 1854. He wrote in June 1851, "we are all tolerably well, except that I am the victim of occasional nervous attacks; a few days ago I fainted after hearing Radecke play the organ." These nervous attacks increased in 1852. He could not think music in rapid tempo and wished everything slow. He heard special tones to the exclusion of all others.

The close of 1853, brought two joyful events to Schumann. In October he met Johann Brahms, whom he had introduced to the world, through his Journal, as the "Messiah of Art." In November he and his wife took a trip through Holland, which was a triumphal procession. He found his music almost as well known in Holland as at home. In Rotterdam and Utrecht his third symphony was performed; in The Hague the second was given, also "The Pilgrimage of the Rose." Clara also played at many concerts.

Just before Christmas the artist pair returned to Düsseldorf.

The hallucinations which had before obsessed him now returned with alarming force. He could no longer sleep—he seemed to be lost in mental darkness.

One day in Febuary 1854, his physician made a noon call upon him. They sat chatting when suddenly Schumann left the room without a word. The doctor and his friends supposed he would return. His wife went in search of him. It seems he had left the house in dressing-gown, gone to the Rhine bridge and thrown himself into the river. Some sailors rescued him.

He now received constant care, and it was found best to place him in a private hospital near Bonn. Here he remained till the end of July, 1856, when the end came.

In his death the world of music lost one of the most highly gifted spirits. His life was important and instructive for its moral and intellectual grandeur, its struggles for the noblest, loftiest subjects as well as for its truly great results.

CHAPTER XII

FREDERIC CHOPIN

WHAT would the piano playing world do without the music of Frederic Chopin? We can hardly think of the piano without thinking of Chopin, since he wrote almost exclusively for the universal instrument. His music touches the heart always rather than the head, the emotional message far outweighs the intellectual meaning. It is vital music—love music, winning the heart by its tenderness, voicing the highest sentiments by its refinement, its purity, its perfection of detail and finish.

And the man who could compose with such refinement, with such appealing eloquence, must have possessed those qualities which shine out in his music. He must have been gentle, chivalrous, high-thoughted. We cannot avoid expressing ourselves in our work—in whatever we do.

The father of this beloved composer was a Frenchman, born in Nancy, Lorraine, in 1770, the same year Beethoven saw the light in Bonn. He was carefully brought up, well-bred and well-educated. When a friend of his in Warsaw, Poland, in the tobacco and snuff trade,

then in high repute with the nobility, needed help with his book-keeping, he sent for the seventeen-year-old lad. Thus it happened that Nicholas Chopin came to Warsaw in 1787. It was a time of unrest, when the nation was struggling for liberty and independence. The young man applied himself to master the language, and study the character and needs of his adopted country, that he might be well informed. During the period of insecurity in political affairs, the tobacco factory had to be closed and Nicholas Chopin looked for other activity. A few years later we find him in the household of Countess Skarbek, as a tutor to her son, Frederic. Here he met his bride, Justina de Krzyzanowska, a young lady of noble but poor family, whom he married in 1806. She became the mother of his four children, three girls and a boy.

The boy Frederic Chopin, was born on March 1, 1809, in the little village of Zelazowa Wola, belonging to the Countess Skarbek, about twenty-eight miles from Warsaw. It is probable the family did not remain here long, for the young husband was on the lookout for more profitable employment. He was successful, for on October 1, 1810, he was appointed Professor of French in the newly founded Lyceum in Warsaw. He also soon organized a boarding school for boys in his own home, which was patronized by the best Polish families of the country.

Surrounded by refined, cultivated people, in an atmosphere at once moral and intellectual, little Frederic passed a fortunate childhood. He soon manifested such fondness for music, especially for the piano, that his parents allowed him to have lessons, his teacher being

Adalbert Zywny, the best-known master of the city. It is related that Zywny only taught his little pupil first principles, for the child's progress was so extraordinary that before long he had mastered all his teacher could impart, and at twelve he was left to shape his own musical destiny.

He early gave proofs of his talents. Before he was eight years old he played at a large evening company, with such surprising cleverness that it was predicted he would become another Mozart. The next year he was invited to take part in a large concert given under distinguished patronage. The boy was a simple, modest child, and played the piano as the bird sings, with unconscious art. When he returned home after this concert, his mother asked: "What did the people like best?" and he answered naïvely: "Oh, mama, every one was looking at my collar."

After this, little Frederic became more than ever the pet of the aristocracy of Warsaw; his charming manners, his unspoiled nature, his musical gifts made him welcome in princely homes. He had also begun to compose; indeed these efforts started soon after he began piano lessons, and before he could handle a pen. His teacher had to write down what the little composer played. Among those early pieces were mazurkas, polonaises, valses and the like. At the age of ten he dedicated a march to Grand Duke Constantine, who had it scored for band and played on parade. He started lessons in composition with Joseph Elsner, a celebrated teacher, who became a life-long adviser and friend.

Up to the age of fifteen, Frederic was taught at home, in his father's school. He now entered the Warsaw Lyceum; and proved a good student, twice carrying off a prize. With this studiousness was joined a gaiety and sprightliness that manifested itself in all sorts of fun and mischief. He loved to play pranks on his sisters, comrades and others, and had a fondness for caricature, taking off the peculiarities of those about him with pose and pen. Indeed it was the opinion of a clever member of the profession, that the lad was born to become a great actor. All the young Chopins had a great fondness for literature and writing; they occasionally tried their hand at poetry, and the production of original one-act plays, written for birthday fêtes and family parties.

The most important event of Frederic's fifteenth year was the publication of his first composition for piano, a Rondo in C minor. This was soon followed by a set of Variations, Op. 2, on an air from Mozart's "Don Giovanni." In these early pieces, written perhaps even before he was fifteen, we find the first stages of his peculiar style. Even at this early time he was pleased with chords that had the tones spread apart in extended harmony. As his hands were small he invented a contrivance which separated the fingers as far apart as possible, in order that he might reach the new chords more easily. This he wore even during the night. The contrivance however, did not result in injury to his hands, as did Schumann's efforts to strengthen his fourth finger.

In 1827, Chopin finished his studies at the Lyceum and determined to adopt music as his profession. He was now seventeen, of slender figure, finely cut features, high forehead, delicate brows above dreamy, soulful eyes. Though not weak or sickly, as some accounts make out, he was never very robust; he would far rather lie under beautiful trees in delightful day dreams, than take long excursions afoot. One of his aversions was smoking or tobacco in any form; he never used it in his whole life. He was vivacious, active, hard working at music and reasonably healthy in early youth, but not of a hardy organism. His mother and sisters constantly cautioned him to wrap up in cold or damp weather, and like an obedient son and good brother, he obeyed.

Young Chopin greatly wished to travel and see something of the world. A much longed-for opportunity to visit Berlin came to him the following year. An old friend of his father's, Dr. Jarocki, Professor in the Warsaw University, was invited to attend a Philosophic Congress, presided over by Alexander von Humboldt, to be held in that city. The good Professor was willing to take his friend's son under his wing, and Frederic was quite beside himself with joy, for now he believed he could meet some of the musical celebrities of Berlin, and hear some great music. As to the latter his hopes were realized, but he did not meet many musicians, and could only gaze at them from a distance. It may have been a certain shyness and reticence that stood in the way, for he wrote home about a concert in the Singakademie: "Spontini, Zelter and Felix Mendelssohn were all there, but I spoke to none of these gentlemen, as I did not think it becoming to introduce myself." Music and things connected with music, music-shops and piano factories, took up most of his time, as he declined to attend the meetings of the Congress.

"At the time of the Berlin visit," writes Niecks, his biographer, "Chopin was a lively, well-educated, well-mannered youth, who walked through life, pleased with its motley garb, but as yet unconscious of the deeper truths, the immensities of joy and sadness, of love and hate, which lie beneath the surface."

After a stay of two weeks in the Prussian capital, Professor Jarocki and Frederic started on their return to Poland. During the journey they were obliged to halt an hour for fresh horses. Chopin began to look about the little inn for some sort of amusement to while away the time. He soon discovered in a corner, an old piano, which proved to be in tune. Of course he lost no time, but sat down and began to improvise on Polish melodies. Soon his fellow passengers of the stage-coach began to drop in one after another; at last came the post master with his wife and pretty daughter. Even when the hour was up and the horses had been put to the chaise, they begged the young musician to go on and on. Although he remonstrated, saying it was now time to go, they protested so convincingly that the boy sat down again and resumed his playing. Afterwards wine was brought in and they all drank to the health of the young master. Chopin gave them a mazurka for farewell, then the tall post master caught him up and carried him out to the coach, and all travelers started away in high spirits.

About the middle of July, 1829, Chopin with three

young friends, started out for Vienna. In those days an artist, in order to make himself and his work known, had to travel about the world and arrange concerts here and there, introduce himself to prominent people in each place and make them acquainted with his gifts. The present journey had for its object Vienna, the city of Beethoven and Schubert and other great masters.

Of course the young musician carried many letters of introduction, both to publishers and influential persons, for whom he played. Every one told him he ought to give a concert, that it would be a disgrace to parents, teachers and to himself not to appear in public. At last Frederic overcame his hesitation. In a letter home he writes: "I have made up my mind; they tell me I shall create a furore, that I am an artist of the first rank, worthy of a place beside Moscheles, Herz and Kalbrenner," well-known musicians of the day. One must forgive the nineteen year old boy, if he felt a little pride in being classed with these older and more famous musicians.

The concert took place in the Imperial Opera House, just ten days after his arrival, and from all accounts was a great success. Chopin was more than satisfied, he was delighted. Indeed his success was so emphatic that a second concert was given the following week. In both he played some of his own compositions and improvised as well.

"It goes crescendo with my popularity here, and this gives me much pleasure," he wrote home, at the end of the fortnight, and on the eve of starting to return. On the way back the travelers visited Prague, Teplitz and Dresden. A couple of days were spent in each, and then the party arrived safely in Warsaw.

With such an intense nature, friendship and love were two vital forces controlling life and action. Chopin was devoted to his friends; he clung to them with effusive ardor, incomprehensible to those less sensitive and romantic. With Titus Woyciechowski he was heart to heart in closest intimacy, and wrote him the most adoring letters when they chanced to be separated. Titus was less demonstrative, but always remained devoted.

Love for women was destined to play a large part in the inner life of Chopin. The first awakening of this feeling came from his admiration of Constantia Gladowska, a beautiful girl and vocal pupil at the Conservatory at Warsaw. Strangely enough he admired the young lady for some time at a distance, and if report be true, never really declared himself to her. But she filled his thoughts by day, and he confessed to dreaming of her each night. When she made her debut in opera, he hung on every note she sang and rejoiced in her success but did not make his feelings known to her. All this pent-up emotion was confined to his piano, in impassioned improvisations.

Seeing no suitable field for his genius in Warsaw and realizing he ought to leave home and strike out for himself, he yet delayed making the break. He continued putting off the evil day of parting from home and friends, and especially putting a wide distance between himself and the object of his adoration, Constantia.

The two years of indecision were fruitful in producing much piano music and in completing the beautiful E minor Concerto, which was rehearsed with orchestra and was performed at the third and last concert he ever gave in Warsaw. This concert was arranged for October 11, 1830. Chopin requested Constantia Gladowska, whom he had never met, to sing an aria. In the success of the evening sorrow was forgotten. He wrote to his friend: "Miss Gladowska wore a white gown with roses in her hair and was wondrously beautiful; she had never sung so well."

After this event, Chopin decided the time had come for him to depart. His trunk was bought, his clothing ready, pocket-handkerchiefs hemmed; in fact nothing remained but the worst of all, the leave-taking. On November 1, 1830, Elsner and a number of friends accompanied him to Wola, the first village beyond Warsaw. There they were met by a group of students from the Conservatory, who sang a cantata, composed by Elsner for the occasion. Then there was a banquet. During this last meal together, a silver goblet filled with Polish earth was presented to Chopin in the name of them all.

We can imagine the tender leave-takings after that. "I am convinced," he said, "I am saying an eternal farewell to my native country; I have a presentiment I shall never return." And so indeed it proved.

Again to Vienna, by way of Breslau, Dresden and Prague. In Vienna all was not as rosy as it had been on his first visit. Haslinger was unwilling to publish more of his compositions, though there were the two concertos, études and many short pieces. The way did not open to give a concert. He was lonely and unhappy, constantly dreaming of home and the beloved Constantia. From graphic letters to one of his dearest friends, a few sentences will reveal his inner life.

"To-day is the first of January (1831). Oh, how sadly this year begins for me! I love you all above all things. My poor parents! How are my friends faring? I could die for you all. Why am I doomed to be here so lonely and forsaken? You can at least open your hearts to each other. Go and see my parents—and—Constantia."

Although it did not seem advisable to give concerts in Vienna, yet Chopin made many pleasant acquaintances among the musicians and prominent people, and was constantly invited. He had planned to go from Vienna to either Italy or France. As there were political troubles in the former country, he decided to start for Paris, stopping on the way at a few places. In Munich he gave a morning concert, in the hall of the Philharmonic, which won him renown. From Munich he proceeded to Stuttgart, and during a short stay there, heard the sad news of the taking of Warsaw by the Russians. This event, it is said, inspired him to compose the C minor Etude, Op. 10, No. 12.

The Poles and everything Polish were at that time the rage in Paris. The young Polish master found ready entrance into the highest musical and literary circles of this most delightful city of the world. All was romance, fantasy, passion, which fitted with Chopin's sensitive and romantic temperament. Little wonder that he became inspired by contact with some of the greatest in the world of arts and letters.

There were Victor Hugo, King of the romanticists, Heine, poet and novelist; De Musset, Flaubert, Zola, Lamartine, Chateaubriand, Baudelaire, Ary Scheffer, Merimée, Gautier, Berlioz, Balzac, Rossini, Meyerbeer, Hiller, Nourrit, to mention a few. Liszt was there too, and George Sand, Mendelssohn and Kalkbrenner. Chopin called on the last named, who was considered the first pianist of the day, and played for him. Kalkbrenner remarked he had the style of Cramer and the touch of Field. He proposed that Chopin should study three years with him, and he would then become a great virtuoso. Of course the young artist might have learned something on the mechanical side, but at the risk of injuring the originality and style of his playing. His old friend and teacher Elsner, kept him from doing this.

The first year in Paris Chopin played at a number of concerts and functions, with ever increasing success. But in spite of the artistic success, his finances ran low, and he began to consider a trip to America. Fortunately he met Prince Radziwill on the street at this time, and was persuaded to play at a Rothschild soirée in the evening. From this moment, it is said, his prospects brightened, and he secured a number of wealthy patrons as pupils. Whether this be true or not, he came to know many titled personages. One has only to turn the pages of his music to note how many pieces are dedicated to Princess This and Countess That. This mode of life was reflected in his music, which became more elegant and aristocratic.

During the season of 1833 and 1834, Chopin continued to make his way as composer, pianist and teacher. A letter to friends in Poland, says: "Frederic looks well and strong; he turns the heads of all the French women, and makes the men jealous. He is now the fashion."

In the spring of 1834 Chopin had been persuaded by Ferdinand Hiller to accompany him to Aix-la-Chapelle, to attend the Lower Rhine Music Festival. Before they started Chopin found he had not the money to go, as it had been spent or given to some needy countryman. Hiller did not like to go alone, and asked if his friend could think of no way out of the dilemma. At last Chopin took the manuscript of the E flat Valse, Op. 18, went with it to Pleyel the publisher, and returned with five hundred francs. They could now go and enjoy the trip they had planned.

In July, 1835, Chopin met his parents at Carlsbad, where his father had been sent by the Warsaw physicians to take the cure. The young musician, now famous, had not seen his parents in nearly five years, and the reunion must have been a happy one. From here he went to Dresden and Leipsic, meeting Schumann and Mendelssohn. Schumann admired the young Pole greatly and wrote much about him in his musical magazine. Mendelssohn considered him a "really perfect virtuoso, whose piano playing was both original and masterly," but he was not sure whether his compositions were right or wrong. Chopin also stopped in Heidelberg on the way to Paris, visiting the father of his pupil Adolph Gutman. He must have been back in Paris about the middle of October, for the papers mention that "M. Chopin, one of the most eminent pianists of our epoch, has just made a tour of Germany, which has been for him a real ovation. Everywhere his admirable talent obtained the most flattering reception and excited much enthusiasm."

The story of Chopin's attraction for Marie Wodzinski and his reported engagement to her, is soon told. During his visit in Dresden, after leaving his parents in Carlsbad, he saw much of his old friends, Count Wodzinski and his family. The daughter, Marie, aged nineteen, was tall and slender, not beautiful but charming, with soft dark hair and soulful eyes. Chopin spent all his evenings at their home and saw much of Marie. The last evening the girl gave him a rose, and he composed a valse for her.

The next summer the two met again at Marienbad, and resumed their walks, talks and music. She drew his portrait, and one day Chopin proposed. She assured him she would always remain his friend, but her family would never consent to their marriage. So that brief romance was over.

An attachment of a different sort was that with Mme. Dudevant, known in literature as George Sand. Books have been written about this remarkable woman. The family at Nohant where she had spent her childhood, where her two children, Maurice and Solange, lived, and where her husband sometimes came, became distasteful to her; she wanted to see life. Paris offered it. Although possessing ample means, she arranged to spend six months in Paris each year, and live on two hundred and fifty francs a month. She came in 1831. Her *ménage* was of the simplest—three small rooms, with meals from a near-by restaurant at two francs; she did the washing herself. Woman's attire was too expensive, so, as she had worn man's attire when riding and hunting at Nohant, she saw nothing shocking in wearing it in Paris.

Her literary student life, as she called it, now began. She went about the streets at all times, in all weathers; went to garrets, studios, clubs, theaters, coffee-houses, everywhere but the *salons*. The romance of society-life as it was lived in the French capital, were the studies she ardently pursued. From these studies of life grew the several novels she produced during the years that followed.

It is said that Chopin met Mme. Sand at a musical matinée, given by the Marquis of C, where the aristocracy of genius, wealth and beauty had assembled. Chopin had gone to the piano and was absorbed in an improvisation, when lifting his eyes from the keys he encountered the fiery glances of a lady standing near. Perhaps the truer account of their first meeting is that given by Chopin's pupil Gutman. Mme. Sand, who had the faculty of subjugating every man of genius she came in contact with, asked Liszt repeatedly to introduce her.

One morning, early in the year 1837, Liszt called on his brother artist and found him in good spirits over some new compositions. He wished to play them to some friends, so it was arranged that a party of them should come to his rooms that evening. Liszt came with his special friend, Mme. d'Agoult and George Sand. Afterwards these meetings were frequently repeated. Liszt poetically describes one such evening, in his "Life of Chopin."

The fastidious musician was not at first attracted to the rather masculine-looking woman, addicted to smoking, who was short, stout, with large nose, coarse mouth and small chin. She had wonderful eyes, though, and her manners were both quiet and fascinating.

Her influence over Chopin began almost at once; they were soon seen together everywhere. Sand liked to master a reserved, artistic nature such as that of the Polish musician. She was not herself musical, but appreciated all forms of art.

In 1838 Mme. Sand's son Maurice became ill, and she proposed a trip to Majorca. Chopin went with the party and fell ill himself. There were many discomforts during their travels, due to bad weather and other inconveniences.

Chopin's health now began to be a source of anxiety to his friends. He had to be very careful, gave fewer lessons during the season, and spent his vacations at Nohant. He played rarely in public, though there were two public concerts in 1841 and '42 at Pleyel's rooms. From 1843 to 1847 he lived quietly and his life was apparently happy. He was fond of the Sand children, and amused himself with them when at Nohant.

But the breach, which had started some years before, between Mme. Sand and Chopin, widened as time passed, and they parted in 1847. It was the inevitable, of course. Chopin never had much to say about it; Sand said more, while the students asserted she had killed their beloved master. Probably it all helped to undermine the master's feeble health. His father passed away in 1844, his sister also, of pulmonary trouble; he was lonely and ill himself. He gave his last concert in Paris, February 16, 1848, Though weak he played beautifully. Some one said he fainted in the artist's room. The loss of Sand, even though he had long wearied of her, was the last drop.

To secure rest and change, he undertook a trip to London, for the second and last time, arriving April 21, 1848. He played at different great houses and gave two matinées, at the homes of Adelaide Kemble and Lord Falmouth, June 23, and July 7. These were attended by many titled personages. Viardot Garcia sang. The composer was thin, pale, and played with "wasted fingers," but the money helped replenish his depleted purse.

Chopin visited Scotland in August of the same year, and stayed with his pupil Miss Jane Stirling, to whom he dedicated the two Nocturnes, Op. 55. He played in Manchester, August 28; his playing was rather weak, but retained all its elegance, finish and grace. He was encored for his familiar Mazurka, Op. 7, No. 1, and repeated it with quite different nuances. One survivor of this audience remarked subsequently in a letter to a friend: "My emotion was so great I was compelled to retire to recover myself. I have heard all the celebrated stars of the musical firmament, but never has one left such an impression on my mind."

Chopin returned to London in November, and left England in January 1849. His purse was very low and his lodgings in the Rue Chaillot, Paris, were represented as costing half their value, the balance being paid by a Russian Countess, who was touched by his need. The generous hearted Miss Stirling raised 25,000 francs for the composer, so his last days were cheered by every comfort. He passed away October 17, 1849, and every writer agrees it was a serene passing. His face was beautiful and young, in the flower-covered casket, says Liszt, for friends filled his rooms with blossoms. He was buried from the Madeleine, October thirtieth. The B flat minor Funeral March, orchestrated by Reber, was given, and during the service Lefébure-Wély played on the organ the E and B minor Preludes. His grave in Père Lachaise is sought out by many travelers who admire his great art. It is difficult to find the tomb in that crowded White City, but no doubt all music lovers seek to bring away at least a leaf—as did the writer— from the earthly resting place of the most ideal pianist and composer who ever lived.

Chopin was preeminently a composer for the piano. With the exception of the Trio, Op. 8 and a book of Polish songs, everything he wrote was for his favorite instrument. There are seventy-one opus numbers in the list, but often whole sets of pieces are contained in one opus number, as is the case with the Études, of which there are twelve in Op. 10, and the same in Op. 25.

These Études take up every phase of piano technic; each one has a definite aim, yet each is a beautiful finished work as music. They have been edited and re-edited by the greatest masters.

The twenty-four Preludes were composed before the trip to Majorca, though they were perfected and polished while there. Written early in his career, they have a youthful vigor not often found in later works. "Much in miniature are these Preludes of the Polish poet," says Huneker.

There are four Impromptus and four Ballades, also four Scherzos. In them the composer is free, fascinating, often bold and daring. The great Fantaisie, Op. 49, is an epic poem, much as the Barcarolle is a poem of love. The two Sonatas, not to mention an early effort in this form, are among the modern classics, which are bound to appear on the programs of every great pianist of the present, and doubtless of the future. The two Concertos are cherished by virtuosi and audience alike, and never fail to make an instant and lasting appeal.

And think of the eleven Polonaises, those courtly dances, the most characteristic and national of his works; the fourteen Valses, beloved of every young piano student the world over; the eighteen Nocturnes, of starry night music; the entrancing Mazurkas, fifty-two in number. One marvels, in merely glancing over the list, that the composer, who lived such a super-sensitive hectic life, whose days were so occupied with lesson giving, ever had the time to create such a mass of music, or the energy to write it.

186

When one considers the amount of it, the beauty, originality and glory of it, one must acknowledge Frederic Chopin as one of the greatest piano geniuses of all time.

CHAPTER XIII

HECTOR BERLIOZ

IN the south of France, near Grenoble, is found a romantic spot, La Côte Saint-André. It lies on a hillside overlooking a wide green and golden plain, and its dreamy majesty is accentuated by the line of mountains that bounds it on the southeast. These in turn are crowned by the distant glory of snowy peaks and Alpine glaciers. Here one of the most distinguished men of the modern movement in French musical art, Hector Berlioz, first saw the light, on December 11, 1803.

He was an only son of a physician. His father, a learned man, with the utmost care, taught his little boy history, literature, geography, languages, even music. Hector was a most romantic, impressionable child, who peopled nature with fairies and elves, as he lay under great trees and dreamed fantastic day dreams. Poetry and romantic tales were his delight and he found much to feed his imagination in his father's large library.

His mother's father lived at Meylan, a little village not far from Grenoble, and there, in this picturesque valley, the family used to spend a part of each summer.

188

HECTOR BERLIOZ

Above Meylan, in a crevice of the mountain, stood a white house amid its vineyards and gardens. It was the home of Mme. Gautier and her two nieces, of whom the younger was called Estelle. When the boy Hector saw her for the first time, he was twelve, a shy, retiring little fellow. Estelle was just eighteen, tall, graceful, with beautiful dusky hair and large soulful eyes. Most wonderful of all, with her simple white gown, she wore pink slippers. The shy boy of twelve fell in desperate love with this white robed apparition in pink slippers. He says himself:

"Never do I recall Estelle, but with the flash of her large dark eyes comes the twinkle of her dainty pink shoes. To say I loved her comprises everything. I was wretched, dumb, despairing. By night I suffered agonies—by day I wandered alone through the fields of Indian corn, or, like a wounded bird, sought the deepest recesses of my grandfather's orchard.

"One evening there was a party at Mme. Gautier's and various games were played. In one of them I was told to choose first. But I dared not, my heart-beats choked me. Estelle, smiling, caught my hand, saying: 'Come, I will begin; I choose Monsieur Hector.' But, ah, she laughed!

"I was thirteen when we parted. I was thirty when, returning from Italy, I passed through this district, so filled with early memories. My eyes filled at sight of the white house: I loved her still. On reaching my old home I learned she was married!"

With pangs of early love came music, that is,

attempts at musical composition. His father had taught him the rudiments of music, and soon after gave him a flute. On this the boy worked so industriously that in seven or eight months he could play fairly well. He also took singing lessons, as he had a pretty soprano voice. Harmony was likewise studied by this ambitious lad, but it was self taught. He had found a copy of Rameau's "Harmony" among some old books and spent many hours poring over those labored theories in his efforts to reduce them to some form and sense.

Inspired by these studies he tried his hand at music making in earnest. First came some arrangements of trios and quartettes. Then finally he was emboldened to write a quintette for flute, two violins, viola and 'cello. Two months later he had produced another quintette, which proved to be a little better. At this time Hector was twelve and a half. His father had set his heart on the boy's following his footsteps and becoming a doctor; the time was rapidly approaching when a decision had to be made. Doctor Berlioz promised if his son would study anatomy and thoroughly prepare himself in this branch of the profession, he should have the finest flute that could be bought. His cousin Robert shared these anatomical lessons; but as Robert was a good violinist, the two boys spent more time over music than over osteology. The cousin, however, really worked over his anatomy, and was always ready at the lessons with his demonstrations, while Hector was not, and thus drew upon himself many a reprimand. However he managed to learn all his father could teach him, and when he was nineteen consented to go to Paris, with Robert, and—though much against his will—become a doctor.

When the boys reached Paris, in 1822, Hector loyally tried to keep his promise to his father and threw himself into the studies which were so repugnant to him. He says he might have become a common-place physician after all, had he not one night gone to the opera. That night was a revelation; he became half frantic with excitement and enthusiasm. He went again and again. Learning that the Conservatoire library, with its wealth of scores, was open to the public, he began to study the scores of his adored Gluck. He read, re-read and copied long parts and scenes from these wonderful scores, even forgetting to eat, drink or sleep, in his wild enthusiasm. Of course, now, the career of doctor must be given up; there was no question of that. He wrote home that in spite of father, mother, relations and friends, a musician he would be and nothing else.

A short time after this the choir master of Saint Roch, suggested that Hector should write a mass for Innocents' Day, promising a chorus and orchestra, with ample rehearsals, also that the choir boys would copy the parts. He set to work with enthusiasm. But alas, after one trial of the completed work, which ended in confusion owing to the countless mistakes the boys had made in copying the score, he rewrote the whole composition. Fearing another fiasco from amateur copyists, the young composer wrote out all the parts himself. This took three months. With the help of a friend who advanced funds, the mass was performed at Saint Roch, and was well spoken of by the press.

The hostility of Hector's family to music as a profession, died down a bit, owing to the success of the
mass, but started up with renewed vigor when the son
and brother failed to pass the entrance examinations at
the Conservatoire. His father wrote that if he persisted
in staying on in Paris his allowance would be stopped.
Lesueur, his teacher, promised to intercede and wrote
an appealing letter, which really made matters worse
instead of better. Then Hector went home himself, to
plead his cause in person. He was coldly received by
his family; his father at last consented to his return to
Paris for a time, but his mother forbade it absolutely.
In case he disobeyed her will, she would disown him
and never again wished to see his face. So Hector at last
set out again for Paris with no kind look or word from
his mother, but reconciled for the time being with the
rest of the family.

The young enthusiast began life anew in Paris, by
being very economical, as he must pay back the loan
made for his mass. He found a tiny fifth floor room,
gave up restaurant dinners and contented himself with
plain bread, with the addition of raisins, prunes or dates.
He also secured some pupils, which helped out in this
emergency, and even got a chance to sing in vaudeville,
at the enormous sum of 50 francs per month!

These were strenuous days for the eager ardent
musician. Teaching from necessity, in order to live,
spending every spare moment on composing; attending
opera whenever he got a free ticket; yet, in spite of
many privations there was happiness too. With score
under arm, he always made it a point to follow the

performance of any opera he heard. And so in time, he came to know the sound—the voice as it were, of each instrument in the orchestra. The study of Beethoven, Weber and Spontini—watching for rare and unusual combinations of sounds, being with artists who were kind enough to explain the compass and powers of their instruments, were the ways and means he used to perfect his art.

When the Conservatoire examinations of 1827, came on, Hector tried again, and this time passed the preliminary test. The task set for the general competition was to write music for Orpheus torn by the Bacchantes. An incompetent pianist, whose duty it was to play over the compositions, for the judges, could seem to make nothing of Hector's score. The six judges, headed by Cherubini, the Director of the Conservatoire, voted against the aspirant, and he was thrown out a second time.

And now came to Berlioz a new revelation—nothing less than the revelation of the art of Shakespeare. An English company of actors had come to Paris, and the first night Hamlet was given, with Henrietta Smithson— who five years later became his wife—as Ophelia.

In his diary Berlioz writes: "Shakespeare, coming upon me unawares, struck me down as with a thunderbolt. His lightning spirit opened to me the highest heaven of Art, and revealed to me the best and grandest and truest that earth can give." He began to worship both the genius of Shakespeare and the art of the beautiful English actress. Every evening found him at the theater, but days were spent in a kind of dumb despair, dreaming of Shakespeare and of Miss Smithson, who had now become the darling of Paris.

At last this sort of dumb frenzy spent itself and the musician in him awoke and he returned to his normal self. A new plan began to take shape in his mind. He would give a concert of his own works: up to that time no French musician had done so. Thus he would compel her to hear of him, although he had not yet met the object of his devoted admiration.

It was early spring of the year 1828, when he set to work with frantic energy, writing sixteen hours a day, in order to carry through the wonderful plan. The concert, the result of so much labor, was given the last of May, with varying success. But alas, Miss Smithson, absorbed in her own affairs, had not even heard of the excitable young composer who had dared and risked so much to make a name that might attract her notice.

As Berlioz père again stopped his allowance, Hector began to write for musical journals. At first ignorant of the ways of journalism, his wild utterances were the despair of his friends; later his trenchant pen was both admired and feared.

For the third time, in June of this year, he entered the Conservatoire contest, and won a second prize, in this case a gold medal. Two years later he won the coveted Prix de Rome, which gives the winner five years' study, free of expense, in the Eternal City.

Before this honor was achieved, however, a new influence came into his life, which for a time overshadowed the passion for Shakespeare and Miss Smithson. It happened on this wise.

Ferdinand Hiller, composer, pianist and one of Hector's intimate friends, fell deeply in love with Marie Moke, a beautiful, talented girl who, later on, won considerable fame as a pianist. She became interested in the young French composer, through hearing of his mental suffering from Hiller. They were thrown together in a school where both gave lessons, she on the piano and he on the—guitar! Meeting so constantly, her dainty beauty won a warm place in the affections of the impressionable Hector. She was but eighteen, while her admirer was twenty-five.

Hiller saw how things were going and behaved admirably. He called it fate, wished the pair every happiness, and left for Frankfort.

Then came the Prix de Rome, which the poor boy had struggled so long to win, and now did not care so much for, as going to Italy would mean to leave Paris. On August 23, 1830, he wrote to a friend:

"I have gained the Prix de Rome. It was awarded unanimously—a thing never known before. My sweet Ariel was dying of anxiety when I told her the news; her dainty wings were all ruffled, till I smoothed them with a word. Even her mother, who does not look too favorably on our love, was touched to tears.

"On November 1, there is to be a concert at the Theater Italien. I am asked to write an Overture and am going to take as subject Shakespeare's Tempest; it will be quite a new style of thing. My great concert, with the

Symphonie Fantastique, will take place November 14, but I must have a theatrical success; Camille's parents insist on that, as a condition of our marriage. I hope I shall succeed."

These concerts were both successful and the young composer passed from deepest anxiety to exuberant delight. He wrote to the same friend;

"The Tempest is to be played a second time at the opera. It is new, fresh, strange, grand, sweet, tender, surprising. Fétis wrote two splendid articles about it for the Revue Musicale.—My marriage is fixed for Easter, 1832, on condition that I do not lose my pension, and that I go to Italy for one year. My blessed Symphonie has done the deed."

The next January Berlioz went home to his family, who were now reconciled to his choice of music as a profession, and deluged him with compliments, caresses and tender solicitude. The parents had fully forgiven their gifted son.

"There is Rome, Signore."

It was true. The Eternal City lay spread out in purple majesty before the young traveler, who suddenly realized the grandeur, the poetry of this heart of the world. The Villa Medici, the venerable ancient palace, centuries old, had been reserved by the Académie of France as home for her students, whose sole obligation was to send, once a year, a sample of their work to the Académie in Paris.

When Hector Berlioz arrived in Rome he was

twenty-seven, and of striking appearance. A mass of reddish auburn hair crowned a high forehead; the features were prominent, especially the nose; the expression was full of sensitive refinement. He was of an excitable and ardent temperament, but in knowledge of the world's ways often simple as a child.

Berlioz, who was welcomed with many humorous and friendly jests on his appearance among the other students, had just settled down to work, when he learned that his Ariel—otherwise Marie Moke—had forsaken him and had married Pleyel. In a wild state of frenzy he would go to Paris at once and seek revenge. He started, got as far as Nice, grew calmer, remained at Nice for a month, during which time the Overture to "King Lear" was written, then returned to Rome by the way of Genoa and Florence.

By July 1832, Berlioz had returned to La Côte Saint-André, for a home visit. He had spent a year in Italy, had seen much, composed a number of important things, but left Rome without regrets, and found the familiar landscape near his home more fascinating than anything Italy could show.

The rest of the summer was spent in the beautiful Dauphiny country, working on the "Damnation of Faust." In the fall he returned to Paris. The vision of his Ophelia, as he used to call Miss Smithson, was seldom long absent from his thoughts, and he now went to the house where she used to live, thinking himself very lucky to be able to find lodging there. Meeting the old servant, he learned Miss Smithson was again in Paris, and would manage a new English theater, which was to open in a few days. But Berlioz was planning a concert of his own compositions, and did not trust himself to see the woman he had so long adored until this venture was over. It happened, however, that some friends induced her to attend the concert, the success of which is said to have been tremendous. The composer had the happiness of meeting the actress the same evening. The next day he called on her. Their engagement lasted nearly a year, opposed by her mother and sister, and also by Hector's family. The following summer Henrietta Smithson, all but ruined from her theatrical ventures, and weak from a fall, which made her a cripple for some years, was married to Hector Berlioz, in spite of the opposition of their two families.

And now there opened to Berlioz a life of stress and struggle, inseparable from such a nature as his. At one moment he would be in the highest heaven of happiness, and the next in the depths of despair. His wife's heavy debts were a load to carry, but he manfully did his best to pay them. We can be sure that every work he ever produced was composed under most trying circumstances, of one kind or another. One of his happiest ventures was a concert of his own compositions, given at the Conservatoire on October 22, 1833. Of it he wrote: "The concert, for which I engaged the very best artists, was a triumphant success. My musicians beamed with joy all evening, and to crown all, I found waiting for me a man with long black hair, piercing eyes and wasted form. Catching my hand, he poured forth a flood of burning praise and appreciation. It was Paganini!"

Paganini commissioned Berlioz to write a solo for his beautiful Strad. viola. The composer demurred for a time, and then made the attempt. While the result was not just what the violinist wished, yet the themes afterward formed the basis for Berlioz' composition "Childe Harold."

The next great work undertaken by Berlioz was the Requiem. It seems that, in 1836, the French Minister of the Interior set aside yearly, 3,000 francs to be given to a native composer, chosen by the Minister, to compose a religious work, either a mass or an oratorio, to be performed at the expense of the Government.

"I shall begin with Berlioz," he announced: "I am sure he could write a good Requiem."

After many intrigues and difficulties, this work was completed and performed in a way the composer considered "a magnificent triumph."

Berlioz, like most composers, always wished to produce an opera. "Benvenuto Cellini" was the subject finally chosen. It took a long time to write, and perhaps would never have been finished, since Berlioz was so tied to bread-winning journalistic labors, if a kind friend—Ernest Legouve—had not offered to lend him two thousand francs. This loan made him independent for a little time, and gave him the necessary leisure in which to compose.

The "Harold" music was now finished and Berlioz advertised both this and the Symphonic Fantastique for a concert at the Conservatoire, December 16, 1838. Paganini was present, and declared he had never been so moved by music before. He dragged the composer back on the platform, where some of the musicians still lingered, and there knelt and kissed his hand. The next day he sent Berlioz a check for twenty thousand francs.

Berlioz and his wife, two of the most highly strung individuals to be found anywhere, were bound to have plenty of storm and stress in their daily life. And so it came about that a separation, at least for a time, seemed advisable. Berlioz made every provision in his power for her comfort, and then started out on various tours to make his compositions known. Concerts were given in Stuttgart, Heckingen, Weimar, Leipsic, and in Dresden two, both very successful. Others took place in Brunswick, Hamburg, Berlin, Hanover, finishing at Darmstadt, where the Grand Duke insisted not only on the composer taking the full receipts for the concert, but, in addition, refused to let him pay any of the expenses.

And now back in Paris, at the treadmill of writing again. Berlioz had the sort of mentality which could plan, and also execute, big musical enterprises on a grand scale. It was proposed that he and Strauss should give a couple of monster concerts in the Exhibition Building. He got together a body of 1022 performers, all paid except the singers from the lyric theaters, who volunteered to help for the love of music.

It was a tremendous undertaking, and though an

artistic success, the exertion nearly finished Berlioz, who was sent south by his physician. Resting on the shores of the Mediterranean, he afterwards gave concerts in Marseilles, Lyons, and Lille and then traveled to Vienna. He writes of this visit:

"My reception by all in Vienna—even by my fellow-plowmen, the critics—was most cordial; they treated me as a man and a brother, for which I am heartily grateful.

"After my third concert, there was a grand supper, at which my friends presented me with a silver-gilt baton, and the Emperor sent me eleven hundred francs, with the odd compliment: 'Tell Berlioz I was really amused.' "

His way now led through Hungary. Performances were given in Pesth and Prague, where he was royally entertained and given a silver cup.

On returning to Paris, he had much domestic trouble to bear. His wife was paralyzed and his only son, Louis, wished to leave home and become a sailor—which he did eventually, though much against the wishes of his parents.

The "Damnation of Faust," now finished, was given at the Opéra, and was not a success. Berlioz then conceived the idea of going to Russia to retrieve his fortunes. With the help of kind friends, who advanced the money, he was able to carry out the plan. He left for Russia on February 14, 1847. The visits to both St. Petersburg and Moscow proved to be very successful financially as well as artistically. To cap the climax, "Romeo and Juliette" was performed at St. Petersburg.

Then the King of Prussia, wishing to hear the "Faust," the composer arranged to spend ten days in Berlin; then to Paris and London, where success was also achieved.

Shadows as well as sunshine filled the next few years. The composer was saddened by the passing of his father. Then a favorite sister also left, and last of all his wife passed quietly away, March 3, 1854. With all these sorrows Berlioz was at times nearly beside himself. But as he became calmer he decided, after half a year, to wed a woman who had been of great assistance to him in his work for at least fourteen years.

The remaining span of Berlioz' life was outwardly more peaceful and happy. He continued to travel and compose. Everywhere he went he was honored and admired.

Among his later compositions were the Te Deum, "Childhood of Christ," "Lelio," "Beatrice and Benedict" and "The Trojans."

At last, after what he called thirty years of slavery, he was able to resign his post of critic. "Thanks to 'The Trojans,' the wretched quill driver is free!"

A touching episode, told in his vivid way, was the meeting, late in life, with his adored Estelle of the pink shoes. He called on her and found a quiet widow, who had lost both husband and children. They had a poignant hour of reminiscence and corresponded for some time afterwards.

Hector Berlioz passed away March 8, 1869. The French Institute sent a deputation, the band of the

National Guard played selections from his Funeral Symphony; on the casket lay wreaths from the Saint Cécilia Society, from the youths of Hungary, from Russian nobles and from the town of Grenoble, his old home.

The music of Berlioz is conceived on large lines, in broad masses of tone color, with new harmonies and imposing effects. He won a noble place in art through many trials and hardships. His music is the expression, the reflection of the mental struggles of a most intense nature. The future will surely witness a greater appreciation of its merits than has up to now been accorded it.

CHAPTER XIV

FRANZ LISZT

FRANZ LISZT, in his day the king of pianists, a composer whose compositions still glow and burn with the fire he breathed into them; Liszt the diplomat, courtier, man of the world—always a conqueror! How difficult to tell, in a few pages, the story of a life so complex and absorbing!

A storm outside: but all was warmth and simple comfort in the large sitting-room of a steward's cottage belonging to the small estate of Raiding, in Hungary.

It was evening and father Liszt, after the labors of the day were over, could call these precious hours his own. He was now at the old piano, for with him music was a passion. He used all his leisure time for study and had some knowledge of most instruments. He had taught himself the piano, indeed under the circumstances had become quite proficient on it. To-night he was playing something of Haydn, for he greatly venerated that master. Adam Liszt made a striking figure as he sat there, his fine head, with its mass of light hair, thrown back, his stern features softened by the music he was making.

At a table near sat his wife, her dark head with its glossy braids bent over her sewing. Hers was a sweet, kindly face, and she endeared herself to every one by her simple, unassuming manners.

Quite near the old piano stood little Franz, not yet six. He was absolutely absorbed in the music. The fair curls fell about his childish face and his deep blue eyes were raised to his father, as though the latter were some sort of magician, creating all this beauty.

When the music paused, little Franz awoke as from a trance.

"Did you like that, Franzerl?" asked his father, looking down at him. The child bent his curly head, hardly able to speak.

"And do you want to be a musician when you grow up?" Franzerl nodded, then, pointing to a picture of Beethoven hanging on the wall, exclaimed with beaming eyes: "I want to be such a musician as he is!"

Adam Liszt had already begun to teach his baby son the elements of music, at the child's earnest and oft-repeated request. He had no real method, being self-taught himself, but in spite of this fact Franz made remarkable progress. He could read the notes and find the keys with as much ease as though he had practised for years. He had a wonderful ear, and his memory was astonishing. The father hoped his boy would become a great musician, and carry out the dream which he had failed to realize in himself.

Little Franz was born in the eventful year of

1811,—the "year of the comet." The night of October 21, the night of his birth, the tail of the meteor seemed to light up the roof of the Liszt home and was regarded as an omen of destiny. His mother used to say he was always cheerful, loving, never naughty but most obedient. The child seemed religious by nature, which feeling was fostered by his good mother. He loved to go to church on Sundays and fast days. The midnight mass on Christmas eve, when Adam Liszt, carrying a lantern, led the way to church along the country road, through the silent night, filled the child's thoughts with mystic awe.

Those early impressions have doubtless influenced the creations of Liszt, especially that part of his "Christus" entitled "Christmas Oratorio."

Before Franz was six, as we have seen, he had already begun his musical studies. If not sitting at the piano, he would scribble notes—for he had learned without instruction how to write them long before he knew the letters of the alphabet, or rudiments of writing. His small hands were a source of trouble to him, and he resorted to all kinds of comical expedients, such as sometimes playing extra notes with the tip of his nose. Indeed his ingenuity knew no bounds, when it came to mastering some musical difficulty.

Franz was an open minded, frank, truth-loving child, always ready to confess his faults, though he seemed to have but few. Strangely enough, though born an Hungarian, he was never taught to speak his native tongue, which indeed was only used by the peasants.

German, the polite language of the country, was alone used in the Liszt home.

The pronounced musical talent of his boy was a source of pride to Adam Liszt, who spoke of it to all his friends, so that the little fellow began to be called "the artist." The result was that when a concert was to be given at the neighboring Oldenburg, Adam was requested to allow his wonder child to play.

When Franz, now a handsome boy of nine, heard of the concert, he was overjoyed at the prospect of playing in public. It was a happy day for him when he started out with his father for Oldenburg. He was to play a Concerto by Reis, and a Fantaisie of his own, accompanied by the orchestra. In this his first public attempt Franz proved he possessed two qualities necessary for success—talent and will. All who heard him on this occasion were so delighted, that Adam then and there made arrangements to give a second concert on his own account, which was attended with as great success as the first.

The father had now fully made up his mind Franz was to be a musician. He decided to resign his post of steward at Raiding and take the boy to Vienna for further study.

On the way to Pressburg, the first stop, they halted to call at Eisenstadt, on Prince Esterházy. The boy played for his delighted host, who gave him every encouragement, even to placing his castle at Pressburg at his disposal for a concert. The Princess, too, was most cordial, and gave the boy costly presents when they left.

At Pressburg Adam Liszt succeeded in arranging a concert which interested all the Hungarian aristocracy of the city. It was given in the spacious drawing-rooms of the Prince's palace, and a notable audience was present. Little Franz achieved a triumph that night, because of the fire and originality of his playing. Elegant women showered caresses upon the child and the men were unanimous that such gifts deserved to be cultivated to the utmost without delay.

When it was learned that father Liszt had not an ample purse, and there would be but little for Franz's further musical education, six Hungarian noblemen agreed to raise a subscription which would provide a yearly income for six years. With this happy prospect in view, which relieved him of further anxiety, the father wrote to Hummel, now in employ of the Court at Weimar, asking him to undertake Franz's musical education. Hummel, though a famous pianist, was of a grasping nature; he wrote back that he was willing to accept the talented boy as a pupil, but would charge a louis d'or per lesson!

As soon as the father and his boy arrived in Vienna, the best teachers were secured for Franz. Carl Czerny was considered head of the piano profession. Czerny had been a pupil of Beethoven, and was so overrun with pupils himself, that he at first declined to accept another. But when he heard Franz play, he was so impressed that he at once promised to teach him. His nature was the opposite of Hummel's, for he was most generous to struggling talent. At the end of twelve lessons, when Adam Liszt wished to pay the debt, Czerny would accept nothing, and for the whole period of instruction—a year and a half—he continued to teach Franz gratuitously.

At first the work with such a strict master of technic as Czerny, was very irksome to the boy, who had been brought up on no method at all, but was allowed free and unrestrained rein. He really had no technical foundation; but since he could read rapidly at sight and could glide over the keys with such astonishing ease, he imagined himself already a great artist. Czerny soon showed him his deficiencies; proving to him that an artist must have clear touch, smoothness of execution and variety of tone. The boy rebelled at first, but finally settled down to hard study, and the result soon astonished his teacher. For Franz began to acquire a richness of feeling and beauty of tone wonderful for such a child. Salieri became his teacher of theory. He was now made to analyze and play scores, also compose little pieces and short hymns. In all these the boy made fine progress.

He now began to realize he needed to know something besides music, and set to work by himself to read, study and write. He also had great opportunity, through his noble Hungarian patrons, to meet the aristocracy of Vienna. His talents, vivacity and grace, his attractive personality, all helped to win the notice of ladies—even in those early days of his career.

After eighteen busy months in Vienna, father Liszt decided to bring his boy out in a public concert. The Town Hall was placed at his disposal and a number of fine artists assisted. With beaming face and sparkling eyes, the boy played with more skill, fire and confidence than he had ever done before. The concert took place December 1, 1822. On January 12, 1823, Franz repeated his success in another concert, again at the Town Hall.

It was after this second concert that Franz's reputation reached the ears of Beethoven, always the object of the boy's warmest admiration. Several times Franz and his father had tried to see the great master, but without success. Schindler was appealed to and promised to do his best. He wrote in Beethoven's diary, as the master was quite deaf:

"Little Liszt has entreated me to beg you to write him a theme for to-morrow's concert. He will not break the seal till the concert begins. Czerny is his teacher— the boy is only eleven years old. Do come to his concert, it will encourage the child. Promise me you will come."

It was the thirteenth of April, 1823. A very large audience filled the Redouten Saal. When Franz stepped upon the platform, he perceived the great Beethoven seated near. A great joy filled him. Now he was to play for the great man, whom all his young life he had worshiped from afar. He put forth every effort to be worthy of such an honor. Never had he played with such fire; his whole being seemed thrilled—never had he achieved such success. In the admiration which followed, Beethoven rose, came upon the platform, clasped the boy in his arms and kissed him repeatedly, to the frantic cheers of the audience.

The boy Franz Liszt had now demonstrated that already at eleven years old, he was one of the leading virtuosi of the time; indeed his great reputation as a pianist dates from this third Vienna concert. The press praised him highly, and many compared him to the wonderful genius, Mozart. Adam Liszt wished him now to see more of the world, and make known his great talents, also to study further. He decided to take the boy to Paris, for there lived the celebrated composer, Cherubini, at that time Director of the Paris Conservatoire.

On the way to Paris, concerts were given in various cities. In Munich he was acclaimed "a second Mozart." In Strassburg and Stuttgart he had great success.

Arrived in Paris, father and son visited the Conservatoire at once, for it would have been a fine thing for the boy to study there for a time, as it was the best known school for counterpoint and composition. Cherubini, however, refused to even read the letters of recommendation, saying no foreigner, however talented, could be admitted to the French National School of Music. Franz was deeply hurt by this refusal, and begged with tears to be allowed to come, but Cherubini was immovable.

However they soon made the acquaintance of Ferdinand Paër, who offered to give the child lessons in composition.

Franz made wonderful progress, both in this new line of study, and in becoming known as a piano virtuoso. Having played in a few of the great houses, he soon found himself the fashion; everybody was anxious for "le petit Litz" as he was called, to attend and play at their soirées. Franz thus met the most distinguished musicians of the day. When he played in public the press indulged in extravagant praise, calling him "the eighth wonder of the world," "another Mozart," and the like. Of course the father was overjoyed that his fondest hopes were being realized. Franz stood at the head of the virtuosi, and in composition he was making rapid strides. He even attempted an operetta, "Don Sancho," which later had several performances.

The eminent piano maker, Erard, who had a branch business in London and was about to start for that city, invited Liszt to accompany him and bring Franz. They accepted this plan, but in order to save expense, it was decided that mother Liszt, who had joined them in Paris, should return to Austria and stay with a sister till the projected tours were over.

Franz was saddened by this decision, but his entreaties were useless; his father was stern. The separation was a cruel one for the boy. For a long time thereafter the mere mention of his mother's name would bring tears.

In May, 1824, father and son, with Erard, started for England, and on June 21 Franz gave his first public concert in London. He had already played for the aristocracy in private homes, and had appeared at Court by command of King George IV. The concert won him great success, though the English were more reserved in their demonstrations, and not like the impulsive, open-hearted French people. He was happy to return to Paris, after the London season, and to resume his playing in the French salons.

The next spring, accompanied by his father, he made a tour of the French provinces, and then set out for a second trip to England. He was now fourteen; a mere boy in years, but called the greatest pianist of the day. He had developed so quickly and was so precocious that already he disliked being called "le petit Litz," for he felt himself full grown. He wished to be free to act as he wished. Adam, however, kept a strict watch on all his movements, and this became irksome to the boy, who felt he was already a man.

But father Liszt's health became somewhat precarious; constant traveling had undermined it. They remained in Paris quietly, till the year 1826, when they started on a second tour of French cities till Marseilles was reached, where the young pianist's success was overwhelming.

Returning to Paris, Franz devoted much of his time to ardent study of counterpoint, under Anton Reicha. In six months' study he had mastered the difficulties of this intricate art.

Adam Liszt and Franz spent the winter of 1826-27 in Switzerland, the boy playing in all important cities. They returned to Paris in the spring, and in May, set out again for England on a third visit. Franz gave his first concert in London on June ninth and proved how much he had gained in power and brilliancy. Moscheles, who was present, wrote: "Franz Liszt's playing surpasses in power and the overcoming of difficulties anything that has yet been heard."

The strain of constant travel and concert playing

was seriously telling on the boy's sensitive, excitable nature. He lost his sunny gaiety, grew quiet, sometimes almost morose. He went much to church, and wanted to take orders, but his father prevented this step. Indeed the father became alarmed at the boy's pale face and changed condition, and took him to the French watering place of Boulogne-sur-Mer. Here both father and son were benefited by the sea baths and absolute rest. Franz recovered his genial spirits and constantly gained in health and strength.

But with Adam Liszt the gain was only temporary. He was attacked with a fever, succumbed in a few days and was buried at Boulogne. The loss of his father was a great blow to Franz. He was prostrated for days, but youth at last conquered. Aroused to his responsibilities, he began to think for the future. He at once wrote his mother, telling her what had happened, saying he would give up his concert tours and make a home for her in Paris, by giving piano lessons.

Looking closer into his finances, of which he had no care before, Franz found the expenses of his father's illness and death had exhausted their little savings, and he was really in debt. He decided to sell his grand piano, so that he should be in debt to no one. This was done, every one was paid off and on his arrival in Paris his old friend Erard invited him to his own home till the mother came.

It was a sweet and happy meeting of mother and son, after such a long separation. The two soon found a modest apartment in the Rue Montholon.

As soon as his intention to give lessons became known, many aristocratic pupils came and found him a remarkable teacher. Among his new pupils was Caroline Saint Cricq, youngest daughter of Count Saint Cricq, then Minister of the Interior, and Madame his wife.

Caroline, scarcely seventeen, the same age as her young teacher, was a beautiful girl, as pure and refined as she was talented. Under the eyes of the Countess, the lessons went on from month to month, and the mother did not fail to see the growing attachment between the young people. But love's young dream was of short duration. The Countess fell ill and the lessons had to be discontinued. Caroline did not see her devoted teacher till all was over.

There was now another bond between them, the sympathy over the loss of their dear ones. The Count had requested that the lessons should be resumed. But when the young teacher remained too long in converse with his pupil after the lessons, he was dismissed by the Count, and all their sweet intercourse came to an abrupt end.

Mme. Liszt did all she could to soothe the grief and despair of her son. For days and weeks he remained at home, neglecting his piano and his work. He again thought of the church with renewed ardor and told his mother he now had decided to become a monk. His spirits sank very low; he became ill, unable to leave the house and it was reported everywhere he had passed away.

Again he rallied and his strong constitution

conquered. As strength slowly returned, so also did his activity and love of life.

During his long convalescence he was seized with a great desire for knowledge, and read everything he could lay hands on. He would often sit at the piano, busying his fingers with technic while reading a book on the desk before him. He had formerly given all his time to music and languages; now he must know literature, politics, history and exact sciences. A word casually dropped in conversation, would start him on a new line of reading. Then came the revolution of 1830. Everybody talked politics, and Franz, with his excitable spirits, would have rushed into the conflict if his mother had not restrained him.

With all this awakening he sought to broaden his art, to make his instrument speak of higher things. Indeed the spirit must speak through the form. This he realized the more as he listened to the thrilling performances of that wizard of the violin, Paganini, who appeared in Paris in 1831. This style of playing made a deep impression on Liszt. He now tried to do on the piano what Paganini accomplished on the violin, in the matter of tone quality and intensity. He procured the newly published Caprices for violin and tried to learn their tonal secrets, also transcribing the pieces for piano.

Liszt became fast friends with the young composer, Hector Berlioz, and much influenced by his compositions, which were along new harmonic lines. Chopin, the young Polish artist, now appeared in Paris, playing his E minor Concerto, his Mazurkas and

Nocturnes, revealing new phases of art. Chopin's calm composure tranquilized Liszt's excitable nature. From Chopin, Liszt learned to "express in music the poetry of the aristocratic salon." Liszt ever remained a true and admiring friend of the Pole, and wrote the poetic study sketch of him in 1849.

Liszt was now twenty-three. Broadened and chastened by all he had passed through, he resumed his playing in aristocratic homes. He also appeared in public and was found to be quite a different artist from what the Parisians had previously known. His bold new harmonies in his own compositions, the rich effects, showed a deep knowledge of his art. He had transcribed a number of Berlioz's most striking compositions to the piano and performed them with great effect.

The handsome and gifted young artist was everywhere the object of admiration. He also met George Sand, and was soon numbered among that wonderful and dangerous woman's best friends. Later he met the young and beautiful Countess Laprunarede, and a mutual attraction ensued. The elderly Count, her husband, pleased with the dashing young musician, invited him to spend the winter at his chateau, in Switzerland, where the witty Countess virtually kept him prisoner.

The following winter, 1833-34, when the salons opened again, Liszt frequented them as before. He was in the bloom of youth and fame, when he met the woman who was to be linked with his destiny for the next ten years.

We have sketched the childhood and youth of this wonderful artist up to this point. We will pass lightly over this decade of his career, merely stating briefly that the lady—the beautiful Countess d'Agoult, captivated by the brilliant talents of the Hungarian virtuoso, left her husband and child, and became for ten years the faithful companion of his travels and tours over Europe. Many writers agree that Liszt endeavored to dissuade her from this attraction, and behaved as honorably as he could under the circumstances. A part of the time they lived in Switzerland, and it was there that many of Liszt's compositions were written.

Of their three children, the boy died very young. Of the girls, Blandine became the wife of Émile Ollivier, a French literary man and statesman. Her sister, Cosima, married first Hans von Bülow and later Richard Wagner.

In 1843 Liszt intended to take Madame with him to Russia, but instead, left her and her children in Paris, with his mother, as the Countess was in failing health. His first concert, in St. Petersburg, realized the enormous sum of fifty thousand francs—ten thousand dollars. Instead of giving one concert in Moscow, he gave six. Later he played in Bavaria, Saxony and other parts of Germany. He then settled in Weimar for a time, being made Grand Ducal Capellmeister. Then, in 1844-45, longing for more success, he toured Spain and Portugal.

A generous act was his labor in behalf of the Beethoven monument, to be erected in the master's birthplace, Bonn. The monument was to be given by subscriptions from the various Princes of Germany. Liszt helped make up the deficit and came to Bonn to organize a Festival in honor of the event. He also composed a Cantata for the opening day of the Festival, and in his enthusiasm nearly ruined himself by paying the heavy expenses of the Festival out of his own pocket.

The political events of 1848 brought him back to Weimar, and he resumed his post of Court Music Director. He now directed his energies toward making Weimar the first musical city of Germany. Greatly admiring Wagner's genius, he undertook to perform his works in Weimar, and to spread his name and fame. Indeed it is not too much to say that without Liszt's devoted efforts, Wagner would never have attained his vogue and fame. Wagner himself testified to this.

While living in Weimar, Liszt made frequent journeys to Rome and to Paris. In 1861 there was a rumor that the object of his visits to Rome was to gain Papal consent to his marriage with the Princess Sayn-Wittgenstein. During a visit to Rome in 1864, the musician was unable to resist longer the mysticism of the church. He decided to take orders and was made an Abbé.

Since that time, Abbé Franz Liszt did much composing. He also continued to teach the piano to great numbers of pupils, who flocked to him from all parts of the world. Many of the greatest artists now before the public were numbered among his students, and owe much of their success to his artistic guidance.

In 1871, the Hungarian Cabinet created him a noble,

with a yearly pension of three thousand dollars. In 1875, he was made Director of the Academy at Budapest. In addition, Liszt was a member of nearly all the European Orders of Chivalry.

Franz Liszt passed away August 1, 1886, in the house of his friend, Herr Frohlich, near Wagner's Villa Wahnfried, Bayreuth, at the age of seventy-five. As was his custom every summer, Liszt was in Bayreuth, assisting in the production of Wagner's masterpieces, when he succumbed to pneumonia. Thus passed a great composer, a world famous piano virtuoso, and a noble and kindly spirit.

For the piano, his chosen instrument, Liszt wrote much that was beautiful and inspiring. He created a new epoch for the virtuoso. His fifteen Hungarian Rhapsodies, B minor Sonata, Concert Études and many transcriptions, appear on all modern programs, and there are many pieces yet to be made known. He is the originator of the Symphonic Poem, for orchestra; while his sacred music, such as the Oratorio "Christus," and the beautiful "Saint Elizabeth," a sacred opera, are monuments to his great genius.

GIUSEPPE VERDI

CHAPTER XV

GIUSEPPE VERDI

In the little hamlet of Le Roncole, at the foot of the Apeninnes, a place that can hardly be found on the map, because it is just a cluster of workmen's houses, Giuseppe Verdi, one of the greatest operatic composers, was born, October 9, 1813.

There were great wars going on in Europe during that time. When Giuseppe was a year old, the Russian and Austrian soldiers marched through Italy, killing and destroying everywhere. Some of them came to Le Roncole for a few hours. All the women and children ran to the church and locked themselves in for safety. But these savage men had no respect for the house of God. They took the hinges off the doors and rushing in murdered and wounded the helpless ones. Luigia Verdi, with the baby Giuseppe in her arms, escaped, ran up a narrow staircase to the belfry, and hid herself and child among some old lumber. Here she stayed in her hiding place, until the drunken troops were far away from the little village.

The babe Giuseppe was born among very poor, ignorant working people, though his father's house was one of the best known and most frequented among the cluster of cottages. His parents Carlo Verdi and Luigia his wife, kept a small inn at Le Roncole and also a little shop, where they sold sugar, coffee, matches, spirits, tobacco and clay pipes. Once a week the good Carlo would walk up to Busseto, three miles away, with two empty baskets and would return with them filled with articles for his store, carrying them slung across his strong shoulders.

Giuseppe Verdi who was to produce such streams of beautiful, sparkling music,—needing an Act of Parliament to stop them, as once happened,—was a very quiet, thoughtful little fellow, always good and obedient; sometimes almost sad, and seldom joined in the boisterous games of other children. That serious expression found in all of Verdi's portraits as a man was even noticeable in the child. The only time he would rouse up, was when a hand organ would come through the village street; then he would follow it as far as his little legs would carry him, and nothing could keep him in the house, when he heard this music. Intelligent, reserved and quiet, every one loved him.

In 1820, when Giuseppe was seven years old, Carlo Verdi committed a great extravagance for an innkeeper; he bought a spinet for his son, something very unheard of for so poor a man to do.

Little Giuseppe practised very diligently on his spinet. At first he could only play the first five notes of the scale. Next he tried very hard to find out chords, and one day was made perfectly happy at having sounded the major third and fifth of C. But the next day he could not find the chord again, and began to fret and fume and got into such a temper, that he took a hammer and tried to break the spinet in pieces. This made such a commotion that it brought his father into the room. When he saw what the child was doing, he gave a blow on Giuseppe's ear that brought the little fellow to his senses at once. He saw he could not punish the good spinet because he did not know enough to strike a common chord.

His love of music early showed itself in many ways. One day he was assisting the parish priest at mass in the little church of Le Roncole. At the moment of the elevation of the Host, such sweet harmonies were sounding from the organ, that the child stood perfectly motionless, listening to the beautiful music, all unconscious of everything else about him.

"Water," said the priest to the altar boy. Giuseppe, not hearing him, the priest repeated the call. Still the child, who was listening to the music, did not hear. "Water," said the priest a third time and gave Giuseppe such a sharp kick that he fell down the steps of the altar, hitting his head on the stone floor, and was taken unconscious into the sacristy.

After this Giuseppe was allowed to have music lessons with Baistrocchi, the organist of the village church. At the end of a year Baistrocchi said there was nothing more he could teach his young pupil, so the lessons came to an end.

Two years later, when old Baistrocchi died, Giuseppe,

who was then only ten, was made organist in his place. This pleased his parents very much, but his father felt the boy should be sent to school, where he could learn to read and write and know something of arithmetic. This would have been quite impossible had not Carlo Verdi had a good friend living at Busseto, a shoemaker, named Pugnatta.

Pugnatta agreed to give Giuseppe board and lodging and send him to the best school in the town, all for a small sum of three pence a day. Giuseppe went to Pugnatta's; and while he was always in his place in school and studied diligently, he still kept his situation as organist of Le Roncole, walking there every Sunday morning and back again to Busseto after the evening service.

His pay as organist was very small, but he also made a little money playing for weddings, christenings and funerals. He also gained a few lire from a collection which it was the habit of artists to make at harvest time, for which he had to trudge from door to door, with a sack upon his back. The poor boy's life had few comforts, and this custom of collections brought him into much danger. One night while he was walking toward Le Roncole, very tired and hungry, he did not notice he had taken a wrong path, when suddenly, missing his footing, he fell into a deep canal. It was very dark and very cold and his limbs were so stiff he could not use them. Had it not been for an old woman who was passing by the place and heard his cries, the exhausted and chilled boy would have been carried away by the current.

After two years' schooling, Giuseppe's father persuaded his friend, Antonio Barezzi of Busseto, from whom he was in the habit of buying wines and supplies for his inn and shop,—to take the lad into his warehouse. That was a happy day for Giuseppe when he went to live with Barezzi, who was an enthusiastic amateur of music. The Philharmonic Society, of which Barezzi was the president, met, rehearsed and gave all its concerts at his house.

Giuseppe, though working hard in the warehouse, also found time to attend all the rehearsals of the Philharmonic, and began the task of copying out separate parts from the score. His earnestness in this work attracted the notice of the conductor, Ferdinando Provesi, who began to take great interest in the boy, and was the first one to understand his talent and advised him to devote himself to music. A Canon in the Cathedral offered to teach him Latin, and tried to make a priest of him, saying, "What do you want to study music for? You have a gift for Latin and it would be much better for you to become a priest. What do you expect from your music? Do you think that some day you will become organist of Busseto? Stuff and nonsense! That can never be."

A short time after this, there was a mass at a chapel in Busseto, where the Canon had the service. The organist was unable to attend, and Verdi was called at the last moment to take his place. Very much impressed with the unusually beautiful organ music, the priest, at the close of the service desired to see the organist. His astonishment was great when he saw his scholar whom he had been seeking to turn from the study of music. "Whose music did you play?" he asked. "It was most beautiful."

"Why," timidly answered the boy, "I had no music, I was playing extempore—just as I felt."

"Ah, indeed," replied the Canon; "well I am a fool and you cannot do better than to study music, take my word for it."

Under the good Provesi, Verdi studied until he was sixteen and made such rapid progress that both Provesi and Barezzi felt he must be sent to Milan to study further. The lad had often come to the help of his master, both at the organ and as conductor of the Philharmonic. The records of the society still have several works written by Verdi at that time—when he was sixteen—composed, copied, taught, rehearsed and conducted by him.

There was an institution in Busseto called the Monte di Pietà, which gave four scholarships of three hundred francs a year, each given for four years to promising young men needing money to study science or art. Through Barezzi one of these scholarships was given to Verdi, it being arranged that he should have six hundred francs a year for two years, instead of three hundred francs for four years. Barezzi himself advanced the money for the music lessons, board and lodging in Milan and the priest gave him a letter of introduction to his nephew, a professor there, who received him with a hearty welcome, and insisted upon his living with him.

Like all large music schools, there were a great

many who presented themselves for admittance by scholarship and only one to be chosen. And Verdi did not happen to be that one, Basili not considering his compositions of sufficient worth. This was not because Verdi was really lacking in his music, but because Basili had other plans. This did not in the least discourage Giuseppe, and at the suggestion of Alessando Rolla, who was then conductor of La Scala, he asked Lavigna to give him lessons in composition and orchestration.

Lavigna was a former pupil of the Conservatoire of Naples and an able composer. Verdi showed him some of the same compositions he had shown Basili. After examining them he willingly accepted the young aspirant as a pupil.

Verdi spent most of his evenings at the home of the master, when Lavigna was not at La Scala and there met many artists. One night it chanced that Lavigna, Basili and Verdi were alone, and the two masters were speaking of the deplorable result of a competition for the position of Maitre di Capelle and organist of the Church of San Giovanni di Monza. Out of twenty-eight young men who had taken part in the competition, not one had known how to develop correctly the subject given by Basili for the construction of a fugue. Lavigna, with a bit of mischief in his eyes, began to say to his friend:—"It is really a remarkable fact. Well, look at Verdi, who has studied fugue for two short years. I lay a wager he would have done better than your eight and twenty candidates."

"Really?" replied Basili, in a somewhat vexed tone.

"Certainly. Do you remember your subject? Yes, you do? Well, write it down."

Basili wrote and Lavigne, giving the theme to Verdi, said:

"Sit down there at the table and just begin to work out this subject."

Then the two friends resumed their conversation, until Verdi, coming to them said simply: "There, it is done."

Basili took the paper and examined it, showing signs of astonishment as he continued to read. When he came to the conclusion he complimented the lad and said: "But how is it that you have written a double canon on my subject?"

"It is because I found it rather poor and wished to embellish it," Verdi replied, remembering the reception he had had at the Conservatoire.

In 1833 his old master Provesi died. Verdi felt the loss keenly, for Provesi was the one who first taught him music and who showed him how to work to become an artist. Though he wished to do greater things, he returned to Busseto to fulfill his promise to take Provesi's place as organist of the Cathedral and conductor of the Philharmonic, rather big positions to fill for a young man of twenty.

And now Verdi fell in love with the beautiful Margherita, the oldest daughter of Barezzi, who did not mind giving his daughter to a poor young man, for Verdi possessed something worth far more than money, and that was great musical talent. The young people were married in 1836, and the whole Philharmonic Society attended.

About the year 1833-34 there flourished in Milan a vocal society called the Philharmonic, composed of excellent singers under the leadership of Masini. Soon after Verdi came to the city, the Society was preparing for a performance of Haydn's "Creation." Lavigna, with whom the young composer was studying composition, suggested his pupil should attend the rehearsals, to which he gladly agreed. It seems that three Maestri shared the conducting during rehearsals. One day none of them were present at the appointed hour and Masini asked young Verdi to accompany from the full orchestral score, adding, "It will be sufficient if you merely play the bass." Verdi took his place at the piano without the slightest hesitation. The slender, rather shabby looking stranger was not calculated to inspire much confidence. However he soon warmed to his work, and after a while grew so excited that he played the accompaniment with the left hand while conducting vigorously with the right. The rehearsal went off splendidly, and many came forward to greet the young conductor, among them were Counts Pompeo Belgiojoso and Renato Borromeo. After this proof of his ability, Verdi was appointed to conduct the public performance, which was such a success that it was repeated by general request, and was attended by the highest society.

Soon after this Count Borromeo engaged Verdi to write a Cantata for chorus and orchestra, to honor the occasion of a marriage in the family. Verdi did so but was never paid a sou for his work. The next request was from Masini, who urged Verdi to compose an opera for the Teatro Filodramatico, where he was conductor. He handed him a libretto, which with a few alterations here and there became "Oberto, Conte di San Bonifacio." Verdi accepted the offer at once, and being obliged to move to Busseto, where he had been appointed organist, remained there nearly three years, during which time the opera was completed. On returning to Milan he found Masini no longer conductor, and lost all hope of seeing the new opera produced. After long waiting however, the impressario sent for him, and promised to bring out the work the next season, if the composer would make a few changes. Young and as yet unknown, Verdi was quite willing. "Oberto" was produced with a fair amount of success, and repeated several times. On the strength of this propitious beginning, the impressario, Merelli, made the young composer an excellent offer—to write three operas, one every eight months, to be performed either in Milan or in Vienna, where he was impressario of both the principal theaters. He promised to pay four thousand lire—about six hundred and seventy dollars—for each, and share the profits of the copyright. To young Verdi this seemed an excellent chance and he accepted at once. Rossi wrote a libretto, entitled "Proscritto," and work on the music was about to begin. In the spring of 1840, Merelli hurried from Vienna, saying he needed a comic opera for the autumn season, and wanted work begun on it at once. He produced three librettos, none of them very good. Verdi did not like them, but since there was no time to lose, chose the least offensive and set to work.

The Verdis were living in a small house near the Porta Ticinesa; the family consisted of the composer, his wife and two little sons. Almost as soon as work was begun on the comic opera, Verdi fell ill and was confined to his bed several days. He had quite forgotten that the rent money, which he always liked to have ready on the very day, was due, and he had not sufficient to pay. It was too late to borrow it, but quite unknown to him the wife had taken some of her most valuable trinkets, had gone out and brought back the necessary amount. This sweet act of devotion greatly touched her husband.

And now sudden sorrow swept over the little family. At the beginning of April one of the little boys fell ill. Before the doctors could understand what was the matter, the little fellow breathed his last in the arms of his desperate mother. A few days after this, the other child sickened and died. In June the young wife, unable to bear the strain, passed away and Verdi saw the third coffin leave his door carrying the last of his dear ones. And in the midst of these crushing trials he was expected to compose a comic opera! But he bravely completed his task. "Un Giorno di Regno" naturally proved a dead failure. In the despondency that followed, the composer resolved to give up composition altogether. Merelli scolded him roundly for such a decision, and promised if, some day, he chose to take up his pen again, he would, if given two months' notice, produce any opera Verdi might write.

At that time the composer was not ready to change his mind. He could not live longer in the house filled with so many sad memories, but moved to a new residence near the Corsia di Servi. One evening on the street, he ran against Merelli, who was hurrying to the theater. Without stopping he linked his arm in that of the composer and made him keep pace. The manager was in the depths of woe. He had secured a libretto by Solera, which was "wonderful, marvelous, extraordinary, grand," but the composer he had engaged did not like it. What was to be done? Verdi bethought him of the libretto "Proscritto," which Rossi had once written for him, and he had not used. He suggested this to Merelli. Rossi was at once sent for and produced a copy of the libretto. Then Merelli laid the other manuscript before Verdi. "Look, here is Solera's libretto; such a beautiful subject! Take it home and read it over." But Verdi refused. "No, no, I am in no humor to read librettos."

"It won't hurt you to look at it," urged Merelli, and thrust it into the coat pocket of the reluctant composer.

On reaching home, Verdi pulled the manuscript out and threw it on the writing table. As he did so a stanza from the book caught his eye; it was almost a paraphrase from the Bible, which had been such a solace to him in his solitary life. He began to read the story and was more and more enthralled by it, yet his resolution to write no more was not altered. However, as the days passed there would be here a line written down, there a melody—until at last, almost unconsciously the opera of "Nabucco" came into being.

The opera once finished, Verdi hastened to Merelli, and reminded him of his promise. The impressario was quite honorable about it, but would not agree to bring the opera out until Easter, for the season of 1841-42, was already arranged. Verdi refused to wait until Easter, as he knew the best singers would not then be available. After many arguments and disputes, it was finally arranged that "Nabucco" should be put on, but without extra outlay for mounting. At the end of February 1842, rehearsals began and on March ninth the first performance took place.

The success of "Nabucco" was remarkable. No such "first night" had been known in La Scala for many years. "I had hoped for success," said the composer, "but such a success—never!"

The next day all Italy talked of Verdi. Donizetti, whose wealth of melodious music swayed the Italians as it did later the English, was so impressed by it that he continually repeated, "It is fine, uncommonly fine."

With the success of "Nabucco" Verdi's career as a composer may be said to have begun. In the following year "I Lombardi" was produced, followed by "Ernani." Then came in quick succession ten more operas, among them "Attila" and "Macbeth."

In 1847, we find Verdi in London, where on July 2, at Her Majesty's Theater, "I Masnadieri" was brought out, with a cast including Lablanche, Gardoni, Colletti, and above all Jenny Lind, in a part composed expressly for her. All the artists distinguished themselves; Jenny Lind acted admirably and sang her airs exquisitely, but the opera was not a success. No two critics could agree as to its merits. Verdi left England in disgust and took his music to other cities.

The advantage to Verdi of his trips through Europe and to England is shown in "Rigoletto," brought out in Vienna in 1851. In this opera his true power manifests itself. The music shows great advance in declamation, which lifts it above the ordinary Italian style of that time. With this opera Verdi's second period begins. Two years later "Trovatore" was produced in Rome and had a tremendous success. Each scene brought down thunders of applause, until the very walls resounded and outside people took up the cry, "Long live Verdi, Italy's greatest composer! Vive Verdi!" It was given in Paris in 1854, and in London the following year. In 1855, "La Traviata" was produced in Vienna. This work, so filled with delicate, beautiful music, nearly proved a failure, because the consumptive heroine, who expires on the stage, was sung by a prima donna of such extraordinary stoutness that the scene was received with shouts of laughter. After a number of unsuccessful operas, "Un Ballo in Maschera" scored a success in Rome in 1859, and "La Forza del Destino," written for Petrograd, had a recent revival in New York.

When Rossini passed away, November 13, 1868, Verdi suggested a requiem should be written jointly by the best Italian composers. The work was completed, but was not satisfactory on account of the diversity of styles. It was then proposed that Verdi write the entire work himself. The death of Manzoni soon after this caused the composer to carry out the idea. Thus the great "Manzoni Requiem" came into being.

In 1869, the Khedive of Egypt had a fine opera house built in Cairo, and commissioned Verdi to write an opera having an Egyptian subject, for the opening. The ever popular "Aida" was then composed and brought out in 1871, with great success. This proved to be the beginning of the master's third period, for he turned from his earlier style which was purely lyric, to one with far more richness of orchestration.

Verdi had now retired to his estate of Sant' Agata, and it was supposed his career as composer had closed, as he gave his time principally to the care of his domain. From time to time it was rumored he was writing another opera. The rumor proved true, for on February 5, 1887, when Verdi was seventy-four years old, "Otello" was produced at La Scala, Milan, amid indescribable enthusiasm. Six years later the musical world was again startled and overjoyed by the production of another Shakespearean opera, "Falstaff," composed in his eightieth year.

In all, his operas number over thirty, most of them serious, all of them containing much beautiful music.

At Sant' Agata the master lived a quiet, retired life. The estate was situated about two miles from Busseto, and was very large, with a great park, a large collection of horses and other live stock. The residence was spacious, And the master's special bedroom was on the first floor. It was large, light and airy and luxuriously furnished. Here stood a magnificent grand piano, and the composer often rose in the night to jot down the themes which came to him in the silence of the midnight hours. Here "Don Carlos" was written. In one of the upper rooms stood the old spinet that Verdi hacked at as a child.

Verdi was one of the noblest of men as well as one of the greatest of musical composers. He passed away in Milan, January 27, 1901, at the age of eighty-eight.

CHAPTER XVI

RICHARD WAGNER

ONE of the most gigantic musical geniuses the world has yet known was Richard Wagner. Words have been exhausted to tell of his achievements; books without number have been written about him; he himself, in his Autobiography, and in his correspondence, has told with minutest detail how he lived and what his inner life has been. What we shall strive for is the simple story of his career, though in the simple telling, it may read like a fairy tale.

Richard Wagner first saw the light on May 22, 1813, in Leipsic. Those were stirring times in that part of the world, for revolution was often on the eve of breaking out. The tiny babe was but six months old when the father passed away. There were eight other children, the eldest son being only fourteen. The mother, a sweet, gentle little woman, found herself quite unable to support her large family of growing children. No one could blame her for accepting the hand of her husband's old friend, Ludwig Geyer, in less than a year after the loss of her first husband. Geyer was a man of much artistic talent, an actor, singer, author and painter. He thought little Richard might become a portrait painter, or possibly a musician, since the child had learned to play two little pieces on the piano.

Geyer found employment in a Dresden theater, so the family removed to that city. But he did not live to see the blossoming of his youngest step-son's genius, as he passed away on September 30, 1821, when the child was eight years old.

Little Richard showed wonderful promise even in those years of childhood. At the Kreuzschule, where his education began, he developed an ardent love for the Greek classics, and translated the first twelve books of the Odyssey, outside of school hours. He devoured all stories of mythology he could lay hands on, and soon began to create vast tragedies. He revelled in Shakespeare, and finally began to write a play which was to combine the ideas of both Hamlet and King Lear. Forty-two persons were killed off in the course of the play and had to be brought back as ghosts, as otherwise there would have been no characters for the last act. He worked on this play for two years.

Everything connected with the theater was of absorbing interest to this precocious child. Weber, who lived in Dresden, often passed their house and was observed with almost religious awe by little Richard. Sometimes the great composer dropped in to have a chat with the mother, who was well liked among musicians and artists. Thus Weber became the idol of the lad's boyhood, and he knew "Der Freischütz" almost by heart. If he was not allowed to go to the theater to listen to his favorite opera, there would be scenes of weeping and beseeching, until permission was granted for him to run off to the performance.

In 1827 the family returned to Leipsic, and it was at the famous Gewandhaus concerts that the boy first heard Beethoven's music. He was so fired by the Overture to "Egmont," that he decided at once to become a musician. But how—that was the question. He knew nothing of composition, but, borrowing a treatise on harmony, tried to learn the whole contents in a week.

It was a struggle, and one less determined than the fourteen-year-old boy would have given up in despair. He was made of different stuff. Working alone by himself, he composed a sonata, a quartette and an aria. At last he ventured to announce the result of his secret studies. At this news his relatives were up in arms; they judged his desire for music to be a passing fancy, especially as they knew nothing of any preparatory studies, and realized he had never learned to play any instrument, not even the piano.

The family, however, compromised enough to engage a teacher for him. But Richard would never learn slowly and systematically. His mind shot far ahead, absorbing in one instance the writings of Hoffmann, whose imaginative tales kept the boy's mind in a continual state of nervous excitement. He was not content to climb patiently the mountain; he tried to reach the top at a bound. So he wrote overtures for orchestras, one of which was really performed in Leipsic—a marvelous affair indeed, with its tympani explosions.

Richard now began to realize the need of solid work, and settled down to study music seriously, this time under Theodor Weinlig, who was cantor in the famous Thomas School.

In less than six months the boy was able to solve the most difficult problems in counterpoint. He learned to know Mozart's music, and tried to write with more simplicity of style. A piano sonata, a polonaise for four hands and a fantaisie for piano belong to this year. After that he aspired to make piano arrangements of great works, such as Beethoven's "Ninth Symphony." Then came his own symphony, which was really performed at Gewandhaus, and is said to have shown great musical vigor.

Intrumental music no longer satisfied this eager, aspiring boy; he must compose operas. He was now twenty, and went to Würzburg, where his brother Albert was engaged at the Würzburg Theater as actor, singer and stage manager. Albert secured for him a post as chorus master, with a salary of ten florins a month.

The young composer now started work on a second opera, the first, called "The Marriage," was found impracticable. The new work was entitled "The Fairies." This he finished, and the work, performed years later, was found to be imitative of Beethoven, Weber, and Marschner; the music was nevertheless very melodious.

Wagner returned to Leipsic in 1834. Soon there came another impetus to this budding genius: he heard for the first time the great singer Wilhelmina Schroeder-Devrient, whose art made a deep impression on him.

It was a time for rapid impressions to sway the ardent temperament of this boy genius of twenty-one. He read the works of Wilhelm Heinse, who depicts both the highest artistic pleasures and those of the opposite sort. Other authors following the same trend made him believe in the utmost freedom in politics, literature and morals. Freedom in everything—the pleasures of the moment—seemed to him the highest good.

Under the sway of such opinions he began to sketch the plot of his next opera, "Prohibition of Love" (Liebesverbot), founded on Shakespeare's "Measure for Measure." This was while he was in Teplitz on a summer holiday. In the autumn he took a position as conductor in a small operatic theater in Magdeburg. Here he worked at his new opera, hoping he could induce the admired Schroeder-Devrient to be his heroine.

Wagner remained in this place about two years and finished his opera there. The performance of it, for which he labored with great zeal, was a fiasco. The theater, too, failed soon after and the young composer was thrown out of work. His sojourn there influenced his after career, as he met Wilhelmina Planer, who was soon to become his wife.

Hearing there was an opening for a musical director at Königsberg, he traveled to that town, and in due course secured the post. Minna Planer also found an engagement at the theater, and the two were married on November 24, 1836; he was twenty-three and she somewhat younger. Kind, gentle, loving, she was quite unable to understand she was linked with a genius. Wagner was burdened with debts, begun in Magdeburg and increased in Königsberg. She was almost as improvident as he. They were like two children playing at life, with fateful consequences. It was indeed her misfortune, as one says, that this gentle dove was mismated with an eagle. But Minna learned later, through dire necessity, to be more economical and careful, which is more than can be said of her gifted husband.

After a year the Königsberg Theater failed and again Wagner was out of employment. Through the influence of his friend Dorn, he secured a directorship at Riga, Minna also being engaged at the theater. At first everything went well; the salary was higher and the people among whom they were placed were agreeable. But before long debts began to press again, and Wagner was dissatisfied with the state of the lyric drama, which he was destined to reform in such a wonderful way. He was only twenty-four, and had seen but little of the world. Paris was the goal toward which he looked with longing eyes, and to the gay French capital he determined to go.

When he tried to get a passport for Paris, he found it impossible because of his debts. Not to be turned from his purpose, he, Minna and the great Newfoundland dog, his pet companion, all slipped away from Riga at night and in disguise. At the port of Pillau the trio embarked on a sailing vessel for Paris, the object of all his hopes. The young composer carried with him one opera and half of a second work—"Rienzi," which he had written during the years of struggle in Magdeburg and Königsberg. In Riga he had come upon Heine's version of the Flying Dutchman legend, and the sea voyage served to make the story more vital.

He writes: "This voyage I shall never forget as long as I live; it lasted three weeks and a half, and was rich in mishaps. Thrice we endured the most violent storms, and once the captain had to put into a Norwegian haven. The passage among the crags of Norway made a wonderful impression on my fancy; the legends of the Flying Dutchman, as told by the sailors, were clothed with distinct and individual color, heightened by the ocean adventures through which we passed."

After stopping a short time in London, the trio halted for several weeks in Boulogne, because the great Meyerbeer was summering there. Wagner met the influential composer and confided his hopes and longings. Meyerbeer received the poor young German kindly, praised his music, gave him several letters to musicians in power in Paris, but told him persistence was the most important factor in success.

With a light heart, and with buoyant trust in the future, though with little money for present necessities, Wagner and his companions arrived in Paris in September, 1839. Before him lay, if he had but known it, two years and a half of bitter hardship and privation; but—"out of trials and tribulations are great spirits molded."

There were many noted musicians in the French capital at that time, and many opportunities for success. The young German produced his letters of introduction and received many promises of assistance from conductors and directors. Delighted with his prospects he located in the "heart of elegant and artistic Paris," without regarding cost.

Soon the skies clouded; one hope after another failed. His compositions were either too difficult for conductors to grasp, or theaters failed on which he depended for assistance. He became in great distress and could not pay for the furniture of the apartment, which he had bought on credit. It was now that he turned to writing for musical journals, to keep the wolf from the door, meanwhile working on the score of "Rienzi," which was finished in November, 1840 and sent to Dresden. In later years it was produced in that city.

But the Wagners, alas, were starving in Paris. One of Richard's articles at this time was called "The End of a Musician in Paris," and he makes the poor musician die with the words; "I believe in God—Mozart and Beethoven." It was almost as bad as this for Wagner himself. He determined to turn his back on all the intrigues and hardships he had endured for over two years, and set out for the homeland, which seemed the only desirable spot on earth.

The rehearsals for "Rienzi" began in Dresden in July 1842. Wagner had now finished "The Flying Dutchman," and had completed the outline of "Tannhaüser," based on Hoffmann's story of the Singers' Contest at the Wartburg.

And now Wagner's star as a composer began to

rise and light was seen ahead. On October 20, 1842 "Rienzi" was produced in the Dresden Opera House and the young composer awoke the next morning to find himself famous. The performance was a tremendous success, with singers, public and critics alike. The performance lasted six hours and Wagner, next day, decided the work must be cut in places, but the singers loudly protested: "The work was heavenly," they assured him, "not a measure could be spared."

With this first venture Wagner was now on the high road to success, and spent a happy winter in the Saxon capital. He could have gone on writing operas like "Rienzi," to please the public, but he aimed far higher. To fuse all the arts in one complete whole was the idea that had been forming in his mind. He first illustrated this in "The Flying Dutchman," and it became the main thought of his later works. This theory made both vocal and instrumental music secondary to the dramatic plan, and this, at that time, seemed a truly revolutionary idea.

"The Flying Dutchman" was produced at the Dresden Opera House January 2, 1843, with Mme. Schroeder-Devrient as Senta. Critics and public had expected a brilliant and imposing spectacle like "Rienzi" and were disappointed. In the following May and June "The Dutchman" was heard in Riga and Cassel, conducted by the famous violinist and composer, Spohr.

In spite of the fact that "The Flying Dutchman" was not then a success, and in Dresden was shelved for twenty years, Wagner secured the fine post of Head Capellmeister, at a salary of nearly twelve hundred dollars. This post he retained for seven years, gaining a great deal of experience in orchestral conducting, and producing Beethoven's symphonies with great originality, together with much that was best in orchestral literature.

"Tannhäuser" was now complete, and during the following summer, at Marienbad, sketches for "Lohengrin" and "Die Meistersinger" were made. During the winter, the book being made he began on the music of "Lohengrin." In March of the exciting year 1848, the music of "Lohengrin" was finished. There was a wide difference in style between that work and "Tannhäuser." And already the composer had in mind a new work to be called "The Death of Siegfried." He wrote to Franz Liszt, with whom he now began to correspond, that within six months he would send him the book of the new work complete. As he worked at the drama, however, it began to spread out before him in a way that he could not condense into one opera, or even two; and thus it finally grew into the four operas of the "Ring of the Nibelungen."

It must not be imagined that Wagner had learned the lesson of carefulness in money matters, or that, with partial success he always had plenty for his needs. He had expensive tastes, loved fine clothing and beautiful surroundings. Much money, too, was needed to produce new works; so that in reality, the composer was always in debt. The many letters which passed between Wagner and Liszt, which fill two large volumes, show how Liszt clearly recognized the brilliant genius of his friend, and stood ready to help him over financial difficulties, and how Wagner came to lean more and more on Liszt's generosity.

Just what part Wagner played in the revolution of 1848 is not quite clear. He wrote several articles which were radical protests for freedom of thought. At all events he learned it would be better for him to leave Dresden in time. In fact he remained in exile from his country for over eleven years.

Wagner fled to Switzerland, leaving Minna still in Dresden, though in due time he succeeded in scraping together funds for her to follow him to Zurich. He was full of plans for composing "Siegfried," while she continually urged him to write pleasing operas that Paris would like. Wagner believed the world should take care of him, while he was composing his great works, whereas Minna saw this course meant living on the charity of friends, and at this she rebelled. But Wagner grew discouraged over these petty trials, and for five years creative work was at a standstill.

How to meet daily necessities was the all absorbing question. A kind friend, who greatly admired his music, Otto Wesendonck, made it possible for him to rent, at a low price, a pretty chalet near Lake Zurich, and there he and Minna lived in retirement, and here he wrote many articles explaining his theories.

During the early years at Zurich Wagner's only musical activity was conducting a few orchestral concerts. Then, one day, he took out the score of his "Lohengrin," and read it, something he rarely did with any of his works. Seized with a deep desire to have this opera brought out, he sent a pleading letter to Liszt, begging him to produce the work. Liszt faithfully accomplished this task at Weimar, where he was conducting the Court Opera. The date chosen was Goethe's birthday, August 28, and the year 1850. Wagner was most anxious to be present, but the risk of arrest prevented him from venturing on German soil. It was not till 1861, in Vienna, that the composer heard this the most popular of all his operas. Liszt was profoundly moved by the beautiful work, and wrote his enthusiasm to the composer.

Wagner now took up his plan of the Nibelung Trilogy, that is the three operas and a prologue. Early in 1853 the poem in its new form was complete, and in February he sent a copy to Liszt, who answered: "You are truly a wonderful man, and your Nibelung poem is surely the most incredible thing you have ever done!"

So Wagner was impelled by the inner flame of creative fire, to work incessantly on the music of the great epic he had planned. And work he must, in spite of grinding poverty and ill health. It was indeed to be the "Music of the Future."

After a brief visit to London, to conduct some concerts for the London Philharmonic, Wagner was back again in Zurich, hard at work on the "Walküre," the first opera of the three, as the "Rheingold" was considered the introduction. By April 1856, the whole opera was finished and sent to Liszt for his opinion. Liszt and his great friend, Countess Wittgenstein, studied out the work together, and both wrote glowing letters to the composer of the deep effect his music made upon them.

And now came a halt in the composition of these tremendous music dramas. Wagner realized that to produce such great works, a special theater should be built, of adaptable design. But from where would the funds be forthcoming? While at work on the "Walküre," the stories of "Tristan" and "Parsifal" had suggested themselves, and the plan of the first was already sketched. He wrote to Liszt: "As I have never in life felt the bliss of real love, I must erect a monument to the most beautiful of all my dreams." The first act of "Tristan and Isolde" was finished on the last day of the year 1857. In his retreat in Switzerland, the composer longed for sympathetic, intellectual companionship, which, alas, Minna could not give him. He found it in the society of Marie Wesendonck, wife of the kind friend and music lover, who had aided him in many ways. This marked attention to another aroused Minna's jealousy and an open break was imminent. The storm, however, blew over for a time.

In June, 1858, Wagner was seized with a desire for luxury and quiet, and betook himself to Venice, where he wrote the second act of "Tristan." Then came the trouble between Wagner and the Wesendoncks which caused the composer to leave Zurich finally, on August 17, 1859. Minna returned to Dresden while Wagner went to Paris, where Minna joined him for a time, before the last break came.

What promised to be a wonderful stroke of good luck came to him here. His art was brought to the notice of the Emperor, Napoleon III, who requested that one of his operas should be produced, promising carte blanche for funds. All might have gone well with music of the accepted pattern. But "Tannhäuser" was different, its composer particular as to who sang and how it was done. The rehearsals went badly, an opposing faction tried to drown the music at the first performance. Matters were so much worse at the second performance that Wagner refused to allow it to proceed. In spite of the Emperor's promises, he had borne much of the expense, and left Paris in disgust, burdened with debt.

From Paris Wagner went to Vienna, where he had the great happiness of hearing his "Lohengrin" for the first time. He hoped to have "Tristan" brought out, but the music proved too difficult for the singers of that time to learn. After many delays and disappointments, the whole thing was given up. Reduced now to the lowest ebb, Wagner planned a concert tour to earn a living. Minna now left him finally; she could no longer endure life with this "monster of genius." She went back to her relatives in Leipsic, and passed away there in 1866.

The concert tours extended over a couple of years, but brought few returns, except in Russia. Wagner became despondent and almost convinced he ought to give up trying to be a composer. People called him a freak, a madman, and ridiculed his efforts at music making. And yet, during all this troublesome time, he was at work on his one humorous opera, "Die Meistersinger." On this he toiled incessantly.

And now, when he was in dire need, and suffering, a marvelous boon was coming to him, as wonderful as any to be found in fairy tale. A fairy Prince was coming to the rescue of this struggling genius. This Prince was the young monarch of Bavaria, who had just succeeded to the throne left by the passing of his father. The youthful Prince, ardent and generous, had long worshiped in secret the master and his music. One of his first acts on becoming Ludwig of Bavaria, was to send for Wagner to come to his capital at once and finish his life work in peace. "He wants me to be with him always, to work, to rest, to produce my works," wrote Wagner to a friend in Zurich, where he had been staying. "He will give me everything I need; I am to finish my Nibelungen and he will have them performed as I wish. All troubles are to be taken from me; I shall have what I need, if I only stay with him."

The King placed a pretty villa on Lake Starnberg, near Munich, at Wagner's disposal, and there he spent the summer of 1864. The King's summer palace was quite near, and monarch and composer were much together. In the autumn a residence in the quiet part of Munich was set apart for Wagner. Hans von Bülow was sent for as one of the conductors; young Hans Richter lived in Munich and later became one of the most distinguished conductors of Wagner's music.

The Bülows arrived in Munich in the early autumn, and almost at once began the attraction of Mme. Cosima von Bülow and Wagner. She, the daughter of Liszt, was but twenty five, of deeply artistic temperament, and could understand the aims of the composer as no other woman had yet done. This ardent attraction led later to Cosima's separation from her husband and finally to her marriage with Wagner.

The first of the Wagner Festivals under patronage of the King, took place in Munich June 10, 13, 19, and July 1, 1865. The work was "Tristan and Isolde," perhaps the finest flower of Wagner's genius; and already eight years old. Von Bülow was a superb conductor and Ludwig an inspired Tristan. Wagner was supremely happy. Alas, such happiness did not last. Enemies sprang up all about him. The King himself could not stem the tide of false rumors, and besought the composer to leave Munich for a while, till public opinion calmed down. So Wagner returned to his favorite Switzerland and settled in Triebschen, near Lucerne, where he remained till he removed to Bayreuth in 1872.

In 1866, the feeling against Wagner had somewhat declined and the King decided to have model per-formances of "Tannhäuser" and "Lohengrin" at Munich. The Festival began June 11, 1867. The following year "Die Meistersinger" was performed—June 21, 1868.

And now the King was eager to hear the "Ring." It was not yet complete but the monarch could not wait and ordered "Das Rheingold," the Introduction to the Trilogy, to be prepared. It was poorly given and was not a success. Not at all discouraged, he wished for "Die Walküre," which was performed the following year, June 26, 1870.

It had long been Wagner's desire to have a theater built, in which his creations could be properly given under his direction. Bayreuth had been chosen, as a quiet spot where music lovers could come for the sole purpose of hearing the music. He went to live there with his family in April, 1872. Two years later they moved into Villa Wahnfried, which had been built according to the composer's ideas. Meanwhile funds were being raised on both sides of the water, through the Wagner Societies, to erect the Festival Theater. The corner stone was laid on Wagner's birthday—his fifty-ninth—May 22, 1872. It was planned to give the first performances in the summer of 1876; by that time Wagner's longed-for project became a reality.

The long-expected event took place in August, 1876. The Festival opened on the thirteenth with "Das Rheingold," first of the Ring music dramas. On the following night "Die Walküre" was heard; then came "Siegfried" and "Götterdämmerung," the third and fourth dramas being heard for the first time. Thus the Ring of the Nibelungen, on which the composer had labored for a quarter of a century at last found a hearing, listened to by Kings and Potentates, besides a most distinguished audience of musicians from all parts of the world.

At last one of Wagner's dreams was realized and his new gospel of art vindicated.

One music drama remained to be written "Parsifal," his last. Failing health prevented the completion of the drama until 1882. The first performance of this noble work was given on July 26, followed by fifteen other hearings. After the exertions attending these, Wagner and his wife, their son Siegfried, Liszt and other friends, went to Italy and occupied the Vendramin Palace, on the Grand Canal, Venice. Here he lived quietly and comfortably, surrounded by those he loved. His health failed more and more, the end coming February 13, 1883.

Thus passed from sight one of the most astonishing musicians of all time. He lives in his music more vitally than when his bodily presence was on earth, since the world becomes more familiar with his music as time goes on. And to know this music is to admire and love it.

CÉSAR FRANCK

CHAPTER XVII

CÉSAR FRANCK

WHATEVER we learn of César Franck endears him to all who would know and appreciate the beautiful character which shines through his art. He was always kind, loving, tender, and these qualities are felt in the music he composed. Some day we shall know his music better. It has been said of this unique composer: "Franck is enamored of gentleness and consolation; his music rolls into the soul in long waves, as on the slack of a moonlit tide. It is tenderness itself."

In Liège, Belgium, it was that César Franck was born, December 10, 1822. Chopin had come a dozen years earlier, so had Schumann, Liszt and other gifted ones; it was a time of musical awakening.

The country about Liège was peculiarly French, not only in outward appearance, but in language and sentiment. Here were low hills covered with pines and beeches, here charming valleys; there wide plains where the flowering broom flourished in profusion. It was the Walloon country, and the Francks claimed descent from a family of early Walloon painters of the same name. The earliest of these painters was Jérome Franck, born away back in 1540. Thus the name Franck had stood for art ideals during a period of more than two and a half centuries.

When César and his brother were small children, the father, a man of stern and autocratic nature—a banker, with many friends in the artistic and musical world—decided to make both his sons professional musicians.

His will had to be obeyed, there was no help for it. In the case of César, however, a musician was what he most desired to become, so that music study was always a delight.

Before he was quite eleven years old, his father took him on a tour of Belgium. It looked then as though he had started on a virtuoso career, as the wonder children—Mozart, Chopin, Thalberg, Liszt and others who had preceded him, had done. The future proved, however, that César's life work was to be composing, teaching and organ playing, with a quiet life, even in busy Paris, instead of touring the world to make known his gifts.

During this youthful tour of Belgium, he met a child artist, a year or two older than himself, a singer, also touring as a virtuoso. The little girl was called Pauline Garcia, who later became famous as Mme. Pauline Viardot Garcia.

When César was twelve he had learned what they could teach him at the Liège Conservatory, and finished his studies there. His father, ambitious for the musical success of his sons, emigrated with his family to Paris, in 1836. César applied for entrance to the Conservatoire, but it was not until the following year, 1837, that he gained admission, joining Leborne's class in composition, and becoming Zimmermann's pupil in piano playing. At the end of the year the boy won a prize for a fugue he had written. In piano he chose Hummel's Concerto in A minor for his test, and played it off in fine style. When it came to sight reading, he suddenly elected to transpose the piece selected a third below the key in which it was written, which he was able to do at sight, without any hesitation or slip.

Such a feat was unheard of and quite against the time-honored rules of competition. And to think it had been performed by an audacious slip of a boy of fifteen! The aged Director, none other than Maestro Cherubini, was shocked out of the even tenor of his way, and declared that a first prize could not be awarded, although he must have realized the lad deserved it. To make amends, however, he proposed a special award to the audacious young pianist, outside the regular competition, to be known as "The Grand Prize of Honor." This was the first time, and so far as is known, the only time such a prize has been awarded.

César Franck won his second prize for fugue composition in 1839. Fugue writing had become so natural and easy for him, that he was able to finish his task in a fraction of the time allotted by the examiners. When he returned home several hours before the other students had finished, his father reproached him roundly for not spending more time on the test upon which so much depended. With his quiet smile the boy answered he thought the result would be all right. And it was! The next year he again secured the first prize for fugue; this was in July 1840. The year following he entered the organ contest, which was a surprise to the examiners.

The tests for organ prizes have always been four. First, the accompaniment of a plain chant, chosen for the occasion; second, the performance of an organ piece with pedals; third, the improvising of a fugue; fourth, improvising a piece in sonata form. Both the improvisations to be on themes set by the examiners. César at once noticed that the two themes could be combined in such a way that one would set off the other. He set to work, and soon became so absorbed in this interweaving of melodies that the improvisation extended to unaccustomed lengths, which bewildered the examiners and they decided to award nothing to such a tiresome boy. Benoist, teacher of this ingenious pupil, explained matters with the result that César was awarded a second prize for organ.

He now began to prepare for the highest honor, the Prix de Rome. But here parental authority interfered. For some unexplained reason, his father compelled him to leave the Conservatoire before the year was up. It may have been the father desired to see his son become a famous virtuoso pianist and follow the career of Thalberg and Liszt. At any rate he insisted his boy should make the most of his talents as a performer and should also compose certain pieces suitable for public playing. To this period of his life belong many of the compositions for piano solo, the showy caprices, fantaisies and transcriptions. Being obliged to write this kind of music, the young composer sought for new forms in fingering and novel harmonic effects, even in his most insignificant productions. Thus among the early piano works, the Eclogue, Op. 3, and the Ballade, Op. 9, are to be found innovations which should attract the pianist and musician of to-day.

His very first compositions, a set of three Trios, Op. 1, were composed while he was still at the Conservatoire, and his father wished them dedicated "To His Majesty, Leopold I, King of the Belgians." He wished to secure an audience with the King and have his son present the composition to his Majesty in person. It may have been for this reason he withdrew the boy so suddenly from the Conservatoire. However this may have been, the Franck family returned to Belgium for two years. At the end of that time, they all returned to Paris, with almost no other resources than those earned by the two young sons, Josef and César, by private teaching and concert engagements.

And now began for César Franck that life of regular and tireless industry, which lasted nearly half a century. This industry was expressed in lesson-giving and composing.

One of the first works written after his return to Paris, was a musical setting to the Biblical story of "Ruth." The work was given in the concert room of the Conservatoire, on January 4, 1846, when the youthful composer was twenty-three. The majority of the critics found little to praise in the music, which, they said, was but a poor imitation of "Le Desert," by David. One critic, more kindly disposed than the others, said: "M. César Franck is exceedingly naïve, and this simplicity we must confess, has served him well in the composition of his sacred oratorio of 'Ruth.'" A quarter of a century later, a second performance of "Ruth" was given, and the same critic wrote: "It is a revelation! This score, which recalls by its charm and melodic simplicity Mehul's 'Joseph,' but with more tenderness and modern feeling, is certainly a masterpiece."

But alas, hard times came upon the Franck family. The rich pupils, who formed the young men's chief clientèle, all left Paris, alarmed by the forebodings of the revolution of 1848. Just at this most inopportune moment, César decided to marry. He had been in love for some time with a young actress, the daughter of a well-known tragedienne, Madame Desmousseaux, and did not hesitate to marry in the face of bad times and the opposition of his parents, who strongly objected to his bringing a theatrical person into the family.

César Franck was then organist in the church of Notre Dame de Lorette, and the marriage took place there, February 22, 1848, in the very thick of the revolution. Indeed, to reach the church, the wedding party were obliged to climb a barricade, helped over by the insurgents, who were massed behind this particular fortification.

Soon after the wedding, Franck, having now lost his pupils—or most of them—and being continually blamed by his father, whom he could no longer supply with funds, decided to leave the parental roof and set up for himself in a home of his own. Of course he had now to work twice as hard, get new pupils and give many more lessons. But with all this extra labor, he made a resolve, which he always kept sacredly, which was to reserve an hour or two each day for composition, or for the study of such musical and literary works as would improve and elevate his mind. Nothing was ever allowed to interfere with this resolution, and to it we owe all his great works.

Franck made his first attempt at a dramatic work in 1851, with a libretto entitled "The Farmer's Man." As he must keep constantly at his teaching during the day, he devoted the greater part of the night to composition. He worked so hard that the opera, begun in December 1851, was finished in two years, but he paid dearly for all this extra labor. He fell ill—a state of nervous prostration— and was unable for some time to compose at all.

It was indeed a time of shadows for the young musician, but the skies brightened after a while. He had the great good fortune to secure the post of organist and choir master in the fine new basilica of Sainte Clothilde, which had lately been erected, and which had an organ that was indeed a masterpiece. This wonderful instrument kept all its fulness of tone and freshness of timbre after fifty years of use. "If you only knew how I love this instrument," Father Franck used to say to the curé of Sainte Clothilde; "it is so supple beneath my fingers and so obedient to all my thoughts."

As Vincent d'Indy, one of Franck's most gifted and famous pupils, writes:

"Here, in the dusk of this organ-loft, which I can never think of without emotion, he spent the best part of his life. Here he came every Sunday and feast day— and toward the end of his life, every Friday morning too, fanning the fire of his genius by pouring out his spirit in wonderful improvisations, which were often far more lofty in thought than many skilfully elaborated compositions. And here, too, he must have conceived the sublime melodies which afterward formed the groundwork of his 'Beatitudes.'"

"Ah, we knew it well, we who were his pupils, the way up to that thrice-blessed organ loft, a way as steep and difficult as that which the Gospels tell us leads to Paradise. But when we at last reached the little organ chamber, all was forgotten in the contemplation of that rapt profile, the intellectual brow, from which seemed to flow without effort a stream of inspired melody and subtle, exquisite harmonies."

César Franck was truly the genius of improvisation. It is said no other modern organist, not excepting the most renowned players, could hold any comparison to him in this respect. Whether he played for the service, for his pupils or for some chosen musical guest, Franck's improvisations were always thoughtful and full of feeling. It was a matter of conscience to do his best always. "And his best was a sane, noble, sublime art."

For the next ten years Franck worked and lived the quiet life of a teacher and organist; his compositions during this time were organ pieces and church music. But a richer inner life was the outgrowth of this period of calm, which was to blossom into new, deeper and more profoundly beautiful compositions.

One of these new works was "The Beatitudes." For years he had had the longing to compose a religious work on the Sermon on the Mount. In 1869, he set to work on the poem, and when that was well under way, began to create, with great ardor, the musical setting.

In the very midst of this absorbing work came the Franco-Prussian war, and many of his pupils must enter the conflict, in one way or another. Then early in 1872, he was appointed Professor of Organ at the Conservatoire, which was an honor he appreciated.

The same year, while occupied with the composition of the "Beatitudes," he wrote and completed his "Oratorio of the Redemption." After this he devoted six years to the finishing of the "Beatitudes," which occupied ten years of his activity, as it was completed in 1879. A tardy recognition of his genius by the Government granted him the purple ribbon as officer of the Academy, while not until five or six years later did he receive the ribbon of a Chevalier of the Legion of Honor.

In consequence of this event his pupils and friends raised a fund to cover expenses of a concert devoted entirely to the master's compositions. These works were given—conducted by Pasdeloup: Symphonic Poem—"Le Chasseur Maudit," Symphonic Variations, piano and orchestra, Second Part of "Ruth." Part II was conducted by the composer and consisted of March and Air de Ballet, with chorus, from "Hulda" and the Third and Eighth Beatitudes.

The Franck Festival occurred January 30, 1887, and was not a very inspiring performance. The artist pupils of the master voiced to him their disappointment that his works should not have been more worthily performed. But he only smiled on them and comforted them with the words: "No, no, you are too exacting, dear boys; for my part I am quite satisfied."

No wonder his pupils called him "Father Franck," for he was ever kind, sympathetic and tender with them all.

During the later years of César Franck's earthly existence, he produced several masterpieces. Among them the Violin Sonata, composed for Eugene and Théophile Ysaye, the D minor Symphony, the String Quartet, the two remarkable piano pieces, Prelude, Chorale and Fugue, Prelude, Aria and Finale, and finally the Three Chorales for organ, his swan song. His health gradually declined, due to overwork and an accident, and he passed quietly away, November 8, 1890.

Chabrier, who only survived Franck a few years, ended his touching remarks at the grave with these words:

"Farewell, master, and take our thanks, for you have done well. In you we salute one of the greatest artists of the century, the incomparable teacher, whose wonderful work has produced a whole generation of forceful musicians and thinkers, armed at all points for hard-fought and prolonged conflicts. We salute, also, the upright and just man, so humane, so distinguished, whose counsel was sure, as his words were kind. Farewell!"

CHAPTER XVIII

JOHANNES BRAHMS

It has been truly said that great composers cannot be compared one with another. Each is a solitary star, revolving in his own orbit. For instance it is impossible to compare Wagner and Brahms; the former could not have written the German Requiem or the four Symphonies any more than Brahms could have composed "Tristan." In the combination of arts which Wagner fused into a stupendous whole, he stands without a rival. But Brahms is also a mighty composer in his line of effort, for he created music that continually grows in beauty as it is better known.

Johannes Brahms was born in Hamburg, May 7, 1833. The house at 60 Speckstrasse still stands, and doubtless looks much as it did seventy years ago. A locality of dark, narrow streets with houses tall and gabled and holding as many families as possible. Number 60 stands in a dismal court, entered by a close narrow passage. A steep wooden staircase in the center, used to have gates, closed at night. Jakob and Johanna lived in the first floor dwelling to the left. It consisted of a sort of lobby or half kitchen, a small living room and a tiny sleeping closet—nothing else. In this and

Johannes Brahms

other small tenements like it, the boy's early years were spent. It certainly was an ideal case of low living and high thinking.

The Brahms family were musical but very poor in this world's goods. The father was a contra bass player in the theater; he often had to play in dance halls and beer gardens, indeed where he could. Later he became a member of the band that gave nightly concerts at the Alster Pavilion. The mother, much older than her husband, tried to help out the family finances by keeping a little shop where needles and thread were sold.

Little Johannes, or Hannes as he was called, was surrounded from his earliest years by a musical atmosphere, and must have shown a great desire to study music. We learn that his father took him to Otto Cossel, to arrange for piano lessons. Hannes was seven years old, pale and delicate looking, fair, with blue eyes and a mass of flaxen hair. The father said:

"Herr Cossel, I wish my son to become your pupil; he wants so much to learn the piano. When he can play as well as you do it will be enough."

Hannes was docile, eager and quick to learn. He had a wonderful memory and made rapid progress. In three years a concert was arranged for him, at which he played in chamber music with several other musicians of Hamburg. The concert was both a financial and artistic success. Not long after this, Cossel induced Edward Marxsen, a distinguished master and his own teacher, to take full charge of the lad's further musical training. Hannes was about twelve at the time.

Marxsen's interest in the boy's progress increased from week to week, as he realized his talents. "One day I gave him a composition of Weber's," he says. "The next week he played it to me so blamelessly that I praised him. 'I have also practised it in another way,' he answered, and played me the right hand part with the left hand." Part of the work of the lessons was to transpose long pieces at sight; later on Bach's Preludes and Fugues were done in the same way.

Jakob Brahms, who as we have seen was in very poor circumstances, was ready to exploit Hannes' gift whenever occasion offered. He had the boy play in the band concerts in the Alster Pavilion, which are among the daily events of the city's popular life, as all know who are acquainted with Hamburg, and his shillings earned in this and similar ways, helped out the family's scanty means. But late hours began to tell on the boy's health. His father begged a friend of his, a wealthy patron of music, to take the lad to his summer home, in return for which he would play the piano at any time of day desired and give music lessons to the young daughter of the family, a girl of about his own age.

Thus it came about that early in May, 1845, Hannes had his first taste of the delights of the country. He had provided himself with a small dumb keyboard, to exercise his fingers upon. Every morning, after he had done what was necessary in the house, Hannes was sent afield by the kind mistress of the household, and told not to show himself till dinner time. Perhaps the good mistress did not know that Hannes had enjoyed himself out of doors hours before. He used to rise at four o'clock and begin his day with a bath in the river. Shortly after this the little girl, Lischen, would join him and they would spend a couple of hours rambling about, looking for bird's nests, hunting butterflies and picking wild flowers. Hannes' pale cheeks soon became plump and ruddy, as the result of fresh air and country food. Musical work went right on as usual. Studies in theory and composition, begun with Marxsen, were pursued regularly in the fields and woods all summer.

When the summer was over and all were back in Hamburg again, Lischen used to come sometimes to Frau Brahms, of whom she soon grew very fond. But it troubled her tender heart to see the poor little flat so dark and dreary; for even the living room had but one small window, looking into the cheerless courtyard. She felt very sorry for her friends, and proposed to Hannes they should bring some scarlet runners to be planted in the court. He fell in with the idea at once and it was soon carried out. But alas, when the children had done their part, the plants refused to grow.

Johannes had returned home much improved in health, and able to play in several small concerts, where his efforts commanded attention. The winter passed uneventfully, filled with severe study by day and equally hard labor at night in playing for the "lokals." But the next summer in Winsen brought the country and happiness once more.

Hannes began to be known as a musician among the best families of Winsen, and often played in their homes. He also had the chance to conduct a small chorus of women's voices, called the Choral Society of Winsen. He was expected to turn his theoretical studies to account by composing something for this choir. It was for them he produced his "A B C" song for four parts, using the letters of the alphabet. The composition ended with the words "Winsen, eighteen-hundred seven and forty," sung slowly and fortissimo. The little piece was tuneful and was a great favorite with the teachers, from that day to this.

The boy had never heard an opera. During the summer, when Carl Formes, then of Vienna, was making a sensation in Hamburg, Lischen got her father to secure places and take them. The opera was the "Marriage of Figaro." Hannes was almost beside himself with delight. "Lischen, listen to the music! there was never anything like it," he cried over and over again. The father, seeing it gave so much pleasure, took the children again to hear another opera, to their great delight.

But the happy summer came to an end and sadness fell, to think Johannes must leave them, for he had found many kind friends in Winsen. He was over fifteen now and well knew he must make his way as a musician, help support the family, and pay for the education of his brother Fritz, who was to become a pianist and teacher. There was a farewell party made for him in Winsen, at which there was much music, speech making and good wishes for his future success and for his return to Winsen whenever he could.

Johannes made his new start by giving a concert

of his own on September 21, 1848. The tickets for this concert were one mark; he had the assistance of some Hamburg musicians. In April next, 1849, he announced a second concert, for which the tickets were two marks. At this he played the Beethoven "Waldstein Sonata," and the brilliant "Don Juan Fantaisie." These two works were considered about the top of piano virtuosity. Meanwhile the boy was always composing and still with his teacher Marxsen.

The political revolution of 1848, was the cause of many refugees crowding into Hamburg on their way to America. One of these was the violinist, Edward Remenyi, a German Hungarian Jew, whose real name was Hofmann. But it seemed Remenyi was really in no haste to leave Hamburg. Johannes, engaged as accompanist at the house of a wealthy patron, met the violinist and was fascinated by his rendering of national Hungarian music. Remenyi, on his side, saw the advantage of having such an accompanist for his own use. So it happened the two played together frequently for a time, until the violinist disappeared from Germany, for several years. He reappeared in Hamburg at the close of the year 1852. He was then twenty-two, while Brahms was nineteen. It was suggested that the two musicians should do a little concert work together. They began to plan out the trip which became quite a tour by the time they had included all the places they wished to visit.

The tour began at Winsen, then came Cella. Here a curious thing happened. The piano proved to be a half tone below pitch, but Brahms was equal to the dilemma.

Requesting Remenyi to tune his violin a half tone higher, making it a whole tone above the piano, he then, at sight, transposed the Beethoven Sonata they were to play. It was really a great feat, but Johannes performed it as though it were an every day affair.

The next place was Lüneburg and there the young musician had such success that a second concert was at once announced. Two were next given at Hildesheim. Then came Leipsic, Hanover and after that Weimar, where Franz Liszt and his retinue of famous pupils held court. Here Johannes became acquainted with Raff, Klindworth, Mason, Prükner and other well-known musicians.

By this time his relations with Remenyi had become somewhat irksome and strained and he decided to break off this connection. One morning he suddenly left Weimar, and traveled to Göttingen. There he met Joseph Joachim, whom he had long wished to know, and who was the reigning violinist of his time. Without any announcement, Johannes walked in on the great artist, and they became fast friends almost at once. Joachim had never known what it was to struggle; he had had success from the very start; life had been one long triumph, whereas Johannes had come from obscurity and had been reared in privation. At this time Johannes was a fresh faced boy, with long fair hair and deep earnest blue eyes. Wollner, the distinguished musician of Cologne, thus describes him: "Brahms, at twenty, was a slender youth, with long blond hair and a veritable St. John's head, from whose eyes shone energy and spirit."

Johannes was at this time deeply engaged on his piano Sonata in F minor, Op. 5. He had already written two other piano sonatas, as yet little known. The Op. 5, is now constantly heard in concert rooms, played by the greatest artists of our time.

In disposition Hannes was kindly and sincere; as a youth merry and gay. A friend in Düsseldorf, where he now spent four weeks, thus describes him:

"He was a most unusual looking young musician, hardly more than a boy, in his short summer coat, with his high-pitched voice and long fair hair. Especially fine was his energetic, characteristic mouth, and his earnest, deep gaze. His constitution was thoroughly healthy; the most strenuous mental exercise hardly fatigued him and he could go to sleep at any hour of the day he pleased. He was apt to be full of pranks, too. At the piano he dominated by his characteristic, powerful, and when necessary, extraordinarily tender playing." Schumann, whom he now came to know in Düsseldorf, called him the "young eagle—one of the elect." In fact Schumann, in his musical journal, praised the young musician most highly. And his kindness did not stop there. He wrote to Hannes' father, Jakob Brahms, in Hamburg, commending in glowing terms his son's compositions. This letter was sent to Johannes and the result was the offering of some of his compositions to Breitkopf and Härtel for publication. He had already written two Sonatas, a Scherzo, and a Sonata for piano and violin. The Sonata in C, now known as Op. 1, although not his first work, was the one in which he introduced himself to the public. For, as he said: "When one first shows one's self, it is to the head and not to the heels that one wishes to draw attention."

Johannes made his first appearance in Leipsic, as pianist and composer, at one of the David Quartet Concerts, at which he played his C major Sonata and the Scherzo. His success was immediate, and as a result, he was able to secure a second publisher for his Sonata Op. 5.

And now, after months of traveling, playing in many towns and meeting with many musicians and distinguished people, Johannes turned his steps toward Hamburg, and was soon in the bosom of the home circle. It is easy to imagine the mother's joy, for Hannes had always been the apple of her eye, and she had kept her promise faithfully, to write him a letter every week. But who shall measure the father's pride and satisfaction to have his boy return a real musical hero?

The concert journey just completed was the bridge over which Johannes Brahms passed from youth to manhood. With the opening year of 1854, he may be said to enter the portals of a new life.

He now betook himself to Hanover, to be near his devoted friend Joachim, plunged into work and was soon absorbed in the composition of his B major Piano Trio. Later Schumann and his charming wife, the pianist, came to Hanover for a week's visit, which was the occasion for several concerts in which Brahms, Joachim and Clara Schumann took part. Soon after this Schumann's health failed and he was removed to a sanatorium. In sympathy for the heavy trial now to be borne by Clara Schumann, both young artists came to Düsseldorf, to be near the wife of their adored master, Robert Schumann. There they remained and by their encouragement so lifted the spirits of Frau Clara that she was able to resume her musical activities.

Johann had been doing some piano teaching when not occupied with composition. But now, on the advice of his musical friends, he decided to try his luck again as a concert pianist. He began by joining Frau Clara and Joachim in a concert at Danzig. Each played solos. Johann's were Bach's "Chromatic Fantaisie" and several manuscript pieces of his own. After this the young artist went his own way. He played with success in Bremen, also in Hamburg. It is said he was always nervous before playing, but especially so in his home city. However all passed off well. He now settled definitely in Hamburg, making musical trips to other places when necessary.

Robert Schumann rallied for a while from his severe malady, and hopes were held out of his final recovery. Frau Clara, having her little family to support, resumed her concert playing in good earnest, and appeared with triumphant success in Vienna, London and many other cities. When possible Brahms and Joachim accompanied her. Then Schumann's malady took an unfavorable turn. When the end was near, Brahms and Frau Clara went to Endenich and were with the master till all was over. On July 31, 1856, a balmy summer evening, the mortal remains of the great composer were laid to rest in the little cemetery at Bonn, on the Rhine. The three chief mourners were: Brahms—who carried a laurel wreath from the wife—Joachim and Dietrich.

Frau Schumann returned to Düsseldorf the next day, accompanied by Brahms and Joachim. Together they set in order the papers left by the composer, and assisted the widow in many little ways. A little later she went to Switzerland to recover her strength, accompanied by Brahms and his sister Elise. A number of weeks were spent in rest and recuperation. By October the three musicians were ready to take up their ordinary routine again. Frau Clara began practising for her concert season, Joachim returned to his post in Hanover, and Johann turned his face toward Hamburg, giving some concerts on the way, in which he achieved pronounced success.

The season of 1856-57, was passed uneventfully by Brahms, in composing, teaching and occasional journeys. He may be said to have had four homes, besides that of his parents in Hamburg. In Düsseldorf, Hanover, Göttingen and Bonn he had many friends and was always welcome.

It may be asked why Brahms, who had the faculty of endearing himself so warmly to his friends, never married. It is true he sometimes desired to found a home of his own, but in reality the mistress of his absorbing passion was his art, to which everything else remained secondary. He never swerved a hair's breadth from this devotion to creative art, but accepted poverty, disappointment, loneliness and often failure in the eyes of the world, for the sake of this, his true love.

Johannes was now engaged as conductor of a Choral Society in Detmold, also as Court Pianist and teacher in the royal family. The post carried with it free rooms and living, and he was lodged at the Hotel Stadt Frankfort, a comfortable inn, exactly opposite the Castle, and thus close to the scene of his new labors.

He began his duties by going through many short choral works of the older and modern masters. With other musicians at Court much chamber music was played, in fact almost the entire repertoire. The young musician soon became a favorite at Court, not only on account of his musical genius but also because of the general culture of his mind. He could talk on almost any subject. "Whoever wishes to play well must not only practise a great deal but read many books," was one of his favorite sayings. One of his friends said, of meetings in Brahms' rooms at night, when his boon companions reveled in music: "And how Brahms loved the great masters! How he played Haydn and Mozart! With what beauty of interpretation and delicate shading of tone. And then his transposing!" Indeed Johann thought nothing of taking up a new composition and playing it in *any* key, without a mistake. His score reading was marvelous. Bach, Handel, Mozart, Haydn, all seemed to flow naturally from under his fingers.

The post in Detmold only required Brahms' presence a part of the year, but he was engaged for a term of years. The other half of the year was spent in Hamburg, where he resumed his activities of composing and teaching. The summer after his first winter in Detmold was spent in Göttingen with warm friends. Clara Schumann was there with her children, and Johann was always one of the family—as a son to her. He was a famous playfellow for the children, too. About this time he wrote a book of charming Children's Folk Songs, dedicated to the children of Robert and Clara Schumann. Johann was occupied with his Piano Concerto in D minor. His method of working was somewhat like Beethoven's, as he put down his ideas in notebooks. Later on he formed the habit of keeping several compositions going at once.

The prelude to Johann's artistic life was successfully completed. Then came a period of quiet study and inward growth. A deeper activity was to succeed. It opened early in the year 1859, when the young musician traveled to Hanover and Leipsic, bringing out his Concerto in D minor. He performed it in the first named city, while Joachim conducted the orchestra. It was said the work "with all its serious striving, its rejection of the trivial, its skilled instrumentation, seemed difficult to understand; but the pianist was considered not merely a virtuoso but a great artist of piano playing."

The composer had now to hurry to Leipsic, as he was to play with the famous Gewandhaus orchestra. How would Leipsic behave towards this new and serious music? Johann was a dreamer, inexperienced in the ways of the world; he was an idealist—in short, a genius gifted with an "imagination, profound, original and romantic." The day after the concert he wrote Joachim he had made a brilliant and decided failure. However he was not a whit discouraged by the apathy of the Leipsigers toward his new work. He wrote: "The Concerto will please some day, when I have made some improvements, and a second shall sound quite different."

It has taken more than half a century to establish the favor of the Concerto, which still continues on upward wing. The writer heard the composer play this Concerto in Berlin, toward the end of his life. He made an unforgettable figure, as he sat at the piano with his long hair and beard, turning to gray; and while his technic was not of the virtuoso type, he created a powerful impression by his vivid interpretation.

After these early performances of the Concerto, Johann returned to Hamburg, to his composing and teaching. He, however, played the Concerto in his native city on a distinguished occasion, when Joachim was a soloist in Spohr's Gesang-Scene, Stockhausen in a magnificent Aria, and then Johann, pale, blond, slight, but calm and self controlled. The Concerto scored a considerable success at last, and the young composer was content.

In the autumn of this year, Johann paid his third visit to Detmold, and found himself socially as well as musically the fashion. It was the correct thing to have lessons from him and his presence gave distinction to any assemblage. But Johann did not wish to waste his time at social functions; when obliged to be present at some of these events he would remain silent the entire evening, or else say sharp or biting things, making the hosts regret they had asked him. His relations with the Court family, however, remained very pleasant. Yet he began to chafe under the constant demands on his time, and the rigid etiquette of the little Court. The next season he definitely declined the invitation to revisit Detmold, the reason given was that he had not the time, as he was supervising the publication of a number of his works. Brahms had become interested in writing for the voice, and had already composed any number of beautiful vocal solos and part songs.

We are told that Frau Schumann, Joachim and Stockhausen came frequently to Hamburg during the season of 1861, and all three made much of Johannes. All four gave concerts together, and Johannes took part in a performance of Schumann's beautiful Andante and Variations, for two pianos, while Stockhausen sang entrancingly Beethoven's Love Songs, accompanied by Brahms. On one occasion Brahms played his Variations on a Handel Theme, "another magnificent work, splendidly long, the stream of ideas flowing inexhaustibly. And the work was wonderfully played by the composer; it seemed like a miracle. The composition is so difficult that none but a great artist can attempt it." So wrote a listener at the time. That was in 1861. We know this wonderful work in these days, for all the present time artists perform it. At each of Frau Schumann's three appearances in Hamburg during the autumn of this year, she performed one of Brahms' larger compositions; one of them was the Handel Variations.

Although one time out of ten Johann might be taciturn or sharp, the other nine he would be agreeable, always pleased—good humored, satisfied, like a child with children. Every one liked his earnest nature, his gaiety and humor.

Johann had had a great longing to see Vienna, the home of so many great musicians; but felt that when the right time came, the way would open. And it did. Early in September, 1862, he wrote a friend: "I am leaving on Monday, the eighth, for Vienna. I look forward to it like a child."

He felt at home in Vienna from the start, and very soon met the leading lights of the Austrian capital. On November 16, he gave his first concert, with the Helmesberger Quartet, and before a crowded house. It was a real success for "Schumann's young prophet." Although concert giving was distasteful, he appeared again on December 20, and then gave a second concert on January 6, 1863, when he played Bach's Chromatic Fantaisie, Beethoven's Variations in C minor, his own Sonata Op. 5, and Schumann's Sonata Op. 11.

Johann returned home in May, and shortly after was offered the post of Conductor of the Singakademie, which had just become vacant. He had many plans for the summer, but finally relinquished them and sent an acceptance. By the last of August he was again in Vienna.

Now followed years of a busy musical life. Brahms made his headquarters in Vienna, and while there did much composing. The wonderful Piano Quintette, one of his greatest works, the German Requiem, the Cantata Rinaldo and many beautiful songs came into being during this period. Every little while concert tours and musical journeys were undertaken, where Brahms often combined with other artists in giving performances of his compositions. A series of three concerts in Vienna in February and March, 1869, given by Brahms and Stockhausen, were phenomenally successful, the tickets being sold as soon as the concerts were announced. The same series was given in Budapest with equal success.

Early in the year 1872, when our composer was nearly forty, we find him installed in the historic rooms in the third floor of Number 4 Carl's Gasse, Vienna, which were to remain to the end of his life the nearest approach to an establishment of his own. There were three small rooms. The largest contained his grand piano, writing table, a sofa with another table in front of it. The composer was still smooth of face and looked much as he did at twenty, judging from his pictures. It was not until several years later, about 1880, that he was adorned by the long heavy beard, which gave his face such a venerable appearance.

The year 1874, was full of varied excitement. Many invitations were accepted to conduct his works in North Germany, the Rhine, Switzerland, and other countries. A tour in Holland in 1876, brought real joy. He played his D minor Concerto in Utrecht and other cities, conducted his works and was everywhere received with honors. But the greatest event of this year was the appearance of his first Symphony. It was performed for the first time from manuscript in Carlsruhe and later in many other cities. In this work "Brahms' close affinity with Beethoven must become clear to every musician, who has not already perceived it," wrote Hanslick, the noted critic.

We have now to observe the unwearied energy with which Brahms, during the years that followed added one after another to his list, in each and every branch of serious music; songs, vocal duets, choral and instrumental works. In the summer of 1877 came the Second Symphony. In 1879 appeared the great Violin Concerto, now acclaimed as one of the few masterpieces for that instrument. It was performed by Joachim at the Gewandhaus, Leipsic, early in the year. There were already four Sonatas for Piano and Violin. The Sonata in G, the Rhapsodies Op. 79 and the third and fourth books of Hungarian Dances, as duets, were the publications of 1880. He now wrote a new Piano Concerto, in B flat, which he played in Stuttgart for the first time, November 22, 1881. In 1883 the Third Symphony appeared, which revealed him at the zenith of his powers. This work celebrated his fiftieth birthday.

The Fourth Symphony was completed during the summer of 1885. Then came the Gipsy Songs.

From 1889 onward, Brahms chose for his summer sojourn the town of Ischl, in the Salzkammergut. The pretty cottage where he stayed was on the outskirts of the town, near the rushing river Traun. He always dined at the "Keller" of the Hotel Elizabeth, which was reached by a flight of descending steps. In this quiet country, among mountain, valley and stream, he could compose at ease and also see his friends at the end of the day.

A visit to Italy in the spring of 1890, afforded rest, refreshment and many pleasant incidents.

The "Four Serious Songs," were published in the summer of 1896. At this time Brahms had been settled in his rooms at Ischl scarcely a fortnight when he was profoundly shaken by news of Clara Schumann's death. She passed peacefully away in Frankfort, and was laid beside her husband, in Bonn, May 24. Brahms was present, together with many musicians and celebrities.

The master felt this loss keenly. He spent the summer in Ischl as usual, composing, among other things, the Eleven Choral Preludes. Most of these have death for their subject, showing that his mind was taken up with the idea. His friends noticed he had lost his ruddy color and that his complexion was pale. In the autumn he went to Carlsbad for the cure.

After six weeks he returned to Vienna, but not improved, as he had become very thin and walked with faltering step. He loved to be with his friends, the Fellingers, as much as possible, as well as with other friends. He spent Christmas eve with them, and dined there the next day. From this time on he grew worse. He was very gentle the last months of his life, and touchingly grateful for every attention shown him. Every evening he would place himself at the piano and improvise for half an hour. When too fatigued to continue, he would sit at the window till long after darkness had fallen. He gradually grew weaker till he passed peacefully away, April 3, 1897.

The offer of an honorary grave was made by the city of Vienna, and he has found resting place near Beethoven and Mozart, just as he had wished.

Memorial tablets have been placed on the houses in which Brahms lived in Vienna, Ischl and Thun, also on the house of his birth, in Hamburg.

CHAPTER XIX

EDWARD GRIEG

"From every point of view Grieg is one of the most original geniuses in the musical world of the present or past. His songs are a mine of melody, surpassed in wealth only by Schubert, and that only because there are more of Schubert's. In originality of harmony and modulation he has only six equals. Bach, Schubert, Chopin, Schumann, Wagner and Liszt. In rhythmic invention and combination he is inexhaustible, and as orchestrator he ranks among the most fascinating."

HENRY T. FINCK

EDWARD HAGERUP GRIEG, "the Chopin of the North," was a unique personality, as well as an exceptional musician and composer. While not a "wonder child," in the sense that Mozart, Chopin and Liszt were, he early showed his love for music and his rapt enjoyment of the music of the home circle. Fortunately he lived and breathed in a musical atmosphere from his earliest babyhood. His mother was a fine musician and singer herself, and with loving care she fostered the desire for it and the early studies of it in her son. She was his first teacher, for she kept up her own musical studies after her marriage, and continued to appear in concerts in

Bergen, where the family lived. Little Edward, one of five children, seemed to inherit the mother's musical talent and had vivid recollections of the rhythmic animation and spirit with which she played the works of Weber, who was one of her favorite composers.

The piano was a world of mystery to the sensitive musical child. His baby fingers explored the white keys to see what they sounded like. When he found two notes together, forming an interval of a third, they pleased him better than one alone. Afterwards three keys as a triad, were better yet, and when he could grasp a chord of four or five tones with both hands, he was overjoyed. Meanwhile there was much music to hear. His mother practised daily herself, and entertained her musical friends in weekly soirées. Here the best classics were performed with zeal and true feeling, while little Edward listened and absorbed music in every pore.

When he was six years old piano lessons began. Mme. Grieg proved a strict teacher, who did not allow any trifling; the dreamy child found he could not idle away his time. As he wrote later: "Only too soon it became clear to me I had to practise just what was unpleasant. Had I not inherited my mother's irrepressible energy as well as her musical capacity, I should never have succeeded in passing from dreams to deeds."

But dreams were turned into deeds before long, for the child tried to set down on paper the little melodies that haunted him. It is said he began to do this at the age of nine. A really serious attempt was made when he was twelve or thirteen. This was a set of variations for piano, on a German melody. He brought it to school one day to show one of the boys. The teacher caught sight of it and reprimanded the young composer soundly, for thus idling his time. It seems that in school he was fond of dreaming away the hours, just as he did at the piano.

The truth was that school life was very unsympathetic to him, very narrow and mechanical, and it is no wonder that he took every opportunity to escape and play truant. He loved poetry and knew all the poems in the reading books by heart; he was fond, too, of declaiming them in season and out of season.

With the home atmosphere he enjoyed, the boy Grieg early became familiar with names of the great composers and their works. One of his idols was Chopin, whose strangely beautiful harmonies were just beginning to be heard, though not yet appreciated. His music must have had an influence over the lad's own efforts, for he always remained true to this ideal.

Another of his admirations was for Ole Bull, the famous Norwegian violinist. One day in summer, probably in 1858, when Edward was about fifteen, this "idol of his dreams" rode up to the Grieg home on horseback. The family had lived for the past five years at the fine estate of Landaas, near Bergen. The great violinist had just returned from America and was visiting his native town, for he too was born in Bergen. That summer he came often to the Griegs' and soon discovered the great desire of young Edward for a musical career. He got the boy to improvise at the piano, and also to show him the little pieces he had already composed. There were consultations with father and mother, and then, finally, the violinist came to the boy, stroked his cheek and announced; "You are to go to Leipsic and become a musician."

Edward was overjoyed. To think of gaining his heart's desire so easily and naturally; it all seemed like a fairy tale, too good to be true.

The Leipsic Conservatory, which had been founded by Mendelssohn, and later directed for a short time by Schumann, was now in the hands of Moscheles, distinguished pianist and conductor. Richter and Hauptmann, also Papperitz, taught theory; Wenzel, Carl Reinecke and Plaidy, piano.

Some of these later gained the reputation of being rather dry and pedantic; they certainly were far from comprehending the romantic trend of the impressionable new pupil, for they tried to curb his originality and square it with rules and customs. This process was very irksome, for the boy wanted to go his own gait.

Among his fellow students at the Conservatory were at least a half dozen who later made names for themselves. They were: Arthur Sullivan, Walter Bache, Franklin Taylor, Edward Dannreuther and J. F. Barnett. All these were making rapid progress in spite of dry methods. So Edward Grieg began to realize that if he would also accomplish anything, he must buckle down to work. He now began to study with frantic ardor, with scarcely time left for eating and sleeping. The result of this was a complete breakdown in the spring of 1860, with several ailments, incipient lung trouble being the most serious. Indeed it was serious enough to deprive Grieg of one lung, leaving him for the remainder of his life somewhat delicate.

When his mother learned of his illness, she hurried to Leipsic and took him back to Bergen, where he slowly regained his health. His parents now begged him to remain at home, but he wished to return to Leipsic. He did so, throwing himself into his studies with great zeal. In the spring of 1862, after a course of four years, he passed his examinations with credit. On this occasion he played some of his compositions—the four which have been printed as Op. 1—and achieved success, both as composer and pianist.

After a summer spent quietly with his parents at Landaas, he began to prepare for coming musical activities. The next season he gave his first concert in Bergen, at which the piano pieces of Op. 1, Four Songs for Alto, and a String Quartet were played. With the proceeds of this concert he bought orchestral and chamber music, and began to study score, which he had not previously learned to do. In the spring of 1863—he was hardly twenty then—he left home and took up his residence in Copenhagen, a much larger city, offering greater opportunties for an ambitious young musician. It was also the home of Niels W. Gade, the foremost Scandinavian composer.

Of course Grieg was eager to meet Gade, and an opportunity soon occurred. Gade expressed a willingness to look at some of his compositions, and asked if he had anything to show him. Edward modestly answered in the negative. "Go home and write a symphony," was the retort. This the young composer started obediently to do, but the work was never finished in this form. It became later Two Symphonic Pieces for Piano, Op. 14.

Two sources of inspiration for Grieg were Ole Bull and Richard Nordraak. We remember that Ole Bull was the means of influencing his parents to send Edward to Leipsic. That was in 1858. Six years later, when Ole Bull was staying at his country home, near Bergen, where he always tried to pass the summers, the two formed a more intimate friendship. They played frequently together, sonatas by Mozart and others, or trios, in which Edward's brother John played the 'cello parts. Or they wandered together to their favorite haunts among mountains, fjords or flower clad valleys. They both worshiped nature in all her aspects and moods, and each, the one on his instrument, the other in his music, endeavored to reproduce these endless influences.

Richard Nordraak was a young Norwegian composer of great talent, who, in his brief career, created a few excellent works. The two musicians met in the winter of 1864 and were attracted to each other at once. Nordraak visited Grieg in his home, where they discussed music and patriotism to their hearts' content. Nordraak was intensely patriotic, and wished to see the establishment of Norse music. Grieg, who had been more or less influenced by German ideas, since Leipsic days, now cast off the fetters and placed himself on the side of Norwegian music. To prove this he composed the Humoresken, Op. 6, and dedicated them to Nordraak. From now on he felt free to do as he pleased in music—to be himself.

In 1864 Grieg became engaged to his cousin, Nina Hagerup, a slender girl of nineteen, who had a lovely voice and for whom he wrote many of his finest songs. He returned to Christiania from a visit to Rome, and decided to establish himself in the Norwegian capital. Soon after his arrival, in the autumn of 1856, he gave a concert, assisted by his financée and Mme. Norman Neruda, the violinist. The program was made up entirely of Norwegian music, and contained his Violin Sonata Op. 8, Humoresken, Op. 6, Piano Sonata, Op. 7. There were two groups of songs, by Nordraak and Kjerulf respectively. The concert was a success with press and public and the young composer's position seemed assured. He secured the appointment of Conductor of the Philharmonic Society, and was quite the vogue as a teacher. He married Nina Hagerup the following June, 1867, and they resided in Christiania for the next eight years.

Grieg could not endure "amateurish mediocrity," and made war upon it, thus drawing jealous attacks upon himself. His great friend and ally, Nordraak, passed away in 1868, and the next year his baby daughter, aged thirteen months, the only child he ever had, left them.

In spite of these discouragements, some of his finest compositions came into being about this period of his life. Songs, piano pieces and the splendid Concerto followed each other in quick succession.

Another satisfaction to Grieg was a most sympathetic and cordial letter from Liszt on making acquaintance with his Sonata for violin and piano, Op. 8, which he praised in high terms. He invited Grieg to come and visit him, that they might become better acquainted. This unsolicitated appreciation from the famous Liszt was a fine honor for the young composer, and was the means of inducing the Norwegian Government to grant him an annuity. This sum enabled him the following year, to go to Rome and meet Liszt personally.

He set out on this errand in October, and later wrote his parents of his visits to Liszt. The first meeting took place at a monastery near the Roman Forum, where Liszt made his home when in town.

"I took with me my last violin Sonata, the Funeral March on the death of Nordraak and a volume of songs. I need not have been anxious, for Liszt was kindness itself. He came smiling towards me and said in the most genial manner:

" 'We have had some little correspondence, haven't we?'

"I told him it was thanks to his letters that I was now here. He eyed somewhat hungrily the package under my arm, his long, spider-like fingers approaching it in such an alarming manner that I thought it advisable to open at once. He turned over the leaves, reading through the Sonata. He had now become interested, but my courage dropped to zero when he asked me to play the Sonata, but there was no help for it.

"So I started on his splendid American Chickering grand. Right in the beginning, where the violin starts in, he exclaimed: 'How bold that is! Look here, I like that; once more please.' And where the violin again comes in *adagio,* he played the part on the upper octaves with an expression so beautiful, so marvelously true and singing, it made me smile inwardly. My spirits rose because of his lavish approval, which did me good. After the first movement, I asked his permission to play a solo, and chose the Minuet, from the Humoresken."

At this point Grieg was brave enough to ask Liszt to play for him. This the master did in a superb manner. To go on with the letter:

"When this was done, Liszt said jauntily, 'Now let us go on with the Sonata'; to which I naturally retorted, 'No thank you, not after this.'

" 'Why not? Then give it to me, I'll do it.' And what does Liszt do? He plays the whole thing, root and branch, violin and piano; nay more, for he plays it fuller and more broadly. He was literally over the whole piano at once, without missing a note. And how he did play! With grandeur, beauty, unique comprehension.

"Was this not geniality itself? No other great man I have met is like him. I played the Funeral March, which was also to his taste. Then, after a little talk, I took leave, with the consciousness of having spent two of the most interesting hours of my life."

The second meeting with Liszt took place soon after this. Of it he writes in part:

"I had fortunately received the manuscript of my Concerto from Leipsic, and took it with me. A number of musicians were present.

" 'Will you play?' asked Liszt. I answered in the negative, as you know I had never practised it. Liszt took the manuscript, went to the piano, and said to the assembled guests: 'Very well, then, I will show you that I also cannot.' Then he began. I admit that he took the first part too fast, but later on, when I had a chance to indicate the tempo, he played as only he can play. His demeanor is worth any price to see. Not content with playing, he at the same time converses, addressing a bright remark now to one, now to another of his guests, nodding from right to left, particularly when something pleases him. In the Adagio, and still more in the Finale, he reached a climax, both in playing and in the praise he bestowed.

"When all was over, he handed me the manuscript, and said, in a peculiarly cordial tone: 'Keep steadily on; you have the ability, and—do not let them intimidate you!'

"This final admonition was of tremendous importance to me; there was something in it like a sanctification. When disappointment and bitterness are in store for me, I shall recall his words, and the remembrance of that hour will have a wonderful power to uphold me in days of adversity."

When Edward Grieg was a little over thirty, in the year 1874, the Norwegian Government honored him with an annuity of sixteen hundred crowns a year, for life. Another good fortune was a request from the distinguished poet, Henrik Ibsen, to produce music for his drama of "Peer Gynt."

With the help of the annuity Grieg was able to give up teaching and conducting and devote himself to composition. He left Christiania, where he and Mme. Grieg had resided for eight years, and came back for a time to Bergen. Here, in January 1874, Ibsen offered him the proposition of writing music for his work, for which he was arranging a stage production.

Grieg was delighted with the opportunity, for such a task was very congenial. He completed the score in the autumn of 1875. The first performance was given on February 24, 1876, at Christiania. Grieg himself was not present, as he was then in Bergen. The play proved a real success and was given thirty-six times that season, for which success the accompanying original and charming music was largely responsible.

Norway is a most picturesque country, and no one could be more passionately fond of her mountains, fjords, valleys and waterfalls than Edward Grieg. For several years he now chose to live at Lofthus, a tiny village, situated on a branch of the Hardanger Fjord. It is said no spot could have been more enchanting. The little study, consisting of one room, where the composer could work in perfect quiet, was perched among the trees above the fjord, with a dashing waterfall near by. No wonder Grieg could write of the "Butterfly," the "Little Bird," and "To the Spring," in such poetical, vivid harmonies. He had only to look from his window and see the marvels of nature about him.

A few years later he built a beautiful villa at Troldhaugen, not far from Bergen, where he spent the rest of his life. Some American friends who visited them in 1901, speak of the ideal existence of the artist pair. Grieg himself is described as very small and frail looking, with a face as individual, as unique and attractive as his music—the face of a thinker, a genius. His eyes were keen and blue; his hair, almost white, was brushed backward like Liszt's. His hands were thin and small; they were wonderful hands and his touch on the piano had the luscious quality of Paderewski's. Mme. Grieg received them with a fascinating smile and won all hearts by her appearance and charm of manner. She was short and plump, with short wavy gray hair and dark blue eyes. Her sister, who resembled her strongly, made up the rest of the family. Grieg called her his "second wife" and they seemed a most united family.

Here, too, Grieg had his little work cabin away from the house, down a steep path, among the trees of the garden, In this tiny retreat he composed many of his unique pieces.

As a pianist, there are many people living who have heard Grieg play, and all agree that his performance was most poetical and beautiful. He never had great power, for a heavy wagon had injured one of his hands, and he had lost the use of one of his lungs in youth. But he always brought out lyric parts most expressively, and had a "wonderfully crisp and buoyant execution in rhythmical passages." He continued to play occasionally in different cities, and with increased frequency made visits to England, France and Germany, to make known his compositions. He was in England in the spring of 1888, for on May 3, the London Philharmonic gave almost an entire program of Grieg's music. He acted in the three-fold capacity of composer, conductor and pianist. It was said by one of the critics: "Mr. Grieg played his own Concerto in A minor, after his own manner; it was a revelation." Another wrote: "The Concerto is very beautiful. The dreamy charm of the opening movement, the long-drawn sweetness of the Adagio, the graceful, fairy music of the final Allegro— all this went straight to the hearts of the audience. Grieg as a conductor gave equal satisfaction. It is to be hoped the greatest representative of 'old Norway' will come amongst us every year."

Grieg did return the next year and appeared with the Philharmonic, March 14, 1889. The same critic then wrote:

"The hero of the evening was unquestionably Mr. Grieg, the heroine being Madame Grieg, who sang in her own unique and most artistic fashion, a selection of her husband's songs, he accompanying with great delicacy and poetic feeling. Grieg is so popular in London, both as composer and pianist, that when he gave his last concert, people were waiting in the street before the doors from eleven in the morning, quite as in the old Rubinstein days."

In only a few cities did the artist pair give their

unique piano and song recitals. These were: Christiania, Copenhagen, Leipsic, Rome, Paris, London and Edinburgh. They were indeed artistic events, in which Nina Grieg was also greatly admired. While not a great singer, it was said she had the captivating abandon, dramatic vivacity and soulful treatment of the poem, which reminded of Jenny Lind.

Mme. Grieg made her last public appearance in London in 1898. After that she sang only for her husband and his friends.

Grieg's sixtieth birthday, June 15, 1903, was celebrated in the cities of Scandinavia, throughout Europe and also in America: thus he lived to see the recognition of his unique genius in many parts of the world.

Grieg was constantly using up his strength by too much exertion. To a friend in 1906, he wrote: "Yes, at your age it is ever hurrah-vivat. At my age we say, sempre diminuendo. And I can tell you it is not easy to make a beautiful diminuendo." Yet he still gave concerts, saying he had not the strength of character to refuse. Indeed he had numerous offers to go to America, which he refused as he felt he could not endure the sea voyage. Always cheerful, even vivacious, he kept up bravely until almost the end of his life, but finally, the last of August, 1907, he was forced to go to a hospital in Bergen. On the night of September 3, his life ebbed away in sleep.

The composer who through his music had endeared himself to the whole world, was granted a touching funeral, at which only his own music was heard, including his Funeral March, which he had composed for his friend Nordraak. The burial place is as romantic as his music. Near his home there is a steep cliff, about fifty feet high, projecting into the fjord. Half way up there is a natural grotto, which can only be reached by water. In this spot, chosen by Grieg himself, the urn containing his ashes was deposited some weeks after the funeral. Then the grotto was closed and a stone slab with the words "Edward Grieg" cut upon it, was cemented in the cliff.

PETER ILYITCH TSCHAIKOWSKY

CHAPTER XX

PETER ILYITCH TSCHAIKOWSKY

RUSSIAN composers and Russian music are eagerly studied by those who would keep abreast of the time. This music is so saturated with strong, vigorous life that it is inspiring to listen to. Its rugged strength, its fascinating rhythms, bring a new message. It is different from the music of other countries and at once attracts by its unusual melodies and its richness of harmony.

Among the numerous composers of modern Russia, the name of Peter Ilyitch Tschaikowsky stands out most prominently. This distinctive composer was born on April 28, 1840, in Votinsk, where his father, who was a mining engineer, had been appointed inspector of the mines at KamskoVotinsk. The position of manager of such important mines carried with it much luxury, a fine house, plenty of servants and an ample salary. Thus the future young musician's home life was not one of poverty and privation, as has been the lot of so many gifted ones, who became creators in the beautiful art of music.

Peter Ilyitch was less than five years old when a

311

new governess came into the family, to teach his elder brother Nicholas and his cousin Lydia. As a little boy he was apt to be untidy, with buttons missing and rumpled hair. But his nature was so affectionate and sympathetic that he charmed every one with his pretty, loving ways. This natural gift he always retained. The governess was a very superior person and her influence over her young charges was healthful and beneficial. The child Peter was most industrious at his lessons; but for recreation often preferred playing the piano, reading, or writing poetry, to playing with other children.

When Peter was eight, the family moved to St. Petersburg, and the two younger boys were sent to boarding school. The parting from his home but especially from his mother—though he saw her once a week—nearly broke his heart. Such a school was no place for a sensitive, high-strung boy like Peter, who needed the most tender fostering care. The work of the school was very heavy, the hours long. The boys often sat over their books till far into the night. Besides the school work, Peter had music lessons of the pianist Philipov, and made rapid progress. At this time music in general excited the boy abnormally; a hand organ in the street would enchant him, an orchestra strangely agitated him. He seemed to live at a high strung, nervous tension, and had frequent ailments, which kept him out of school.

In 1849 the father secured another appointment, this time at Alapaiev, a little town, where, though there was not so much luxury, the family tried to revive the home life of Votinsk.

No one at Alapaiev seemed to take any interest in the boy Peter's music. He was really making great progress, for he had learned much in the lessons he had taken in St. Petersburg. He studied many pieces by himself, and often improvised at the piano. His parents did nothing to further his musical education; this may have been because they were afraid of a return of the nervous disorders that the quiet of the present home surroundings had seemed to cure.

From the fact that the father had held government appointments, his sons were eligible for education at the School of Jurisprudence. Peter was accordingly entered there as a scholar, and completed his course at the age of nineteen. In those nine years the child Peter developed into maturity. During this period he suffered the loss of his mother, a handsome and very estimable woman, whom he adored with passionate devotion, and from whom he could never bear to be separated.

While attending the Law School, music had to be left in the background. His family and companions only considered it as a pastime at best, and without serious significance; he therefore kept his aspirations to himself. The old boyish discontent and irritability, which were the result of his former nervous condition, had now given place to his natural frankness of character and charm of manner, which attracted all who came in contact with him.

In 1859, when Peter had finished his studies at the School of Jurisprudence, he received an appointment in the Ministry of Justice, as clerk of the first class. This would have meant much to some young men, but did not greatly impress Peter, as he did not seem to take his work very seriously. During the three years in which he held the post, he followed the fashion of the day, attended the opera and theater, meanwhile receiving many impressions which molded his character and tastes. The opera "Don Giovanni," Mozart's masterpiece, made a deep impression upon him, also the acting of Adelaide Ristori and the singing of Lagrona.

The new Conservatoire of Music was founded at St. Petersburg in 1862, with Anton Rubinstein as director, and Tschaikowsky lost no time in entering as a pupil, studying composition and kindred subjects with Professor Zaremba. His progress was so rapid in the several branches he took up—piano, organ and flute—that Rubinstein advised him to make music his profession, and throw his law studies to the winds. Thanks to Rubinstein, he secured some pupils and also engagements as accompanist. Meanwhile he worked industriously at composition, and one of his pieces was a Concert Overture in F, scored for small orchestra. In 1865 he took his diploma as a musician and also secured a silver medal for a cantata. One year after this the Moscow Conservatoire was founded, with Nicholas Rubinstein at its head. The position of Professor of Composition and Musical History was offered to Tschaikowsky, then only twenty-six. It was a flattering offer for so young a man, when many older heads would have liked to secure such an honor. He moved to Moscow, and retained his position in the Conservatoire for at least twelve years, in the meantime making many friends for himself and his art, as his fame as a composer grew. One of these friends was the publisher Jurgenson, who was to play rather an important part in the composer's life, through accepting and putting forth his compositions.

During those first years in Moscow, Tschaikowsky made his home with Nicholas Rubinstein. His life was of the simplest, his fare always so. Later on when money was more abundant, and he had his own house in the country, he lived with just the same simplicity. One would think that all this care and thought for expense would have taught him the value of money. Not at all. He never could seem to learn its value, never cared for it, and never could keep it. He liked to toss his small change among groups of street boys, and it is said he once spent his last roubles in sending a cablegram to von Bülow in America, to thank him for his admirable performance of his first Piano Concerto. Often his friends protested against this prodigality, but it was no use to protest, and at last they gave up in despair.

Soon after he began his professorship in Moscow, he composed a Concert Overture in C minor. To his surprise and disappointment, Rubinstein disapproved of the work in every way. This was a shock, after the lack of encouragement in St. Petersburg. But he recovered his poise, though he made up his mind to try his next work in St. Petersburg instead of Moscow. He called the new piece a Symphonic Poem, "Winter Daydreams," but it is now known as the First Symphony, Op. 13. About the end of 1866, he started out with it, only to be again rebuffed and cast down. The two men whose good opinion he most desired, Anton Rubinstein and Professor Zaremba, could find nothing good in his latest work, and the young composer returned to Moscow to console himself with renewed efforts in composition. Two years later the "Winter Daydreams" Symphony was produced in Moscow with great success, and its author was much encouraged by this appreciation. He was, like most composers, very sensitive to criticism and had a perfect dread of controversy. Efforts to engage him in arguments of this sort only made him withdraw into himself.

Tschaikowsky held the operas of Mozart before him as his ideal. He cared little for Wagner, considering his music dramas to be built on false principles. Thus his first opera, "Voivoda," composed in 1866, evidently had his ideal, Mozart, clearly in mind. It is a somewhat curious fact that Tschaikowsky, who was almost revolutionary in other forms of music, should go back to the eighteenth century for his ideal of opera. Soon after it was completed "Voivoda" was accepted to be produced at the Moscow Grand Theater. The libretto was written by Ostrowsky, one of the celebrated dramatists of the day. The first performance took place on January 30, 1869. We are told it had several performances and considerable popular success. But the composer was dissatisfied with its failure to win a great artistic success, and burnt the score. He did the same with his next work, an orchestral fantaisie, entitled "Fatum." Again he did the same with the score of a complete opera, "Undine," finished in 1870, and refused at the St. Petersburg

Opera, where he had offered it.

"The Snow Queen," a fairy play with music, was the young Russian's next adventure; it was mounted and produced with great care, yet it failed to make a favorable impression. But these disappointments did not dampen the composer's ardor for work. Now it was in the realm of chamber music. Up to this time he had not seemed to care greatly for this branch of his art, for he had always felt the lack of tone coloring and variety in the strings. The first attempt at a String Quartet resulted in the one in D major, Op. 11. Today, fifty years after, we enjoy the rich coloring, the characteristic rhythms of this music; the Andante indeed makes special appeal. A bit of history about this same Andante shows how the composer prized national themes and folk tunes, and strove to secure them. It is said that morning after morning he was awakened by the singing of a laborer, working on the house below his window. The song had a haunting lilt, and Tschaikowsky wrote it down. The melody afterwards became that touching air which fills the Andante of the First String Quartet. Another String Quartet, in F major, was written in 1814, and at once acclaimed by all who heard it, with the single exception of Anton Rubinstein.

Tschaikowsky wrote six Symphonies in all. The Second, in C minor was composed in 1873; in this he used themes in the first and last movements, which were gathered in Little Russia. The work was produced with great success in Moscow in 1873. The next orchestral composition was a Symphonic Poem, called "The Tempest," with a regular program, prepared by Stassow.

It was brought out in Paris at the same time it was heard in Moscow. Both at home and in France it made a deep impression. The next work was the splendid piano Concerto in B flat minor, Op. 23, the first of three works of this kind. At a trial performance of it, his friend and former master, Nicholas Rubinstein, to whom it was dedicated, and who had promised to play the piano part, began to criticize it unmercifully and ended by saying it was quite unplayable, and unsuited to the piano.

No one could blame the composer for being offended and hurt. He at once erased the name of Nicholas Rubinstein from the title page and dedicated the work to Hans von Bülow, who not long after performed it with tremendous success in America, where he was on tour. When we think of all the pianists who have won acclaim in this temperamental, inspiring work, from Carreno to Percy Grainger, to mention two who have aroused special enthusiasm by their thrilling performance of it, we can but wonder that his own countrymen were so short sighted at the time it was composed. Later on Nicholas Rubinstein gave a superb performance of the Concerto in Moscow, thus making some tardy amends for his unkindness.

Tschaikowsky was now thirty-five. Most of his time was given to the Conservatoire, where he often worked nine hours a day. Besides, he had written a book on harmony, and was contributing articles on music to two journals. In composition he had produced large works, including up to this time, two Symphonies, two Operas, the Concerto, two String Quartets and numerous smaller pieces. To accomplish such an amount of work, he must have possessed immense energy and devotion to his ideals.

One of the operas just mentioned was entitled "Vakoula the Smith." It bears the date of 1874, and was first offered in competition with others. The result was that it not only was considered much the best work of them all but it won both the first and second prizes. "Vakoula" was splendidly mounted and performed in St. Petersburg, at the Marinsky Theater at least seventeen times. Ten years later, in January 1887, it appeared again. The composer meanwhile had re-written a good part of it and now called it "Two Little Shoes." This time Tschaikowsky was invited to conduct his own work. The invitation filled him with alarm, for he felt he had no gift in that direction, as he had tried a couple of times in the early years of his career and had utterly failed. However, he now, through the cordial sympathy of friends, decided to make the attempt. Contrary to his own fears, he obtained a successful performance of the opera.

It proved an epoch-making occasion. For this first success as conductor led him to undertake a three months' tour through western Europe in 1888. On his return to St. Petersburg he conducted a program of his own compositions for the Philharmonic Society, which was also successful, in spite of the intense nervousness which he always suffered. As a result of his concert he received offers to conduct concerts in Hamburg, Dresden, Leipsic, Vienna, Copenhagen and London, many of which he accepted.

To go back a bit in our composer's life story, to an affair of the heart which he experienced in 1868. He became engaged to the well-known singer Désirée Artôt; the affair never went further, for what reason is not known. He was not yet thirty, impressionable and intense. Later on, in the year 1877, at the age of thirty-seven, he became a married man. How this happened was doubtless told in his diaries, which were written with great regularity: but unfortunately he destroyed them all a few years before his death. The few facts that have been gleaned from his intimate friend, M. Kashkin, are that he was engaged to the lady in the spring of this year, and married her a month or so afterward. It was evidently a hasty affair and subsequently brought untold suffering to the composer. When the professors of his Conservatoire re-assembled in the autumn, Tschaikowsky appeared among them a married man, but looking the picture of despair. A few weeks later he fled from Moscow, and when next heard of was lying dangerously ill in St. Petersburg. One thing was evident, the ill-considered marriage came very near ruining his life. The doctors ordered rest and change of scene, and his brother Modeste Ilyitch took him to Switzerland and afterward to Italy. The peaceful life and change of scene did much to restore his shattered nerves. Just at this time a wealthy widow lady, Madame von Meek, a great admirer of Tschaikowsky's music, learning of his sad condition, settled on him a generous yearly allowance for life. He was now independent and could give his time to composition.

The following year he returned to Moscow and

seemed quite his natural self. A fever of energy for work took possession of him. He began a new opera, "Eugen Onégin," and completed his Fourth Symphony, in F minor. The score of the opera was finished in February, 1878, and sent at once to Moscow, where the first performance was given in March 1879. In the beginning the opera had only a moderate success, but gradually grew in favor till, after five years, it was performed in St. Petersburg and had an excellent reception. It is considered Tschaikowsky's most successful opera, sharing with Glinka's "Life of the Tsar" the popularity of Russian opera. In 1881 he was invited to compose an orchestral work for the consecration of the Temple of Christ in Moscow. The "Solemn Overture 1812," Op. 49, was the outcome of this. Later in the year he completed the Second Piano Concerto. The Piano Trio in A minor, "To the memory of a great artist," Op. 50, refers to his friend and former master, Nicholas Rubinstein, who passed away in Paris, in 1881.

Tschaikowsky's opera, "Mazeppa," was his next important work. In the same year the Second Orchestral Suite, Op. 53, and the Third, Op. 55, followed. Two Symphonic Poems, "Manfred" and "Hamlet" came next. The latter of these was written at the composer's country house, whose purchase had been made possible by the generosity of his benefactress, and to which he retired at the age of forty-five, to lead a peaceful country life. He had purchased the old manor house of Frovolo, on the outskirts of the town of Klin, near Moscow. Here his two beautiful ballets and two greatest Symphonies, the Fifth and Sixth, were written. The Fifth Symphony was composed in 1888 and published the next year. On its first hearing it made little impression and was scarcely heard again till Nikisch, with unerring judgment, rescued it from neglect; then the world discovered it to be one of the composer's greatest works.

Tschaikowsky's two last operas, the "Pique Dame" (Queen of Spades), Op. 68, and "King Rene's Daughter" are not considered in any way distinctive, although the former was performed in New York, at the Metropolitan. The Third Piano Concerto, Op. 75, occupied the master during his last days at Frovolo; it was left unfinished by him and was completed by the composer Taneiev. The wonderful Sixth Symphony, Op. 74, is a superb example of Tschaikowsky's genius. It was composed in 1893, and the title "Pathetic" was given it by the composer after its first performance, in St. Petersburg, shortly before his death, as the reception of it by the public did not meet his anticipations. In this work the passion and despair which fill so many of the master's finest compositions, rise to the highest tragic significance. The last movement, with its prophetic intimation of his coming death, is heart-breaking. One cannot listen to its poignant phrases without deep emotion. The score is dated August 31, 1893. On October twelfth, Tschaikowsky passed away in St. Petersburg, a victim of cholera.

A couple of years before he passed away, Tschaikowsky came to America. In May, 1891, he conducted four concerts connected with the formal opening of Carnegie Hall, New York. We well remember his interesting personality, as he stood before the orchestra, conducting many of his own works, with Adele Aus der Ohe playing his famous Concerto in B flat minor.

The music of this representative Russian composer has made rapid headway in the world's appreciation, during the last few years. Once heard it will always be remembered. For we can never forget the deeply human and touching message which is brought to us through the music of Peter Ilyitch Tschaikowsky.

CHAPTER XXI

EDWARD MACDOWELL

EDWARD MACDOWELL has been acclaimed America's greatest composer. If we try to substitute another name in its place, one of equal potency cannot be found.

Our composer's ancestors were Irish and Scotch, though his father was born in New York City and his mother was an American girl. Edward was their third son, and appeared December 18, 1861; this event happened at the home of his parents, 220 Clinton Street, New York.

The father was a man of artistic instincts, and as a youth, fond of drawing and painting. His parents had been Quakers of a rather severe sort and had discouraged all such artistic efforts. Little Edward seems to have inherited his father's artistic gifts, added to his own inclination toward music.

The boy had his first piano lessons when he was about eight years old, from a family friend, Mr. Juan Buitrago, a native of Bogota, South America. Mr. Buitrago became greatly interested in Edward

EDWARD   MACDOWELL

and asked permission to teach him his notes. At that time the boy was not considered a prodigy, or even precocious, though he seemed to have various gifts. He was fond of covering his music and exercise books with little drawings, which showed he had the innate skill of a born artist. Then he liked to scribble bits of verses and stories and invent fairy tales. He could improvise little themes at the piano, but was not fond of technical drudgery at the instrument in those early days.

The lessons with Mr. Buitrago continued for several years, and then he was taken to a professional piano teacher, Paul Desvernine, with whom he remained till he was fifteen. During this time he received occasional lessons from the brilliant Venezuelan pianist, Teresa Carreño, who admired his gifts and later played his piano concertos.

Edward was now fifteen, and his family considered he was to become a musician. In those days and for long after, even to the present moment, it was thought necessary for Americans to go to Europe for serious study and artistic finish. It was therefore determined the boy should go to Paris for a course in piano and theory at the Conservatoire. In April, 1876, accompanied by his mother, he left America for France.

He passed the examinations and began the autumn term as a pupil of Marmontel in piano and of Savard in theory and composition.

Edward's knowledge of French was very uncertain, and while he could get along fairly well in the piano class, he had considerable trouble in following the lessons in theory. He determined to make a special study of the language, and a teacher was engaged to give him private lessons.

His passion for drawing was liable to break out at any moment. During one of the lesson hours he was varying the monotony by drawing, behind his book, a picture of his teacher, whose special facial characteristic was a very large nose. Just as the sketch was finished he was detected and was asked to show the result. The professor, instead of being angry, considered it a remarkable likeness and asked to keep it. Shortly after this the professor called on Mrs. MacDowell, telling her he had shown the drawing to an eminent painter, also an instructor at the École des Beaux Arts. The painter had been so greatly impressed with the boy's talent that he offered him a three years' course of free instruction, under his own supervision. He also promised to be responsible for Edward's support during that time.

This was a vital question to decide; the boy's whole future hung in the balance. Mrs. MacDowell, in her perplexity, laid the whole matter before Marmontel, who strongly advised against diverting her son from a musical career. The decision was finally left to Edward himself, and he chose to remain at the Conservatoire.

Conditions there, however, were not just to his liking, and after two years he began to think the school was not the place for him. It was the summer of 1878, the year of the Exposition. Edward and his mother attended a festival concert and heard Nicholas Rubinstein play the Tschaikowsky B flat minor piano Concerto. His performance was a revelation. "I can never learn to play the piano like that if I stay here," exclaimed Edward, as they left the hall.

They began to consider the merits of the different European schools of music, and finally chose Stuttgart. Mrs. MacDowell and her son went there in November hoping that in this famous Conservatory could be found the right kind of instruction.

But alas, MacDowell soon found out his mistake. He discovered that he would have to unlearn all he had acquired and begin from the beginning. And even then the instruction was not very thorough.

They now thought of Frankfort, where the composer Joachim Raff was the director and Carl Heymann, a very brilliant pianist, was one of the instructors.

After months of delay, during which young MacDowell worked under the guidance of Ehlert, he at last entered the Frankfort Conservatory, studying composition with Raff, and piano with Heymann. Both proved very inspiring teachers. For Heymann he had the greatest admiration, calling him a marvel, whose technic was equal to anything. "In hearing him practise and play, I learned more in a week than I ever knew before."

Edward MacDowell remained in close study at the Frankfort Conservatory for two years, his mother having in the meantime returned to America. He had hoped to obtain a place as professor on the teaching staff of the institution. Failing to do this he took private pupils. One of these, Miss Marian Nevins, he afterwards married. He must have been a rather striking looking youth at this time. He was nineteen. Tall and vigorous, with blue eyes, fair skin, rosy cheeks, very dark hair and reddish mustache, he was called "the handsome American." He seemed from the start, to have success in teaching, though he was painfully shy, and always remained so.

In 1881, when he was twenty, he applied for the position of head piano teacher in the Darmstadt Conservatory, and was accepted. It meant forty hours a week of drudgery, and as he preferred to live in Frankfort, he made the trip each day between the two towns. Besides this he went once a week to a castle about three hours away, and taught some little counts and countesses, really dull and sleepy children, who cared but little if anything for music. However the twelve hours spent in the train each week, were not lost, as he composed the greater part of his Second Modern Suite for piano, Op. 14; the First Modern Suite had been written in Frankfort the year before. He was reading at this period a great deal of poetry, both German and English, and delving into the folk and fairy lore of romantic Germany. All these imaginative studies exerted great influence on his subsequent compositions, both as to subject and content.

MacDowell found that the confining labors at Darmstadt were telling on his strength, so he gave up the position and remained in Frankfort, dividing his time between private teaching and composing. He hoped to secure a few paying concert engagements, as those he had already filled had brought in no money.

One day, as he sat dreaming before his piano, some one knocked at the door, and the next instant in walked his master Raff, of whom the young American stood in great awe. In the course of a few moments, Raff suddenly asked what he had been writing. In his confusion the boy stammered he had been working on a concerto. When Raff started to go, he turned back and told the boy to bring the concerto to him the next Sunday. As even the first movement was not finished, its author set to work with vigor. When Sunday came only the first movement was ready. Postponing the visit a week or two, he had time to complete the work, which stands today, as he wrote it then, with scarcely a correction.

At Raff's suggestion, MacDowell visited Liszt in the spring of 1882. The dreaded encounter with the master proved to be a delightful surprise, as Liszt treated him with much kindness and courtesy. Eugen D'Albert, who was present, was asked to accompany the orchestral part of the concerto on a second piano. Liszt commended the work in warm terms: "You must bestir yourself," he warned D'Albert, "if you do not wish to be outdone by our young American." Liszt praised his piano playing too, and MacDowell returned to Frankfort in a happy frame of mind.

At a music Convention, held that year in Zurich, in July, MacDowell played his First Piano Suite, and won a good success. The following year, upon Liszt's recommendation, both the First and Second Modern Suites were brought out by Breitkopf and Härtel. "Your two Piano Suites are admirable," wrote Liszt from Budapest, in February, 1883, "and I accept with sincere pleasure and thanks the dedication of your piano Concerto."

The passing of Raff, on June 25, 1882, was a severe blow to MacDowell. It was in memory of his revered teacher that he composed the "Sonata Tragica," the first of the four great sonatas he has left us. The slow movement of this Sonata especially embodies his sorrow at the loss of the teacher who once said to him: "Your music will be played when mine is forgotten."

For the next two years MacDowell did much composing. Then in June 1884 he returned to America, and in July was married to his former pupil, Miss Marian Nevins, a union which proved to be ideal for both. Shortly after this event the young couple returned to Europe.

The next winter was spent in Frankfort, instructing a few private pupils, but mostly in composing, with much reading of the literature of various countries, and, in the spring, with long walks in the beautiful woods about Frankfort. Wiesbaden became their home during the winter of 1885-86. The same year saw the completion of the second Piano Concerto, in D minor.

In the spring of 1887, MacDowell, in one of his walks about the town, discovered a deserted cottage on the edge of the woods. It overlooked the town, with the Rhine beyond, and woods on the other side of the river. Templeton Strong, an American composer, was with him at the time, and both thought the little cottage an ideal spot for a home. It was soon purchased, and the young husband and wife lived an idyllic life for the next year. A small garden gave them exercise out of doors, the woods were always enticing and best of all, MacDowell was able to give his entire time to composition. Many beautiful songs and piano pieces were the result, besides the symphonic poem "Lamia," "Hamlet and Ophelia," the "Lovely Aidâ," "Lancelot and Elaine," and other orchestral works.

In September, 1888, the MacDowells sold their Wiesbaden cottage and returned to America, settling in Boston. Here MacDowell made himself felt as a pianist and teacher. He took many pupils, and made a conspicuous number of public appearances. He also created some of his best work, among which were the two great Sonatas, the "Tragica" and "Eroica." One of the important appearances was his playing of the Second Concerto with the Philharmonic Orchestra of New York, under Anton Seidl, in December, 1894.

In the spring of 1896 a Department of Music was founded at Columbia University, of New York, the professorship of which was offered to MacDowell. He had now been living eight years in Boston; his fame as a pianist and teacher was constantly growing; indeed more pupils came to him than he could accept. The prospect of organizing a new department from the very beginning was a difficult task to undertake. At first he hesitated; he was in truth in no hurry to accept the offer, and wished to weigh both sides carefully. But the idea of having an assured income finally caused him to decide in favor of Columbia, and he moved from Boston to New York the following autumn.

He threw himself into this new work with great

ardor and entire devotion. With the founding of the department there were two distinct ideas to be carried out. First, to train musicians who would be able to teach and compose. Second, to teach musical history and aesthetics.

All this involved five courses, with many lectures each week, taking up form, harmony, counterpoint, fugue, composition, vocal and instrumental music, both from the technical and interpretative side. It was a tremendous labor to organize and keep all this going, unaided. After two years he was granted an assistant, who took over the elementary classes. But even with this help, MacDowell's labors were increasingly arduous. He now had six courses instead of five, which meant more classes and lectures each week. Perhaps the most severe drain on his time and strength was the continual correction of exercise books and examination papers, a task which he performed with great patience and thoroughness. Added to all this, he devoted every Sunday morning to his advanced students, giving them help and advice in their piano work and in composition.

Amid all this labor his public playing had to be given up, but composition went steadily on. During the eight years of the Columbia professorship, some of the most important works of his life were produced; among them were, Sea Pieces, the two later Sonatas, the Norse and the Keltic, Fireside Tales, and New England Idyls. The Woodland Sketches had already been published and some of his finest songs. Indeed nearly one quarter of all his compositions were the fruit of those eight years while he held the post at Columbia.

In 1896 he bought some property near Peterboro, New Hampshire—fifteen acres with a small farmhouse and other buildings, and fifty acres of forest. The buildings were remodeled into a rambling but comfortable dwelling, and here, amid woods and hills he loved, he spent the summer of each year. He built a little log cabin in the woods near by, and here he wrote some of his best music.

In 1904 MacDowell left Columbia, but continued his private piano classes, and sometimes admitted free such students as were unable to pay. After his arduous labors at Columbia, which had been a great drain on his vitality, he should have had a complete rest and change. Had he done so, the collapse which was imminent might have been averted. But he took no rest though in the spring of 1905 he began to show signs of nervous breakdown. The following summer was spent, as usual, in Peterboro but it seemed to bring no relief to the exhausted composer. In the fall of that year his ailment appeared worse. Although he seemed perfectly well in body, his mind gradually became like that of a child. The writer was privileged to see him on one occasion, and retains an ineffaceable memory of the composer in his white flannels, seated in a large easy chair, taking little notice of what was passing about him, seldom recognizing his friends or visitors, but giving the hand of his devoted wife a devoted squeeze when she moved to his side to speak to him.

This state continued for over two years, until his final release, January 23, 1908, as he had just entered his forty-seventh year. The old Westminster Hotel had been the MacDowell home through the long illness. From here is but a step to St. George's Episcopal Church, where a simple service was held. On the following day the composer was taken to Peterboro, his summer home, a spot destined to play its part, due to the untiring efforts of Mrs. MacDowell, in the development of music in America.

Mr. Gilman tells us:

"His grave is on an open hill-top, commanding one of the spacious and beautiful views he had loved. On a bronze tablet are these lines of his own, used as a motto for his 'From a Log Cabin,' the last music he ever wrote:

> 'A house of dreams untold
> It looks out over the whispering tree-tops
> And faces the setting sun.'"

CLAUDE ACHILLE DEBUSSY

CHAPTER XXII

CLAUDE ACHILLE DEBUSSY

"I love music too much to speak of it otherwise than passionately."

DEBUSSY

"Art is always progressive; it cannot return to the past, which is definitely dead. Only imbeciles and cowards look backward. Then—Let us work!"

DEBUSSY

IT is difficult to learn anything of the boyhood and youth of this rare French composer. Even his young manhood and later life were so guarded and secluded that few outside his intimate circle knew much of the man, except as mirrored in his music. After all that is just as the composer wished, to be known through his compositions, for in them he revealed himself. They are transparent reflections of his character, his aims and ideals.

Only the barest facts of his early life can be told. We know that he was born at Saint Germain-en-Laye, France, August 22, 1862. From the very beginning he seemed precociously gifted in music, and began at a very early age to study the piano. His first lessons on

337

the instrument were received from Mme. de Sivry, a former pupil of Chopin. At ten he entered the Paris Conservatoire, obtaining his Solfège medals in 1874, '75, and '76, under Lavignac; a second prize for piano playing from Marmontel in 1877, a first prize for accompanying in 1880; an accessory prize for counterpoint and fugue in 1882, and finally the Grande Prix de Rome, with his cantata, "L'Enfant Prodigue," in 1884, as a pupil of Guirand.

Thus in twelve years, or at the age of twenty-two, the young musician was thoroughly furnished for a career. He had worked through carefully, from the beginning to the top, with thoroughness and completeness, gaining his honors, slowly, step by step. All this painstaking care, this overcoming of the technical difficulties of his art, is what gave him such complete command and freedom in using the medium of tone and harmony, in his unique manner.

While at work in Paris, young Debussy made an occasional side trip to another country. In 1879 he visited Russia, where he learned to know the music of that land, yet undreamed of by the western artists. When his turn came to go to Rome, for which honor he secured the prize, he sent home the required compositions, a Symphonic Suite "Spring," and a lyric poem for a woman's voice, with chorus and orchestra, entitled "La Demoiselle Elue."

From the first Claude Debussy showed himself a rare spirit, who looked at the subject of musical art from a different angle than others had done. For one thing he must have loved nature with whole souled devotion, for he sought to reflect her moods and inspirations in his compositions. Once he said: "I prefer to hear a few notes from an Egyptian shepherd's flute, for he is in accord with his scenery and hears harmonies unknown to your treatises. Musicians too seldom turn to the music inscribed in nature. It would benefit them more to watch a sunrise than to listen to a performance of the Pastorale Symphony. Go not to others for advice but take counsel of the passing breezes, which relate the history of the world to those who can listen."

Again he says, in a way that shows what delight he feels in beauty that is spontaneous and natural:

"I lingered late one autumn evening in the country, irresistibly fascinated by the magic of old world forests. From yellowing leaves, fluttering earthward, celebrating the glorious agony of the trees, from the clangorous angelus bidding the fields to slumber, rose a sweet persuasive voice, counseling perfect oblivion. The sun was setting solitary. Beasts and men turned peacefully homeward, having accomplished their impersonal tasks."

When as a youth Debussy was serving with his regiment in France, he relates of the delight he experienced in listening to the tones of the bugles and bells. The former sounded over the camp for the various military duties; the latter belonged to a neighboring convent and rang out daily for services. The resonance of the bugles and the far-reaching vibrations of the bells, with their overtones and harmonics, were specially noted by the young musician, and used by him later in his music. It is a well-known fact that every tone or sound is accompanied by a whole series of other sounds; they are the vibrations resulting from the fundamental tone. If the tone C is played in the lower octave of the piano, no less than sixteen overtones vibrate with it. A few of these are audible to the ordinary listener, but very keen ears will hear more of them. In Claude Debussy's compositions, his system of harmony and tonality is intimately connected with these laws of natural harmonics. His chords, for instance, are remarkable for their shifting, vapory quality; they seem to be on the border land between major and minor—consonance and dissonance; again they often appear to float in the air, without any resolution whatever. It was a new aspect of music, a new style of chord progression. At the same time the young composer was well versed in old and ancient music; he knew all the old scales, eight in number, and used them in his compositions with compelling charm. The influence of the old Gregorian chant has given his music a certain fluidity, free rhythm, a refinement, richness and variety peculiarly its own.

We can trace impressions of early life in Debussy's music, through his employment of the old modes, the bell sounds which were familiar to his boyhood, and also circumstances connected with his later life. As a student in Rome, he threw himself into the study of the music of Russian composers, especially that of Moussorgsky; marks of the Oriental coloring derived from these masters appear in his own later music. When he returned to Paris for good, he reflected in music the atmosphere of his environment. By interest and temperament he was in sympathy with the impressionistic school in art, whether it be in painting, literature or in music. In Debussy's music the qualities of impressionism and symbolism are very prominent. He employs sounds as though they were colors, and blends them in such a way as literally to paint a picture in tones, through a series of shaded, many-hued chord progressions. Fluid, flexible, vivid, these beautiful harmonies, seemingly woven of refracted rays of light, merge into shadowy melody, and free, flowing rhythm.

What we first hear in Debussy's music, is the strangeness of the harmony, the use of certain scales, not so much new as unfamiliar. Also the employment of sequences of fifths or seconds. He often takes his subjects from nature, but in this case seems to prefer a sky less blue and a landscape more atmospheric than those of Italy, more like his native France. His music, when known sufficiently, will reveal a sense of proportion, balance and the most exquisite taste. It may lack strength at times, it may lack outbursts of passion and intensity, but it is the perfection of refinement.

Mr. Ernest Newman, in writing of Debussy, warmly praises the delightful naturalness of his early compositions. "One would feel justified in building the highest hopes on the young genius who can manipulate so easily the beautiful shapes his imagination conjures up."

The work of the early period shows Debussy developing freely and naturally. The independence of his thinking is unmistakable, but it does not run into wilfulness. There is no violent break with the past, but simply the quickening of certain French qualities by the infusion of a new personality. It seemed as if a new and charming miniaturist had appeared, who was doing both for piano and song what had never been done before. The style of the two Arabesques and the more successful of the Ariettes oubliées is perfect. A liberator seemed to have come into music, to take up, half a century later, the work of Chopin—the work of redeeming the art from the excessive objectivity of German thought, of giving it not only a new soul but a new body, swift, lithe and graceful. And that this exquisitely clear, pellucid style could be made to carry out not only gaiety and whimsicality but emotion of a deeper sort, is proved by the lovely "Clair de Lune."

Among Debussy's best known compositions are "The Afternoon of a Faun," composed in 1894 and called his most perfect piece for orchestra, which he never afterward surpassed. There are also Three Nocturnes for orchestra. In piano music, as we have briefly shown, he created a new school for the player. All the way from the two Arabesques just mentioned, through "Gardens in the Rain," "The Shadowy Cathedral," "A Night in Granada," "The Girl with Blond Hair," up to the two books of remarkable Preludes, it is a new world of exotic melody and harmony to which he leads the way. "Art must be hidden by art," said Rameau, long ago, and this is eminently true in Debussy's music.

Debussy composed several works for the stage, one of which was "Martyrdom of Saint Sebastien," but his

"Pélleas and Mélisande" is the one supreme achievement in the lyric drama. As one of his critics writes: "The reading of the score of Pélleas and Mélisande' remains for me one of the most marvelous lessons in French art: it would be impossible for him to express more with greater restraint of means." The music, which seems so complicated, is in reality very simple. It sounds so shadowy and impalpable, but it is really built up with as sure control as the most classic work. It is indeed music which appeals to refined and sensitive temperaments.

This mystical opera was produced in Paris, at the Opéra Comique, in April, 1902, and at once made a sensation. It had any number of performances and still continues as one of the high lights of the French stage. Its fame soon reached America, and the first performance was given in New York in 1907, with a notable cast of singing actors, among whom Mary Garden, as the heroine gave an unforgettable, poetic interpretation.

Many songs have been left us by this unique composer. He was especially fond of poetry and steeped himself in the verse of Verlaine, Villon, Baudelaire and Mallarmé. He chose the most unexpected, the most subtle, and wedded it to sounds which invariably expressed the full meaning. He breathed the breath of life into these vague, shadowy poems, just as he made Maeterlinck's "Pélleas" live again.

As the years passed, Claude Debussy won more and more distinction as a unique composer, but also gained the reputation of being a very unsociable man. Physically it has been said that in his youth he seemed like an Assyrian Prince; through life he retained his somewhat Asiatic appearance. His eyes were slightly narrowed, his black hair curled lightly over an extremely broad forehead. He spoke little and often in brusque phrase. For this reason he was frequently misunderstood, as the irony and sarcasm with which he sometimes spoke did not tend to make friends. But this attitude was only turned toward those who did not comprehend him and his ideals, or who endeavored to falsify what he believed in and esteemed.

A friend of the artist writes:

"I met Claude Debussy for the first time in 1906. Living myself in a provincial town, I had for several years known and greatly admired some of the songs and the opera, 'Pelleas and Mélisande,' and I made each of my short visits to Paris an opportunity of improving my acquaintance with these works. A young composer, André Caplet, with whom I had long been intimate, proposed to introduce me to Debussy; but the rumors I had heard about the composer's preferred seclusion always made me refuse in spite of my great desire to know him. I now had a desire to express the feelings awakened in me, and to communicate to others, by means of articles and lectures, my admiration for, and my belief in, the composer and his work. The result was that one day, in 1906, Debussy let me know through a friend, that he would like to see me. From that day began our friendship." Later the same friend wrote:

"Debussy was invited to appear at Queen's Hall

with the London Symphony Orchestra, on February 1, 1908, to conduct his 'Afternoon of a Faun,' and 'The Sea.' The ovation he received from the English public was exceptional. I can still see him in the lobby, shaking hands with friends after the concert, trying to hide his emotion, and saying repeatedly: 'How nice they are— how nice they are!' "

He went again the next year to London, but the state of his health prevented his going anywhere else. For a malady, which finally proved fatal, seemed to attack · the composer when in his prime, and eventually put an end to his work. We cannot guess what other art works he might have created. But there must be some that have not yet seen the light. It is known that he was wont to keep a composition for some time in his desk, correcting and letting it ripen, until he felt it was ready to be brought out.

One of his cherished dreams had been to compose a "Tristan."

The characters of Tristan and Iseult are primarily taken from a French legend. Debussy felt the story was a French heritage and should be restored to its original atmosphere and idea. This it was his ardent desire to accomplish.

Debussy passed away March 26, 1918.

Since his desire to create a Tristan has been made impossible, let us cherish the rich heritage of piano, song and orchestral works, which this original French artist and thinker has left behind, to benefit art and his fellow man.